BEYOND THE CALL OF DUTY

ALSO BY STEPHEN L. MOORE

Strike of the Sailfish*: Two Sister Submarines and the Sinking of a Japanese Aircraft Carrier*

Blood and Fury: The World War II Story of Tank Sergeant Lafayette "War Daddy" Pool

Patton's Payback: The Battle of El Guettar and General Patton's Rise to Glory

Battle Stations: How the USS Yorktown *Helped Turn the Tide at Coral Sea and Midway*

Rain of Steel: Mitscher's Task Force 58, Ugaki's Thunder Gods, and the Kamikaze War off Okinawa

Uncommon Valor: The Recon Company That Earned Five Medals of Honor and Included America's Most Decorated Green Beret

As Good as Dead: The Daring Escape of American POWs from a Japanese Death Camp

The Battle for Hell's Island: How a Small Band of Carrier Dive-Bombers Helped Save Guadalcanal

Texas Rising: The Epic True Story of the Lone Star Republic and the Rise of the Texas Rangers, 1836–1846

Pacific Payback: The Carrier Aviators Who Avenged Pearl Harbor at the Battle of Midway

Battle Surface!: Lawson P. "Red" Ramage and the War Patrols of the USS Parche

Presumed Lost: The Incredible Ordeal of America's Submarine POWs During the Pacific War

Relic Quest: A Guide to Responsible Relic Recovery Techniques with Metal Detectors

Savage Frontier: Rangers, Riflemen, and Indian Wars in Texas, Volume IV: 1842–1845

Last Stand of the Texas Cherokees: Chief Bowles and the 1839 Cherokee War in Texas

War of the Wolf: Texas' Memorial Submarine, World War II's Famous USS Seawolf

Savage Frontier: Rangers, Riflemen, and Indian Wars in Texas, Volume III: 1840–1841

Spadefish*: On Patrol with a Top-Scoring World War II Submarine*

Savage Frontier: Rangers, Riflemen, and Indian Wars in Texas, Volume II: 1838–1839

Eighteen Minutes: The Battle of San Jacinto and the Texas Independence Campaign

Savage Frontier: Rangers, Riflemen, and Indian Wars in Texas, Volume I: 1835–1837

Taming Texas: Captain William T. Sadler's Lone Star Service

The Buzzard Brigade: Torpedo Squadron Ten at War (with William J. Shinneman and Robert Gruebel)

BEYOND THE CALL OF DUTY

The Life of Colonel Robert Howard, America's Most Decorated Green Beret

STEPHEN L. MOORE

CALIBER

CALIBER
An imprint of Penguin Random House LLC
penguinrandomhouse.com

LIBRARY OF CONGRESS CATALOGING-IN-PUBLICATION DATA
has been applied for.

ISBN 9780593475843 (paperback)
ISBN 9780593475850 (ebook)

Printed in the United States of America
1st Printing

★ CONTENTS ★

PROLOGUE

Sergeant First Class Robert Howard pressed his face into the damp jungle floor as bullets hit all around him. Explosions from rocket-propelled grenades (RPG) flung green foliage and red-hot steel in every direction. A fragment ripped into his right clavicle, fracturing the bone. Minutes later, another fragment or a ricocheting bullet gashed his right cheek.

The injuries just made Bob Howard more determined. Thirty yards away, a North Vietnamese Army (NVA) machine-gun nest threatened his life and those of his Green Beret comrades. Minutes earlier, he had led an assault on the NVA position. Using a single magazine of his automatic rifle, he had gunned down four charging enemy soldiers. But then the camouflaged machine-gun bunker had roared to life. Crawling carefully forward, Howard successfully shot down a sniper. Then he stood and charged, using his M16 to mow down all of the NVA gunners in the bunker.

As he moved back to safety, another unseen bunker commenced firing. Howard called in air strikes to silence this other gun emplacement, then eased forward to assess the bomb damage. But surviving North Vietnamese soldiers had remanned the gun. Chattering machine-gun fire filled the air. Bullets and RPG shrapnel bloodied his face and broke his collarbone. Then a ricocheting bullet slammed into his head above his left eye. It failed to penetrate his skull, but Howard was knocked senseless for several seconds.

At six feet and 170 pounds, the athletically built Howard made a prime target. His forehead pierced, his shoulder separated, and his face bloodied, Bob Howard was angry. While a child, he had been taught by his Granny Callie to always face his threats head-on. Never run. Bob's only goal now was to save lives. He scooted ahead, a steady stream of lead zipping just six inches above his head.

As he neared the North Vietnamese bunker, he pulled a fragmentation grenade from his web gear (or load-carrying equipment) and removed the pin. He lobbed the explosive into the enemy's emplacement and pressed his face into the soil as a red-orange burst of flame erupted in the pillbox. Once again, he had wiped out an enemy gun team.

Howard stood and dashed back across the clearing to check on his recon platoon comrades. Their mission was to destroy a sizable NVA supply dump that a besieged MACV-SOG recon team had discovered. But they had encountered a much larger force that had no intention of allowing the American Special Forces men to further damage their cache of weapons and food.

Within minutes, NVA soldiers returned to one of the many nearby machine-gun nests. The SOG team was pinned down by bullets once again.

While others took cover and fired back, Howard crept over to one of his indigenous grenadiers. Bullets thumped into the soil and jungle foliage all around him as he grabbed an anti-tank rocket launcher.

"Cover me!" Howard shouted.

Another Green Beret rose and began spraying the bunker with automatic weapon fire. Struggling with his injured clavicle and wiping blood from his eyes, Howard stood up and tried to keep as low a profile as possible. As machine-gun bullets zipped around him, he charged toward the new target.

HOWARD'S ACTIONS ON this mission were heroic. But for this Special Forces recon man, they were merely typical of his nature. His senior commanders thought enough of Howard's valor this day to write him up for the Medal of Honor. And after subsequent missions, Howard's superiors would submit his name for the Medal of Honor a second and third time.

Time and time again, Bob Howard survived missions that should have claimed his life. Others wondered if he had a special charm or maybe even a deal with the devil. In the most dire of situations, he often ignored his own wounds and charged the enemy. It was the only way he knew how to fight.

During one recon mission, Howard was rendered unconscious by the explosion of a rifle grenade that tossed his body like a rag doll. He awoke to find his right ankle too injured for him to walk. His legs and groin had been ripped by shrapnel. Blood poured into his eyes from head lacerations, and his CAR-15 automatic rifle (Colt Automatic Rifle-15 Commandos, designed in 1966 as a lighter-weight and controllable carbine version of the M16A1) had been blasted apart. As Howard struggled to pull himself up, he was suddenly aware of a horrifying sight and a stomach-turning smell. Just yards away, a North Vietnamese soldier had emerged from the brush with a flamethrower. The NVA killer methodically moved among the writhing bodies of Howard's injured comrades, incinerating them with liquid fire. Howard was practically defenseless as the enemy soldier approached him and swung the flamethrower in his direction.

On another mission, already wounded by shrapnel, Howard and his company commander ran across an open field to help rescue survivors of an American Huey helicopter that had been shot down near them. Howard calmly shot down charging NVA soldiers as he worked to pull wounded aviators from the blazing wreckage.

His SOG comrades were impressed as stories of Bob Howard began to circulate on base in the wake of successful operations. They learned how the sergeant had been shot through the shoulder during a firefight but refused to be extracted by a medevac chopper. Howard remained on the ground with his team for two more days to complete the mission. During a different operation, his comrades watched in awe as Howard raced forward to tackle and subdue a North Vietnamese soldier. Covered by his team, Howard raced back with the NVA man slung over his shoulder and deposited him before the team's interpreter for interrogation.

Howard's military medical records would later show that, over the course of his service, he suffered multiple gunshot wounds to his face, head, both legs, and right foot. He endured spinal injuries, a nasal fracture, and shrapnel and blast wounds to his neck, face, buttocks, hands, and legs. By his own count, Bob Howard was wounded in action fourteen different times during his four tours of duty in Vietnam. The U.S. Army officially processed only eight Purple Hearts for his wounds, as he never bothered to submit paperwork for some of them. Valor medals meant far less to Howard than the feeling of completing a mission successfully.

Howard is one of a little over 3,500 U.S. service veterans as of this date to have received the nation's highest honor, the Medal of Honor. He holds the distinction of being the only soldier nominated for the Medal of Honor three times over a thirteen-month period. He is the most decorated Green Beret, with more than fifty awards and ribbons for valor and distinctive service in combat.

Other servicemen have collected more total medals for valor, leaving historians to debate who is truly the most decorated American soldier based on rank of commendations. But Robert Lewis Howard's accomplishments rank him in the same class as American military heroes such as World War II's Audie Murphy and World War I's Alvin York.

Recon commanders who ran MACV-SOG missions with Howard in Vietnam would later declare him to be the bravest man they had ever met. They said he was a man any leader would want to have on his mission, because Howard simply acted without an ounce of fear under fire. A man of faith, Bob Howard more than once offered his own perspective on his survival.

"I ran with the devil, but God always had my back."

★ ONE ★

"RUN TOWARDS YOUR PROBLEMS"

The preteen boy was panting heavily as he reached the porch of his family's modest, whitewashed wood-frame house. Sitting atop a hill inside the little town of Opelika, Alabama, the Howard home was accessed by a single road that led back into town to the school campus.

Bob Howard was relieved. For five straight days, he had successfully evaded several older boys—the school bullies—who lived downhill from his family. Bob's family was dirt-poor, and good things rarely came to him. But he was proudly sporting a new pair of tennis shoes. The shoes were not brand-new, but they were new to him. The bullies had taunted him at school, promising that he wouldn't be keeping them for long.[1]

As grade school let out each day, Bob decided his only chance to avoid a fight was to utilize his speed. He was physically fit, and running was something that had always come naturally to him. As he neared the neighboring homes of the boys, Bob broke into a full sprint. He was only lightly sweating as he outraced them up the hill and reached his home. Once again, he had dodged the older boys.

The boys shouted jeers and went on their way as Bob reached the porch. He was surprised when his Granny Callie appeared from around the corner of the house. Only later did he learn that she had been secretly spying on him each day as he ran up the hill away from the bigger boys.

Callie Elizabeth Bowen Nichols, a petite woman in her early fifties, was a tough-as-nails, no-nonsense person. With Bob's parents struggling to make ends meet and with several small children in the Howard home, she had long been a big help for the family. Callie's husband, Virgil, had passed away in 1938, leaving her with two children to raise. In 1939, when Callie's daughter, Martha, gave birth to her first child, Callie was still raising her own seven-year-old son, Virgil Wesley Nichols. Once Virgil was old enough to strike out on his own, Callie devoted her time to helping her daughter raise her own large family in Opelika. Her grandson Robert, known as "Bob," was the oldest, followed by his sister Betty Jean ("Jeannie") and younger brother Charlie, who was known as "Bo." Three other Howard children—Frances, Judith, and Steve—were still too young for grade school, and Martha was pregnant again. Martha's husband, Charlie, was rarely home to assist with the kids.

Callie helped tend to the little ones and instilled values and morals in the older Howard kids. Bob Howard would always remember his Granny Callie as a devout Christian; she was one of the few positive role models young Bob and his eldest sister, Jeannie, had. She taught the two children how to read from the Bible and empowered Bob with the drive to make something of himself. The Howard kids respected their Granny Callie. So it was no small matter when she grabbed young Bob by his ear.

"Boy, what have you been running from?" she said.

Between gasps for breath, Bob began relating his story. Callie waved him quiet with her hand. She was not a fan of fighting, but she knew that her grandson would not be able to avoid conflict through the rest of the school year.

Granny Callie stared into his bright blue eyes. "I'd better never catch you running from something ever again," she said. "If you're going to run, you best run towards your problems, not away!"[2]

"Yes, ma'am," he said.

Her succinct advice would stick with Bob Howard through the rest of his life.

The following day, Bob tied up his new shoes and headed off to school. That afternoon on the way home, he steeled his nerves as he approached the homes of the older boys. When he was confronted by the Opelika bullies, he looked them straight in the eyes. He did not run up the hill.

Granny Callie wasn't sure what to say at first when her grandson arrived home. His clothes were dirty and torn and he was sweaty. His face, arms, and fists had scratches and bruises. Young Bob didn't offer many details on how well he had stood his ground. He merely smiled and pointed at his feet.

He was still wearing his new sneakers.

ROBERT LEWIS HOWARD was born on July 11, 1939, in Opelika, Alabama. His parents were young and struggled to make ends meet in their little community. Opelika, the county seat of Lee County, was located a hundred miles southwest of Atlanta and only twenty minutes from the Georgia border. Opelika was chartered as a town in 1854; its population in 1939 was just greater than six thousand souls.

Robert's father, Charlie C. Howard, had been born in Lee County in 1920 to Barney Howard and Nettie Brown. One of seven kids, Charlie was raised in a poor farming family who rode out the Great Depression in Alabama. During World War II, Charlie and his three brothers—Barney, Palmer, and Homer—each enlisted or were drafted into the U.S. Army and fought for their country. All returned home, although Palmer Howard was wounded in action in the Mediterranean Theater in the spring of 1944. Charlie married Martha Nichols, who gave birth to their first son, Robert Lewis Howard, before she reached the age of fifteen.

By the time Charlie Howard enlisted in the Army in 1944, he and Martha had two more children, Betty Jean and Charles Howard Jr. Their marriage would eventually produce seven kids. During the war, Martha Howard helped provide for her growing family by working at a local textile mill. Oldest son Robert and some of his siblings helped work the farm and pick cotton in their youth while attending grade school in Opelika.

Charlie Howard was a hard-drinking, unpleasant man after he returned from the war. He became a taxi driver for a local company where others from his family worked. His long work hours and bouts with alcohol left little time for raising his kids.

As Bob reached his teen years, school was far from the most important thing in his life. He was powerfully built and athletic and involved in football and other sports, but he had a larger purpose—to escape from Opelika, blaze his own trails, and avoid ending up like his father.

Bob remembered that when he was a young boy, people delivered government-assistance milk and cheese to his home. Although the family was dirt-poor, he was impressed that his Granny Callie always managed to help provide for the Howard boys who had gone off to war. She would pack one-gallon syrup cans full of homemade cookies to ship overseas.

Callie instilled a strong sense of patriotism in her grandchildren. "She taught me in a simple old way to appreciate my country and the love of our country," Bob later recalled.

"Every time you see the American flag, you see freedom, liberty, and Almighty God," she told her grandson. This belief would remain with Bob Howard throughout his life. Another was "Never have hate in your heart."

During high school, Bob worked for the same taxi company as his father. He served as a "taxicab starter" and as a dispatcher, sending out cabbies for patrons who had requested a ride. The thirty dollars per month he earned was enough to convince him that he did not need to finish high school. Like many other teenage boys in prewar America, he quit school to help provide for his family. But by 1956, Bob returned to school long enough to earn his high-school-equivalency diploma.

When Howard turned seventeen on July 11, 1956, he already

had a plan for his escape from Opelika. The U.S. Army base at Fort Benning, Georgia, near Columbus, was only a forty-five-minute drive from Opelika. As a little boy, he had seen young paratroopers marching past his home. Standing by the road-side, Bob had marveled at their khaki uniforms and the glider patches some wore on their hats and shoulders.

As he approached his seventeenth birthday, he had become convinced of a new purpose.

I'd like to be a paratrooper, he thought. *I want to jump out of airplanes.*

★ TWO ★

AIRBORNE

Charlie Howard was furious. His oldest son, Bob, had just earned his high-school-equivalency diploma in June 1956. But one evening in July, Bob returned home and announced to his father that he had met with an Army recruiter and was interested in enlisting. Since he was only seventeen, he would need a parent's approval—and his father didn't approve. Charlie wished for his son to take a regular job and avoid the hell of war that he had endured.

Charlie's hot temper flared, and he stormed down to the recruiter's office to berate him for more than an hour. Once Charlie cooled down a few days later, Bob was able to change his father's mind. He enlisted on July 20, 1956, a little more than a week after his birthday.[1]

Bob Howard's Basic training commenced at Fort Jackson, South Carolina. Originally created in 1917 as Camp Jackson when the U.S. entered World War I, the facility was reactivated for World War II as one of the country's largest training bases. Howard learned further skills at the Advanced Individual Training (AIT) school at Fort Gordon, Georgia. Powerfully built, Bob did not find Basic to be overly challenging.

"I was in good shape, physically," he recalled. "It was a lot of harassment, hollering and screaming, and making you do push-ups and physical things. I enjoyed firing the weapons. It was not difficult." The hardest part for Howard was seeing fellow recruits who were not in shape struggle with the physical demands and the mental challenges. For him, the most rewarding part of his months of training was coaching the weaker ones in his platoon. "I kinda catered to the underprivileged," he remembered.[2]

Standing six feet tall and weighing 170 pounds, he was by nature a gentle man with a warrior's heart. Years later, some would say he resembled the actor Clint Eastwood, with his sardonic smile, chiseled features, and blue eyes. His stern look was often enough to turn away a challenger, but those who knew Bob well understood that he would give all to protect another in need.

During his Basic training, Howard became friends with Stephen Day from Spokane, Washington; the twenty-one-year-old had been drafted around the time that Bob volunteered to go into the Army. During one of their liberties, Howard took his buddy Steve back to Opelika with him to visit his family. He introduced his friend to his younger sister Jeannie, and the two soon became an item They later married and would live together for thirty-one years until Steve passed away in 1990. Although Howard and his brother-in-law Steve would not spend time together in combat, they would remain very close friends throughout their military careers.[3]

At Fort Gordon, Howard found that weapons and ammunition were somewhat scarce during the Cold War era. During drills, he was often issued only a wooden weapon. For firing practice, Bob and his squad mates were given the semiautomatic M1 Garand rifle, which had been used since before World War II. "They gave us only three rounds of ammunition to zero our rifles," Howard recalled. "The ones that had good weapons and could qualify with two rounds, we passed the ammunition to guys that couldn't qualify with three rounds." The Garand would be replaced in March 1958 by the selective-fire M14.[4]

Howard endured rough treatment throughout Basic. But thanks to the morals instilled in him about the military and patriotism, Bob never argued with his sergeants, even when called on to pick up trash and cigarette butts around the base, mow grass, or pull KP duty. He never complained, even when the first boots he was issued were too large for him and his first uniform was untailored. He learned to improvise and overcome every challenge.

The Army offered three square meals a day, a far cry from his years as a poor boy in Opelika, when hot meals were not taken for granted. Upon graduation from AIT in 1957, Private Howard was assigned to Fort Hood, Texas, near Killeen. Located about halfway between Waco and Austin, Fort Hood initially comprised more than 158,000 acres and could billet more than 88,000 officers and men.

By 1954, the U.S. Army III Corps had made Fort Hood its headquarters, where officers supervised the training of combat units. (During Bob Howard's time at the base, perhaps the most famous trainee to come through was one Elvis Aaron Presley, already a rock and roll and movie star before being drafted.) Howard spent 1958 and 1959 alternately engaged as a power-man, an automobile maintenance helper, and a power generator operator with the 53rd Signal Battalion and later with the 54th Signal Company. Although this work was not a combat military occupation specialty (MOS), Bob's previous experience with the taxi company helped guide his early assignments. He soon rose in rank from private to private first class up to specialist fourth class (pay grade E-4).

But there his progress would stall for several years. His enthusiasm waned, and his dream of becoming a paratrooper did not materialize. Finally, one of his sergeants advised him sternly, "You're going to get kicked out if you don't show that you can be mature." Bob wanted to be promoted, so he decided it was high time to lay off having fun and drinking too much and become a family man.[5]

One young lady he had met at the local dance hall had caught his eye. Her name was Tina LaRuth Dickenson, a twenty-one-year-old brunette. Tall, slender, and attractive, she pronounced her first name "Tie-nah." Bob learned that she was a local girl who lived in nearby Temple, Texas, where she had been raised by her parents, Rufus and Emma Mae "Molly" Holley Dickenson. Like Bob, she had not yet found the right person, but she seemed ready for a change in her life.

Bob explained his desire to change his ways and become serious. "I need to marry somebody," he said. "You want out?"[6]

Although his proposal was blunt, Tina saw a future with

Bob Howard and agreed that they should get married. Their wedding in Bell County on March 21, 1959, was simple, but their union was solid. Bob moved from the bunkhouse to married quarters at Fort Hood, and the change seemed to motivate him.

When his initial enlistment expired, Bob traveled to Montgomery, Alabama, in early April 1959 after his honeymoon and reenlisted in the U.S. Army for six more years. He listed his job occupation as "professional soldier," and he was now more committed than ever to provide for his wife and future family.

Per his reenlistment request, Howard was assigned to the 426th Supply and Transportation Battalion of the 101st Airborne Division, stationed at Fort Campbell, Kentucky. Bob's dream of becoming a paratrooper like his father, Charlie, and uncles Homer, Palmer, and Barney was finally realized. "The first time I flew on an airplane, I jumped out of it," he later recalled.[7] As part of the fabled 101st of World War II fame, Bob Howard successfully completed his three-week qualification course.

Being Airborne qualified also meant extra pay. Whereas a buck private earned only eighty-three dollars and twenty cents a month, an Airborne assignment added fifty-five dollars per month. After graduating from Airborne School, Howard was sent to a three-week parachute rigger course at Fort Lee, Virginia. Every one of his initial parachute jumps was a thrill.

"It just seemed like up there, I was a little closer to God," he said. "For a few seconds in life, there was just nobody up there but me and my Maker." As a rigger, he fully appreciated the need for triple-checking everything. When one of the old chutes failed to open, he knew he had only seconds to respond with his emergency chute. As Howard would later tell his friends, "I've never seen an atheist on a battlefield or getting ready to jump out of an airplane."[8]

Specialist Fourth Class Howard was assigned as a parachute rigger with the 612th Quartermaster Company at Fort Bragg, North Carolina. He and his wife, Tina, settled into base life on the massive 251-square-mile base that bordered the towns of Fayetteville, Spring Lake, and Southern Pines. He remained there into 1961, when he was assigned his first overseas tour of duty as a rigger with the 557th Quartermaster Company in France. During the two years he was stationed in Europe, Bob would miss out on plenty with his family.

On September 21, 1961, Tina gave birth to their first child, daughter Denicia. With her husband away for an extended period, Tina returned to Bell County, Texas, to be near her father, Rufus Dickenson, in his Temple home. Her mother had passed away in 1957, but her aunt, Annie Marie Shiplett, and her cousins helped with raising her daughter in the modest rental house that she secured. Denicia was more than a year old before her father returned Stateside as part of A Company of the 5th Supply and Transportation Battalion of the 5th Infantry Division.

Howard served in this role at Fort Carson, Colorado, until early 1964, when he was transferred to Fort Campbell, Kentucky, to serve as a senior parachute packer for B Company of the 426th Supply and Transportation Battalion. During that year, Bob Howard enjoyed two particular events more than anything else. The first was news of the birth of his second daughter, Melissa, on April 2, 1964. During the latter stages of her pregnancy, Tina had remained with her extended family in

Texas for assistance with two-year-old Denicia. Howard would later admit to his younger daughter that the unique pronunciation of her name ("Mah-lisa") was in honor of an old French girlfriend he'd had while stationed in Europe.[9]

The other noteworthy 1964 event for Bob Howard was his promotion to sergeant (pay grade E-5). By early 1965, he was serving as a senior parachute packer with the 104th Quartermaster Company of the 101st Airborne Division. Although far removed from the world crisis in Vietnam, Sergeant Howard was very aware that American forces could be deployed at any time. And as a member of the 101st Airborne, known as the "Screaming Eagles," he knew his number could be called sooner than others.

Following strikes on U.S. naval ships in the summer of 1964, Congress had approved the Gulf of Tonkin Resolution in August. President Lyndon Johnson was granted permission to use all necessary measures to repel armed attacks against U.S. forces in order to prevent further aggression. In the wake of an attack on a U.S. Army base in Pleiku, South Vietnam, American air strikes commenced, and more ground troops were moved into the area. The beginning of the American ground war in Vietnam came in March 1965, when the first U.S. Marines landed near Da Nang, South Vietnam.

Charlie Howard's concerns about his son joining the military and being shipped off to war were now legitimate. By May 5, the 173rd Airborne Brigade became the first U.S. Army ground unit committed to the conflict. It was only the start of what would be a significant buildup of U.S. troops in the region.

"I didn't know much about Vietnam at the time, but I knew

we were at war," Howard recalled. Reality sank in when in June 1965 the division was alerted that it would soon be deployed. The base went into lockdown mode as troops, equipment, and supplies were readied for movement overseas. An advance party of the 101st was flown to Nha Trang, while the bulk of the brigade prepared to fly from Fort Campbell, Kentucky, to the Army terminal in Oakland, California.[10]

Bob Howard's family was prepared. His wife, Tina, with her daughters, Denicia and Melissa, had settled back into the Temple area in an apartment near her father. There they would be looked after by other family members, including Tina's aunt, Annie, until Sergeant Howard could return from the war. After nine years of noncombat military life, Bob fully understood the risks involved in where he was heading.

His introduction to the hell of ground warfare was just weeks away.

★ THREE ★

INTO THE GRAVE

Sergeant Bob Howard was awake long before dawn on July 7, 1965. He and his fellow troops of the 101st Airborne Division were herded like cattle onto trucks for the ride from their Fort Campbell barracks to the airfield. Then he hauled his heavy duffel bags and combat gear on the civilian airliner and readied himself for the cross-country flight to San Francisco International Airport.[1]

Several hours later, Howard and hundreds of other Airborne soldiers crammed into buses for the ride to the dock at the Oakland Army Terminal. Clutching his duffel bags, eager to head toward overseas action, Howard shuffled toward the waiting ship. There he walked up the gangplank and boarded a 510-foot rusting transport vessel named the *General LeRoy Eltinge.* During the Second World War, the aging Liberty ship had often carried twenty-five hundred men, but it was now packed with thirty-seven hundred paratroopers from the 101st's 1st Brigade. Howard was one of the 792 men of the 1st Battalion, 327th Infantry Regiment, 1st Brigade, 101st Airborne Division.

He was sent three decks below in the *Eltinge,* where the men were stacked like cordwood in four-high racks for their voyage to the Vietnam War. At 0600 on July 8, the troopship was underway from her dock without much fanfare. An Army band blared out martial melodies, but there were no throngs of cheering civilians to bid Howard and his comrades goodbye.[2]

The following morning, the *Eltinge* plowed through heavy seas that left many of the young soldiers unable to keep down their chow. The sights and smells often caused more men to get sick. Howard did his best to maintain his physical shape with calisthenics, but space was limited. He passed his twenty-sixth birthday on board. Six days out of port, the brigade's executive officer (XO, or second officer in command), Lieutenant Colonel Charles Rogers, announced they were heading for South Vietnam. He concluded his speech by chanting the Screaming Eagles division slogan, "We have a rendezvous with destiny!"[3]

Howard considered the voyage "a lifetime experience." After the first seventeen days on the ship, water rationing was in place. The troops took "hard water" baths in salt water. "It seemed like you couldn't stay clean," he remembered. "You'd get in the shower and the soap wouldn't lather." Meals were even a challenge, with the men standing in line with food trays as the *Eltinge* rolled about in the open ocean. "I was eager to get to war, to get off that ship," Howard said.[4]

On July 24, the *Eltinge* reached the American naval base at Subic Bay in the Philippines for refueling. Underway the following day, the ship steamed into the South China Sea and made her approach to the coast of Indochina. By the morning of July 29, the *Eltinge* had reached the beautiful blue waters of Cam Ranh Bay on South Vietnam's central shores. The American troops going ashore would be charged with helping to repel a Communist insurgency that seemed close to toppling the South Vietnamese government.

After weeks of training for a true amphibious landing, Howard was disappointed to find that his company would be floated off their troopship on transports and then run up to the beach. With his loaded rifle in hand and his personal gear on his back, Howard joined his unit in climbing down rope ladders to reach the LCVPs (landing craft vehicle personnel) bobbing in the waves below. "People were falling off the ropes into the China Sea trying to get into the troop transport," he remembered.

By the time his squad was on board the small vessel, rifles at the ready, it was nearly two a.m. on July 30. Their beachhead was fully secured, so there was no mass panic of storming ashore under enemy gunfire. But in the darkness, Howard had no idea of the water's depth when the vessel's ramp crashed down into the water. It had not pulled all the way up onto the beach, as the men had been led to believe. Leading his squad, he charged forward and stepped off into the ocean. Heavily weighted, he plunged some twelve feet deep before his boots hit the sand. Howard struggled to bounce forward and kick himself upward to gasp for a breath of air.

I'm going to drown before I even get on the beach! he thought.

Some members of his squad dropped their weapons and

other gear as they struggled to reach shallow water. "If there had been any enemy there, they would have killed us all," Howard recalled, exasperated.

Howard and his fellow paratroopers helped unload the *Eltinge* during the following hours. He was impressed that Generals William C. Westmoreland and Maxwell D. Taylor, both former commanders of the Screaming Eagles, were on hand to greet the 101st Division. Howard's battalion advanced across the bay from the Cam Ranh peninsula to establish their base camp near the hamlet of Dong Ba Thin along Highway 1. The ensuing days were spent establishing the camp and training at the various squad, platoon, and company levels.[5]

After sorting out supply issues, Bob Howard's brigade moved forward to seek and destroy Viet Cong forces west of Nha Trang. No enemy contact was made during the mid-August Operation Anvil, but the 101st gained valuable experience in conducting large operations. Next, the brigade began movement to An Khe in Binh Dinh Province to provide security for the arrival of the 1st Cavalry Division. By August 24, Howard's 1st Battalion of the 327th Infantry Regiment moved its equipment by sea to the coastal town of Qui Nhon, where the paratroopers would screen the arrival of Korean units.

During his early weeks in Vietnam, Sergeant Howard found himself leading his squad on various search-and-clear operations. Once one area was declared clear, the group advanced to another, gradually moving beyond the zone already secured by the 1st Infantry Division. "We didn't get much information at my level as a sergeant," he recalled. In a constant state of confusion, he was discouraged as he learned that his force would cover the arrival of other military groups. "What for?" he asked one of his comrades. "There's no war going on here. We haven't made any contact with any enemy."[6]

Howard would find action soon enough. But his first six weeks were annoying at best.

This is not what I was trained to do, he thought. Without solid intelligence, he had little knowledge of where his enemy was located. Even worse, he was being ordered around by fresh lieutenants younger than he was who were equally uninformed. At one point, he told one of the lieutenants, "Tell the captain the men are frustrated. They want to fight. Where's the enemy? Let's go fight the enemy."

That wish began to slowly materialize as his battalion pushed forward into the area beyond Qui Nhon and conducted infantry operations. "We started making contact with the enemy forces and started to experience hasty ambushes and people being shot by snipers as we moved to an area," he recalled. "Then we started seeing the Vietnamese people in the villages, and we started getting serious. We knew we were at war."

Without quality maps of the region, Sergeant Howard was often baffled by precisely where his C Company was moving. At night, sporadic gunfire and mortar rounds became more common. One day, his battalion was tasked with clearing a large area to set up a battalion-sized base camp. Large tents, each sizable enough to hold an infantry squad of about ten men, were erected during the late afternoon. Howard had scarcely gotten to sleep that night when explosions suddenly began rocking his company's perimeter around two a.m.

Mortar explosions sporadically lit up the area, and the ground trembled. Excited soldiers charged out of their tents and began firing. Bob's company commander announced that they were being assaulted by a North Vietnamese Army (NVA) force, but Bob would later learn that their immediate enemies were in fact Viet Cong soldiers. Officially the National Liberation Front of South Vietnam, this armed Communist organization fighting under the direction of North Vietnam included both regular army and guerrilla units, all known as Viet Cong (or "VC" to most American soldiers). In the confusion of the moment, it mattered little to Howard. *They all dress in black uniforms,* he thought. *We're not going to be able to identify them, much less even see them in the dark.* For the moment, he was more concerned that American troops might be firing on one another. After gathering his squad, Howard hurried over to his platoon leader.

"What's my mission?" he demanded. "We're being attacked. Just give me a position on the ground and I'll defend it!"

The lieutenant assigned Howard to set up an outer base perimeter, just beyond the platoon's new base camp. The late-evening hours had been spent erecting the camp, so Howard had not been afforded the luxury of scouting about the immediate area to learn the terrain. To his surprise, as his squad moved forward, they found themselves in a local cemetery outside Qui Nhon.

Rifles continued firing from all directions, each creating

brief muzzle flashes that further challenged good night vision. Howard, directing his men to various defensive points, stood exposed as bullets zinged by and ricocheted off unseen objects. The next instant, he felt a powerful blow to his face that knocked him off his feet.

Howard fell backward, then tumbled into a hole with fresh dirt pushed up all around it. As he hit the ground, his body struck a large, heavy object just below the soil. When he felt his face, he found his hands suddenly covered with warm liquid. *I'm bleeding! I've been hit!*

Bob was stunned, and he wondered if half his head had been blown away. He probed the right side of his face and felt an opening. A bullet had pierced his cheek beside his nose and smashed through some of his upper and lower teeth before exiting through his lower-right jaw. Spitting blood, he feared that he was mortally wounded. For the moment, at least, he was alive. With mortar explosions erupting some distance away and bullets zinging about him in all directions, he felt terribly exposed.

He had no idea whether he had been shot by a Viet Cong or an American. His only immediate thought was to keep his head down to avoid being hit again. Howard clawed into the dirt mound he had disturbed and pressed his face into the soil. As he wriggled about to attain the lowest possible profile, he found himself lying against a solid body.

In the brief flashes of light, he suddenly realized he had tumbled into a Vietnamese grave. The locals buried their dead partially upright, with a mound above ground level, and the corpse in a vertical burial position. As Howard pressed himself tighter into the mound, he was mortified to find that he was hugging the rotting corpse of a recently deceased Vietnamese person.

But he dared not crawl away and become a prime target. He decided that it was better to dig in and lie still until the shooting subsided. But doing so was stomach turning. Each movement smeared rotting flesh from the corpse across his face and body. The stench was unbearable. And he could feel maggots crawling all over him.

Touching his face was painful and only further smeared the gore, which made him sick. As he vomited to one side, sharp pain raced through his head like a lightning strike. That hurt worse than being shot in the face.

Semiconscious, he lay in agony for the next few hours. Maggots crawled over his face and under his collar. But he decided to wait until the shooting died down. When the first rays of dawn began illuminating the area, and Howard's company moved forward to check on the wounded, they found him pressed against the decaying corpse, his own face covered in blood and other ooze.

"The company commander found me," Howard recalled. "They realized I was not dead, so they got some medics over there and started treating me."

Sergeant Howard's first big firefight in Vietnam was nearly his last. He would later come to believe that his life had been spared because the bullet that struck him had apparently ricocheted off a tree, lessening the impact to some degree.

Medics administered morphine and hustled him in a stretcher back toward the division hospital established at Qui Nhon.

★ FOUR ★

SPECIAL FORCES

His face heavily bandaged, Bob Howard lay on a cot in the Qui Nhon field evacuation hospital. The medics treating him said that the round that struck his face was from a 7.62mm weapon, likely an AK-47 assault rifle. Surgeons replaced teeth broken on both the upper and the lower right side of his mouth, and they reconstructed part of his face.

His rehab would take weeks, but he was able to speak with only minor difficulty. He found that the wounded man lying in the bunk next to him was a sergeant from the 5th Special Forces Group Airborne (SFGA). He was a twenty-nine-year-old New Yorker named John Curtin, and the two had first met during their Airborne training. Howard and Curtin discussed their wounds and soon became engaged in a long conversation about their military specialties. To Howard, Special Forces had a certain appeal: covert missions into enemy territory, the chance to grab Viet Cong prisoners, and plenty of action. It all sounded better than blindly patrolling into poorly mapped villages and having firefights in the dead of night when opponents could not even be seen.[1]

As Howard and Curtin talked one day, the medical staff came to attention as a senior officer entered the facility. Howard learned from his friend that it was Colonel William McKean, commander of the 5th SFGA and Curtin's CO (commanding officer). As the colonel made his rounds, he stopped to check on the Special Forces sergeant to see how his wounds were healing.

I'm shot up worse than him! Howard thought. *And nobody's coming around here to check on me.*

As Curtin chatted with McKean, he suddenly said, "I've got a good friend here named Sergeant Howard. He's with the 101st. He got shot in Qui Nhon. We need a guy like him in Special Forces."[2]

McKean turned to Howard. "What unit are you in, son?"

"I'm in the First Brigade, 101st Airborne Division, First Battalion, 327th Infantry Regiment, Charlie Company, sir," Howard replied in his slow Alabama drawl through his shattered jaw.

The colonel duly made note of Howard's unit, name, and serial number, and asked him if he was interested in Special Forces.

"My God, if I can get out of the 101st, I'd really like that," said Howard. "You know, I can train. I can fight. We're a little bit disorganized and don't know what we're doing. So if you've got a job for an infantry sergeant, I'll volunteer for it."

"Well, all right, son," said McKean. "The Fifth can always use another good warrior. Let's get you healed up."

"Yes, sir."

Howard gave little thought to the chance meeting with the Special Forces (SF) colonel until he was discharged from the field hospital days later. His face still bandaged, he climbed into a two-and-a-half-ton truck (a "deuce and a half" in Army lingo) for the ride back to the 101st's base camp. Upon reporting to his battalion's first sergeant, he was floored by his news.

"Howard, you've been transferred to Special Forces. Get your gear. You've gotta go to Saigon for a special mission."

"What do you mean?" Howard asked.

"Well, you've got to have top secret clearance," said the sergeant. "You've been selected to be in the Special Forces now."

"Okay, sir."

"How did they pick your name?" the first sergeant said.

"I don't know," said Howard. He didn't have the desire to tell his superior about how he had met with Colonel McKean.

With that, Sergeant Howard found himself being flown to Saigon to the headquarters of the Military Assistance Command, Vietnam (MACV) in late fall 1965. "I didn't even know what Special Operations was at that time," Howard later admitted.

In 1964, MACV had established a joint unconventional warfare task group that was code-named the Studies and Observations Group (SOG). It was composed strictly of volunteers—Army Green Berets, a few Navy SEALs (sea, air, and land), Central Intelligence Agency (CIA) field agents, and indigenous personnel. The newly formed SOG reported directly to the Joint Chiefs of Staff (JCS) and to the White House. Their top secret operations ("black ops") were so classified that the very existence of this covert unit was denied by the U.S. government. Operating in small teams, SOG operatives were charged with conducting strategic reconnaissance missions, capturing enemy soldiers for intelligence, identifying targets for bombing missions, wiretapping enemy communication lines, attempting to rescue American prisoners of war, and conducting psychological missions, such as sabotaging enemy ammunition.

During 1965, SOG operations were still being organized by General William Westmoreland, the MACV commander in charge of all U.S. forces deployed in South Vietnam. Originally commanded by Colonel Clyde Russell and then Colonel Donald Blackburn, who had led a guerrilla network during World War II, MACV-SOG operated out of Saigon, with its command and control (C and C) headquarters at Da Nang Air Base on the eastern coast of Vietnam.

Upon arriving in Saigon, Howard found himself with a group of other sergeants who had been selected for potential processing into Special Forces duty. The group was first run through a series of lie detector tests and several screenings by CIA field agents to assess their mental and physical prowess. Potential new recruits were then advised that their service was strictly voluntary. Many of their operations would be conducted behind enemy lines, and the U.S. government would deny any knowledge of their activities should they be killed or captured. Casualty rates would be high, so anyone not willing to accept such risk could bow out—he would be reassigned to other duties without any questions asked.

Howard was told that he would be assigned to an SF unit, but full training to become an official Green Beret would require Stateside courses. With a half year remaining on his one-year tour of duty in Vietnam, he would be assigned to Detachment B-52 of Project Delta to run special long-range reconnaissance missions inside the country of South Vietnam. Such B-52 missions included bomb-damage assessments, wiretapping of enemy communication lines, psychological operations, and mining of enemy transportation routes.[3]

From Saigon, Bob Howard flew down to Nha Trang, the current headquarters for Colonel McKean's 5th Special Forces Group in Vietnam. He quickly found his job there more appealing than his last one. "We ran small-unit operations," Howard recalled. "We went into areas and sought the enemy." With each in-country mission came the potential to storm a Viet Cong camp in guerrilla-warfare style, with the aim of bringing back in a live prisoner of war for interrogation.

Little is recorded of Sergeant Howard's exact Detachment B-52 missions while operating from Nha Trang, but it was certainly more attractive to him than his previous life as a parachute rigger and infantry soldier. Near the completion of his service period, he was issued the Combat Infantryman Badge (CIB) on May 3, 1966, by headquarters, 5th Special Forces Group. The CIB was issued only to infantrymen and SF soldiers who had fought in active ground combat in a brigade or a smaller-sized unit.

To Howard, there were no bad soldiers, just misguided soldiers. With Special Forces, he felt he was now working with people who had a mission in mind—true professionals. "They were much better trained than normal Airborne or infantry soldiers I had trained with," he remembered. "They taught me that you can take a small number of people, and if you've got cohesion and good training, you know you can defeat a much larger foe."[4]

The next step in Bob Howard's induction into the life of a Green Beret was to complete additional Stateside training courses. On June 6, 1966, upon completing his first tour in Vietnam, he was flown back to the United States to begin that journey.

But first came a heartwarming reunion with his family in Temple, Texas, during his granted liberty period. He had little interest in seeing his parents in Opelika, but his grandmother and his own family were another story. His daughter Denicia was soon to be five, and Melissa was two. To Bob, his kids were precious. But to them, he was more like a stranger.

More than a year had passed since they had seen him, and Melissa had been in diapers at that point. Her mother, Tina, had given Melissa a small photo of her daddy that she treasured. She kept it hidden away under a carpet so no one could take it from her. When Bob returned home, he tried to give Melissa a hug. The husky man with the scarred face did not match the look of the young soldier she knew from her photo. She pulled away from him. Tina announced, "Your daddy is home!"[5]

Melissa ran from the room. A shy girl who did not speak during her first four years of life, Melissa was obviously troubled. When her parents found her, she was clutching her photo of Bob Howard and pointing to it, as if to say, *THIS is my daddy!*

For the next nine months, Sergeant Howard's kids had more opportunities to see their father. Tina Howard moved the girls from Texas to North Carolina, where they lived in married housing near the base. Howard returned to work in July 1966 as a senior parachute rigger and supply sergeant for the 6th Special Forces Group at Fort Bragg, North Carolina. His lengthy schooling to become a Green Beret commenced. During the early months of 1967, many of his courses were at the adjacent Camp Mackall—the special North Carolina training base that had been in use by the U.S. Army since 1943. The Special Forces Qualification Course (SFQC) was simply known as the "Q Course" to most new recruits.

For Bob, it was all exciting and new. His body was built for the physical challenges ahead and his mind was clear. "They had a seven-week Special Forces enlistment course," he recalled. "Once we finished that, the emphasis was on demolition: to train to storm units, patrolling, shooting up weapons, and setting up base camp for small-unit operation."[6]

Phase Two training, which took up to eight weeks, allowed Howard to achieve MOS in weapons and demolition. Upon completion, he was gathered into a small team for another eight-week block of instructions on unconventional warfare. The team was dropped into a rural part of North Carolina where they linked up with other groups to learn guerrilla-force tactics by practicing small-unit operations against organized Army units already secured in their patrol area.

"The training after that was extremely rigorous," he remembered. Some days his team would run miles, carrying heavy pack loads. To Howard, physical endurance was crucial. It was not uncommon for his unit to be given two hours to run six miles wearing eighty-pound gear packs, and then immediately be secured in a proper fighting position.[7]

In addition to his early military training during the 1960s, Howard made cameo appearances in two John Wayne films. The first, *The Longest Day,* was a black-and-white film about the D-Day landings at Normandy. Filmed in 1962, the picture included Howard as one of the soldiers making a parachute jump. While in SF training during 1967, Howard also made a brief appearance as an Airborne trooper in Wayne's film *The Green Berets,* which was released the following year.

Special Forces training required each new recruit to learn how to be a teacher. It was imperative that a qualified team leader could instruct others in the field how to improvise and survive under the harshest of conditions. Those who completed the grueling course were finally eligible to don a green beret, the soft cap that President John F. Kennedy had approved in October 1961 when he visited Fort Bragg.

That Special Forces cap was a badge of courage to Howard and a mark of distinction in the fight for freedom. He remembered JFK's remarks on this subject, and he was immensely proud in early April 1967 when he officially became a member of this elite group. By that time, he had also been promoted to staff sergeant (SSG; E-6 pay grade).

When his Special Forces training was complete, the U.S. Army decided it was time to put SSG Howard to the test. At Fort Bragg, he received new orders sending him back to Vietnam. Once again, Tina would return to Texas, where she could enjoy the help of her extended family in raising her daughters.

Their father had a new calling with an elite group known as MACV-SOG.

★ FIVE ★

FOB-2 KONTUM

Bob Howard grabbed his duffel bags and headed toward the waiting jeep. Another noncom greeted him at the modest Kontum airfield and assured him it was a short ride to the base. Howard's chiseled face was that of a seasoned poker veteran. The young sergeant driving the jeep had no idea how excited Howard felt as he was escorted to the forward MACV-SOG base.

Twenty-seven-year-old Howard's second tour of duty in Vietnam commenced on April 24, 1967. He was now a Green Beret attached to the 5th Special Forces Group. Upon his arrival in-country for processing, he had received orders to hop another flight to a SOG forward operating base (FOB) in the Central Highlands region of South Vietnam. He could not have asked for more.

SOG had three FOBs in operation in the spring of 1967; each was strategically located in a key area that allowed recon men to be inserted into enemy territory. The base that Bob Howard was assigned to, FOB-2, was located just south of Kontum City, about forty miles southeast of the tri-border area where Cambodia, Laos, and South Vietnam met. Howard learned that his new base had been in operation less than one year. In May 1966, the first thirty-three Green Berets assigned to build out the base had arrived. Calling themselves the "original 33" of Kontum, these SF men had made significant improvements to what had once been an Army of the Republic of Vietnam (ARVN) truck compound during the French Indochina War.

A short distance from the airfield, Howard's jeep came to a halt within FOB-2. The base lay on either side of local Highway 14, and it consisted of a few dozen clapboard buildings and vehicle sheds. Some of the Green Berets there had spent as much time constructing permanent housing and buildings as they had done performing recon work. Bob quickly absorbed all he could from the Special Forces men who greeted him.

In its first year, FOB-2 had supported as many as nine small-unit operation groups. These were called "spike teams," but were alternatively referred to as "recon teams" by many of the Green Berets. In fact, in less than a year's time, MACV-SOG would formally change the spike team (ST) reference to recon team (RT). Naming designation aside, each spike team consisted of two or three Americans (Special Forces Green Berets) and a small number of local tribesmen to fill out their ranks. The early teams from FOB-2 all ran with indigenous Chinese Nungs, ethnic Chinese who had long since immigrated to Vietnam from China's Kwangsi Province.

Kontum SF men quickly began actively recruiting other

indigenous mountain people (known as Montagnards, French for "mountain dwellers") to help run recon missions with the Americans. Montagnards comprised a diverse group of tribes inhabiting the Central Highlands region. Although some were sympathetic to the North Vietnamese Army, the majority of the Montagnards were eager to fight the enemy that had invaded their homeland. Invariably shortened to "Yards" by Green Berets, these indigenous men proved to be loyal and able fighters. They were well adapted to moving stealthily through the jungle and were excellent at tracking the movements of other forces. Spike Team Colorado had been the first recon team to begin running missions with Yards, but other teams followed suit by the fall of 1966. Captain Edward Lesesne, commander of the FOB-2 recon company, had his Green Berets help build a proper camp for their Montagnards about two miles from Kontum, just off Highway 14.

Upon Howard's arrival, FOB-2 was in a transition period between permanent commanding officers of the base. Major Frank Sova, who had been in charge of the Kontum base for the past seven months, had orders for a new command. While Howard and the other men awaited a new senior officer, Sova's place as base CO was filled temporarily during May and June by one of his senior officers, Major Jerry Kilburn.

Kilburn, who hailed from West Virginia, was a by-the-book kind of commander. In 1950, he had deployed as an infantryman to Korea, where he was captured and spent three years as a prisoner of war. Kilburn recovered from his injuries, completed officers' school in 1956, and was commissioned as a second lieutenant. By 1961, he had completed the Special Forces Officers'

Qualification Course at Fort Bragg, North Carolina, and he had since held various commands within the 5th SFG and MACV-SOG.

As the new FOB-2 base commander, Kilburn put in some requests that his Green Berets found peculiar. In one such case, he had noted in older U.S. Army regulations that a forward base such as his was authorized to use draft animals for moving equipment. Kilburn put his base XO, Major Frank Jaks, to the task of finding said draft animals. Jaks managed to have his resourceful SF men purchase from the locals a horse that became an instant source of amusement for his recon company. But Kilburn was not amused when one of his team leaders rode the horse into Kontum City and left it hitched to a post while he sought the service of a local prostitute. The team commander returned to find that the FOB-2 service animal had been rustled.[1]

When Staff Sergeant Howard reported to Major Kilburn's office, the new base commandant reviewed Howard's papers. Seeing that Howard had most recently served as a supply sergeant with the 6th SFG at Fort Bragg, Kilburn assigned him to the S-4 division (supply) at Kontum. In recon lingo, Howard was a "FNG," or "f**king new guy." He knew better than to complain. He accepted his new assignment willingly—tackling the supply room, doing the base paperwork, and even managing the base kitchen—with pride. But inside, he yearned to find a way back into long-range recon missions.

The supply room, made of simple wood framing and plywood sheets, contained a wide variety of equipment. It held an ample supply of older 9mm Swedish K submachine guns, which had been the main weapon that the recon teams had carried on missions in 1966. Some SOG men now carried Colt M16s, and a select few were beginning to get their hands on CAR-15s (Colt Automatic Rifle-15 Commandos, designed in 1966 as a lighterweight and controllable carbine version of the M16A1). Regardless of rifle type, each recon man generally carried 350 to 450 rounds of ammunition, along with two or more fragmentation hand grenades, one CS (tear gas) grenade, and at least two smoke grenades. Each team of six to ten men would also carry at least two M79 grenade launchers—a single-shot, shoulder-fired, break-action grenade launcher. Howard's supply area, located on the east side of the camp compound near the road, afforded a wide array of other specialty weapons, in addition to communications gear, canned rations, and any other items needed to conduct a mission.

The supply room was near the FOB-2 command area, including the tactical operations center (TOC) and the base helipad. If a hot action was going down, Howard would be one of the first to know, as his shack was used to help outfit both the base's smaller recon teams and FOB-2's larger exploitation group. Major Kilburn's base was authorized to house as many as sixty Green Berets, and his American SF men were almost equally split between the two groups at that point. Each 138-man "Hatchet Force" company of the exploitation group was formed by three platoons, the smaller units often called "Hornet Forces." Four Green Berets and forty-two indigenous troops made up a Hornet Force, which was commanded by an American lieutenant. In due time, Bob Howard would see action with both spike teams and Hornet Forces.

A selection of weapons carried by MACV-SOG recon men. Top row: the most desired gun, a Colt CAR-15, with a twenty-round magazine and a weapon sling. Second row: a 40mm M79 grenade launcher. Third row: an M79 ammo pouch with rounds, a 40mm tear gas round, and a high-explosive round (with a gold tip); and a sawed-off M79 with a rappelling D ring in the trigger guard. Bottom row: a Claymore mine with a connector wire and a detonator; a Browning 9mm semiautomatic pistol; and a mini grenade. Courtesy of Alan R. Wise

Recon work from FOB-2 was a little different in procedure from the long-range recon work Howard had done in 1966 with Project Omega. Project Omega B-50 was formed by 5th Special Forces Group Airborne (SFGA) to accomplish clandestine reconnaissance in hostile controlled territory—special ground operations. Recon teams inserted into Laos could communicate with their own Special Forces personnel thanks to an ingenious communications relay site that FOB-2 men had manned since mid-January 1967. Spike Team Colorado, hoping its radio signals would be clearly heard at the Dak To launch site miles away, was shocked to find that its first broadcasts were also received at their own, more distant FOB-2. Known by the radio call name of "Heavy Drop," the mountaintop site was referred to by the Green Berets as "Eagle's Nest." The name Heavy Drop would later be changed to "Leghorn."

Howard learned that men from FOB-2 had already been submitted for the nation's highest military awards for their valor, including the Medal of Honor. Two Kontum Green Berets had been written up for the Medal of Honor from the same mission on February 7, 1967. Lieutenant George "Ken" Sisler had perished during the mission, and his medal would be presented to his widow on June 27, 1968—a year and a half after his death. Sergeant First Class (SFC) Leonard Tilley, who took command of the recon team when Sisler fell mortally wounded, had his MOH recommendation downgraded to the second-highest military decoration, the Distinguished Service Cross (DSC).

Tilley was the second Kontum recon man to have earned the DSC. Sergeant First Class Morris "Mo" Worley had been written up for his in January 1967, following a mission in which Worley had been badly wounded. A third man from Howard's sixty-man recon company had earned a DSC just weeks prior, on March 29. Sergeant First Class Billy Evans had single-handedly fought off surging NVA soldiers until his recon team could be extracted from a nearby landing zone.

At the time of Howard's arrival, the bulk of the SOG missions run from his base were being sent into southern Laos. When FOB-2 had first opened in 1966, missions conducted inside Laos were dubbed "Operation Shining Brass" missions. In March 1967, Shining Brass inserts had been renamed "Prairie Fire" target operations, in hopes of confusing outsiders who had somehow learned the meaning of Shining Brass. The operational phrase "Prairie Fire" was also used by recon teams to request emergency air support and extraction when they faced overwhelming enemy assaults.

Aside from Prairie Fire missions into Laos, Kontum recon men also ran targets in North Vietnam, sometimes staging from another forward operating base. These missions were code-named "Nickel Steel" targets. The North Vietnamese Army had long moved weapons and food supplies through neighboring Cambodia, but it was not until May 1967 that General William Westmoreland convinced Washington that SOG missions should be run into Cambodia to disrupt NVA operations. Commencing in June from FOB-2, missions into Cambodia were known as "Daniel Boone" operations.

Howard learned that the spike teams running from Kontum were named after states, including Colorado, Hawaii, Iowa, Maine, Nevada, New York, Ohio, and Texas. By late spring 1967, Major Kilburn's base was also serving as host to eight B-50 recon teams of Project Omega, in which Howard had participated in the spring of 1966. The Project Omega teams running from FOB-2 were each named after tools, such as ST Auger, ST Brace, ST Hatchet, and ST Saw.

These B-50 teams helped handle the increasingly heavy load of Daniel Boone missions, which quickly became hotly contested operations. The teams penetrating Cambodia uncovered

NVA communication lines, base camps, and ammunition caches and dozens of enemy trails. One of the most fearless team leaders Howard met during the summer of 1967 was Sergeant First Class Jerry Shriver. Known in the SOG community as "Mad Dog," Shriver was the leader of ST Brace, and his team was almost constantly in heated battles with NVA forces in the toughest target areas. In his brief months at FOB-2, Shriver would earn a Silver Star, three Bronze Stars, and an Army Commendation Medal (ACM) with "Valor" device.

These eight B-50 teams would run missions from Kontum until November 1967, when the detachment was transferred to a new FOB at Ban Me Thuot. Before their departure, Bob Howard would learn a great deal from these warriors, and he even managed to substitute in with some of them when a team had a man ill or injured.

Outside of his supply shack duties, Howard regularly monitored the procedures utilized by the more effective Kontum spike teams. Running recon in denied enemy territory was known as going "across the fence" by his fellow Green Berets. Each recon team generally consisted of three Green Berets and as many as a half dozen indigenous troops, either Chinese Nungs or Montagnards. The senior American serving as team leader was code-named a "one-zero." His rank was often staff sergeant or sergeant first class, although some recon teams were occasionally commanded by a specialist fourth class (spec-4).

Rank was far less important on a spike team than experience. Any Green Beret who had been across the fence on a half dozen missions against NVA troops was respected. Those who kept their cool, accomplished the mission, and still had the stomach to go back on more missions were quickly promoted. Those unable to handle such life-threatening work could simply request a transfer. Howard soon learned that skill and bravery put men into team leadership positions, and a one-zero's rank was never questioned when across the fence in action.

The Green Beret on a spike team who served as the assistant team leader was code-named the "one-one." A third American SF man was called the "one-two." Meanwhile, for each spike team's indigenous personnel (called "indig" in slang by the Americans), the senior Nung or Yard team leader, responsible for the actions of all his indig, was code-named the zero-one and generally served as the point man. The second-most-senior indig on a team, often the team interpreter, was the zero-two, and so on.

Insertion areas in Laos were divided up on the command operations map into four-mile (or six-kilometer) grid squares and assigned a single word from the military alphabet: Alpha, Bravo, Charlie, Delta, Echo, on through Juliett. Howard was quick to learn which target grids were the most dangerous with the greatest concentrations of enemy forces. "Each team was briefed on the mission, and it was the one-zero's responsibility to work out the mission," Howard remembered. In preparation for a mission, the assigned team would go into isolation days in advance. "You couldn't take a bath," said Howard. "You couldn't brush your teeth. You didn't wear deodorant to the field." Enemy trackers, some using specially trained recon dogs, could sniff out an ill-prepared U.S. team miles away.[2]

One of the most important training scenarios that each

one-zero taught was the immediate action drill. Such worst-case maneuvers could mean life or death. Team leaders stressed the specific role of each team member should they be surprised by an enemy attack. Some practiced against opposing "enemy" teams. Others ran the maneuvers with markers designating each team member in a sandbox, not unlike a football coach scheming up special plays.

Howard found the lifestyle at FOB-2 to be more relaxed than the normal military discipline enforced on other Army bases. It was not uncommon to see Green Berets unshaven and others with longer hair styles. Teams returning from missions went on stand-down for days, allowing them to live it up at the base bar with casual dress and ample drinking. Bob quickly learned that base officers allowed a certain slack to combatants freshly returned from the stress and death of across-the-fence missions.

Sergeant Billy Greenwood was assigned to FOB-2 briefly in 1967, as he was getting Special Forces A-teams ready to go into Laos. While there, he ran into Bob Howard for the first time. Over the next three years, their paths would cross again, and Greenwood would become good friends with the new supply sergeant. He learned that Howard was a soldier's soldier. He never complained, and his disposition was almost always positive during his early months at the base. Greenwood could tell that this former infantryman was burning with desire to fight enemy forces.

Howard hadn't gone through Special Forces training to spend the whole war filling out paperwork and tackling requisitions. But he applied himself to those tasks without complaint.

"Everybody in the outfit, above and below, had the utmost respect for him," Greenwood recalled.[3]

Respect from peers was one thing. But what Robert Lewis Howard wanted more than respect was the chance to get out of the supply shack and across the fence. His wish would soon be fulfilled.

★ SIX ★

STRAPHANGER

Joe Messer was the first Green Beret to give Bob Howard a chance.

At age twenty-five, Sergeant First Class Messer was two years younger than Howard. But they had plenty in common. Messer came from a strong military family. Two of his uncles had fought in World War II, and at age seventeen, he had joined the Army Reserve and left behind the rural coal mining country of Kentucky. By 1963, Messer had completed Jump School, SF training, and his first tour in Vietnam.

During 1964 and 1965, he had served two more six-month tours of duty in Vietnam with Special Forces A-teams operating out of Okinawa. During the early years of the Vietnam War, such A-teams had rotated into the Central Highlands of South Vietnam on temporary assignments to help train irregular soldiers on how to fight the Viet Cong. Messer had returned for yet another tour and was assigned to Kontum in early 1967. He and another SFC, Tom Corbett, were assigned to head up ST Wyoming.

Howard, who preferred to maintain a clean-shaven, more traditional Army look, still struggled to wrap his head around the ways of the recon men. They wore their hair longer, rarely shaved, and refused to shower for two days prior to being inserted into enemy territory. They lived life on the edge, both in the field and during their downtime.

Joe Messer was quite the opposite of Howard. His long hair framed a dark Fu Manchu mustache, which dripped down the sides of his mouth all the way to his chin. Other SOG veterans about the base had dubbed him "Dirty Joe" due to his ragged complexion. In addition, his skin color and stature helped Messer blend right in with the indigenous Montagnards who ran with the recon teams. "I was Yard size, and had a tan as dark as a Yard," Joe recalled.[1]

Messer and Corbett had run a couple missions together previously, including one with a hot insertion on April 22. As their Sikorsky H-34 Choctaw helicopter had settled into the landing zone (LZ), enemy gunfire stitched the chopper and one of the bullets passed through Messer's leg. The wound was minor and did nothing to slow him down. Dirty Joe had since stepped into the one-zero role with ST Wyoming when his former team leader, Corbett, was assigned to oversee a construction project.

Bob Howard had been in supply for a few weeks when his chance to join Messer's team for an operation came. In mid-May 1967, Messer was preparing for a Prairie Fire mission into Laos. While he had a new one-one, SFC Gaetano "Guy" Albre-

Joe Messer (standing second from left) *in early 1967 with Montagnards of his ST Wyoming squad. Equipped with untraceable Swedish Ks and grenade launchers, they are posing before a CH-34 Kingbee chopper. Sergeant Messer was the first to take Bob Howard on a recon mission from FOB-2.* JOE MESSER

gio, Messer was still in need of an extra American to carry a radio for him.

"I'll do it," Howard offered.

As a key member of the base supply operations, Howard was not in a position to become a full-time, or regular, member of a recon team. But teams were often in need of a qualified volunteer. Recon men had a name for a substitute or volunteer Green Beret: "straphanger." When an SF man went along with a regularly organized team as its one-one (second-in-command) or one-two, he was straphanging.

Messer explained that their team would be inserted on a

recon mission along a large river that NVA forces were known to frequent due to the well-worn foot trails they left behind. The main objective was to go in, survey the trail, and report back on enemy activity. As Messer explained it to Howard, their job was to "snoop and poop, and come on back."

Mixing it up with the enemy was not top priority.

To Howard, it was still exciting. Whether he was carrying the PRC-25 team radio or heading an indigenous point squad mattered little. The thrill of being dropped into enemy territory was enough for him.

Joe Messer generally ran a "large team," meaning three American Green Berets and up to nine Yards. On missions like this river recon, a heavy force was not required, so Joe would leave behind a few of his Montagnards while maintaining three Americans.

On May 15, Howard had his first chance to operate with an MACV-SOG team. Once properly equipped with gear, ST Wyoming was flown by chopper to Dak To, an SF-manned airfield about thirty miles northwest of FOB-2. Dak To was little more than an airstrip with three buildings in a small compound surrounded by barbed wire. A staging area, or launch site, for SF operations, it was located just minutes from potential team insertion areas. From Dak To, teams were routinely transferred into landing zones within the tri-border area of Cambodia, Laos, and North Vietnam. During the first year of operation, FOB-2 special ops missions had been serviced by South Vietnamese Air Force (VNAF) pilots. Messer, Howard, and their team boarded one of the old Sikorsky Choctaw helicopters, which the Green Berets had nicknamed "Kingbees." Larger than the

U.S. Army's UH-1 "Huey" choppers, the Kingbees had older radial, nine-cylinder Wright Aeronautical Corporation "Cyclone" R-1820 engines. They were the same engines used in WWII B-17 bombers, and they were notorious for leaking hydraulic fluid.

The big Kingbee choppers were flown by VNAF pilots of the 219th Helicopter Squadron, many of whom were young, college-educated men who flew the American Green Berets in to earn extra combat pay. The pilots of the 219th were paid five hundred Vietnam piastres for every twelve hours of service away from their home station, plus a bonus of three thousand piastres (roughly twenty-five U.S. dollars) each time they crossed the border into North Vietnam.[2]

Howard had packed six extra magazines for his Swedish K submachine gun, and he had plenty of extra 9mm rounds that could be used for his Browning Hi-Power semiautomatic pistol. Like the rest of Messer's spike team, he was dressed in regular green military fatigues. The main difference this day was that he wore absolutely nothing to show that he was U.S. Army.

In recon terms, the team was going in "sterile." This meant that Howard had left behind all personal belongings, including dog tags, U.S. military patches, insignia, and even any weapons with serial numbers that could be traced to the American military. If he was killed or captured, his presence in forbidden enemy territory would simply be denied by his government. It was a risk that Bob Howard had been fully briefed on.

Spike Team Wyoming's target was several miles from Dak To, beyond the border of Laos. As their Kingbee roared low above the lush green jungle, Howard made a final check of his gear. Aside from his guns, he was also carrying a Bowie knife, a smoke grenade, fragmentation grenades, food rations, and other survival gear, including plastic water bottles that would not clink if brushed against metal. In the event a firefight separated the team in the jungle, each Green Beret was equipped with devices to help aid his own emergency extraction: a small URC-10 survival radio, a signaling mirror, a fluorescent red-and-orange reversible signal panel, a strobe light, and a pen flare.

In filling the third American slot on ST Wyoming, Howard was the one-two for this mission, or third senior Green Beret. He was also the "commo" man, meaning that he would be toting the bricklike radio, an AN/PRC-25 (or "Prick Twenty-five" in SF lingo). The radio gear, including radio and battery pack, meant humping an extra twenty-three pounds in his rucksack, plus another five pounds of spare radio batteries.

As one-zero, Joe Messer was the first to exit the chopper as it nestled onto an open LZ in the mountainous Laotian terrain. The team leader was responsible for doing reconnaissance work for his team target area prior to insert. This often meant aerial flights over the area to locate more than one acceptable LZ. These were usually areas where previous bomb damage or fires had erased enough jungle foliage and tree cover to allow a helicopter to settle in low to deposit a recon team. Less desired LZs in jungle recon were "slash and burns," or primitive agricultural areas used by mountain tribesmen where ash from burned vegetation provided nitrogen and nutrients for crops. An active slash and burn was a bad place for an LZ, as the food grown there was often taken by nearby NVA units.

As the Kingbee spiraled downward to the LZ, Howard felt

pressure in his ears due to the rapid descent. He swung his Swedish K back and forth, watching for signs of enemy activity as the first members of his team made their exits.

As the acting one-two carrying the radio, Howard was the second American to exit the chopper. He jumped down from his Kingbee into the tall grass several feet below the chopper. He did not look back as his insert "bird" lifted away. It was vital that the group quickly cleared the LZ, headed into the thick jungle, scanned for enemy opposition, and regrouped for its mission. Many SOG teams were surprised by waiting North Vietnamese soldiers at their insertion points, so immediate firefights were always threats. Recon teams unable to be landed at their primary LZ due to extreme gunfire were said to have been "shot out" of their landing zone.

"We went into a fairly rough area, terrain-wise," Messer recalled of this mission. "We didn't run into any enemy on our insert." Spike Team Wyoming's objective was to determine levels of enemy troop movements and potential NVA company locations. Messer cautioned Howard to avoid obvious footpaths that might have been booby-trapped with explosives or that might have caused them to run directly into an enemy patrol.

As Bob moved through the jungle terrain, he carefully followed the procedures that he had been taught. The team advanced for about ten minutes at a time, then paused for several minutes to listen. During each hiatus, he noted that animal and bird noises increased in volume. Howard knew that chatter was a good thing. Absence of such jungle clamor could indicate the presence of other humans who had spooked the creatures. He sometimes learned more from hearing than from seeing. When all appeared normal, Howard's team continued its cautious advance, avoiding open areas as much as possible.

During the day, SOG recon teams were assisted by a U.S. Air Force forward air controller (FAC) code-named "Covey." Operating small aircraft from forward bases in South Vietnam, Covey pilots directly supported cross-border missions and helped call in air strikes when a team was in trouble with enemy forces. Assisting each Covey pilot was an experienced recon man whose position was code-named "Covey Rider." Generally an experienced Green Beret who was a former team leader, these Covey Riders helped select LZs, looked for targets, scouted for suitable emergency extraction points, and maintained radio contact with the recon teams on the ground. Each evening and early morning, recon teams across the fence checked in with their FAC to report on the unit's condition.

Clear of the LZ, Messer's team moved quietly through the dense terrain. Shielded from any breeze and marching in thick humidity, the recon men sweated profusely. Darkness settled over the lush Laotian jungle quickly. As team leader, Messer was responsible for deciding where his men would rest until dawn. SOG men called this a "remain overnight," or RON, position. Generally, this was a spot in the densest patch of jungle where trackers would have been unable to see the hidden men unless they stepped on them. Before settling down to rest, some one-zeros had their teams place Claymore mines around their perimeters. Other team leaders had individuals stay awake for hours at a time on guard duty to prevent their teams from being overrun by NVA troops while resting. Dirty Joe Messer grouped

ST Wyoming into a tight semicircle at the RON spot in the jungle. "Nobody ever really slept," Messer recalled. "You'd rest but you had to keep from rolling around."[3]

Howard tried to sleep, but the thought of an enemy ambush hitting his team at any moment was always present. Before first light, Team Wyoming was back on the move, continuing to survey the enemy's use of the river area. Howard's regular green fatigues worked well in this terrain to help him blend in. The area was thick with jungle growth, something that Messer and other recon men called "triple canopy."

The first layer of jungle growth was vines, brush, and grass. Some of the elephant grass in open areas could be waist high on Sergeant Howard and chest high on the shorter Montagnard soldiers moving with him. The second canopy level was formed by all the small trees rising above the floor layer of jungle foliage. They created a heavy blanket that prevented most sunlight from filtering through. In the third level, towering large trees reached as high as a hundred feet above the jungle forestation. The three layers of canopy could help recon men on a mission, but they could also prove fatal in an emergency extraction.

"If we run into anybody, we'll be in a world of shit," Messer explained to Howard. "With this triple canopy, a chopper won't be able to get in low enough to pull us out." This meant that ST Wyoming would be forced to fight its way back to the same LZ where they had inserted, nearly two miles back.

The recon area had obviously been heavily used by North Vietnamese troops. The team found many foxholes dug in along the sides of trails that skirted the large river that they were following. There would be no crossing the river to check the other side, though. It was springtime in Laos, monsoon season, and heavy rains had caused the river to become swollen and angry.

Messer found the main trail to be well-defined: a dirt path four to six feet wide in places as it snaked through the dense green jungle. The NVA had obviously cleared the area, as Messer was not even aware of trackers following his team. Bob Howard was notably disappointed at the lack of enemy resistance in this area. "He seemed to always be looking for a fight," Messer recalled. "It was just his nature."

Howard even suggested following some of the trails deeper into the hills in hopes of surprising an NVA patrol. His years of infantry training had given him a natural desire to want to fight. Messer had to remind him that their job was not to initiate a fight in this triple canopy. "He wanted to mix it up," said Messer. "Howard was much more at home on a Hatchet Force team than he was on a recon team."

Kontum's Hatchet Force teams were most often sent into hot areas to directly contest enemy forces. Howard would find the opportunity to join some of these missions in due time. But for now, his first run with Joe Messer ended successfully; the team returned with intelligence about the enemy's use of a particular grid, or target area. After four days of moving through the jungle without enemy contact, ST Wyoming was safely extracted from its original LZ.

Upon return to base, SOG recon men were traditionally handed a cold welcome-home beer by their comrades, while many of their Montagnards preferred to celebrate with iced Coca-Colas. Once the team was deposited at FOB-2, Messer and Howard were pulled into the TOC for the usual debriefing. The S-2 (intelligence) team collected all valuable intelligence notes and forwarded them on to MACV-SOG headquarters in Saigon. Following their reports, most recon men showered and then hit the small base club to drink off their stress and unwind.

Messer found that Bob Howard did not want to partake in as many drinks as some of the other men. Bob did not share that he was on a different path. His own drinking and wild living had put his Army career on hold years before. He was now a married man with children back home to think about. He shared drinks with others at FOB-2 while smoking his trademark Lucky Strikes, but he chose not to overindulge at the base bar. He had survived his first full insert into Laos with an MACV-SOG team, and he had learned plenty.

Messer remembered that due to the lack of action, Bob "was probably a little disappointed coming out of that one with me." But Robert Howard would find a fight soon enough.

★ SEVEN ★

DISTINGUISHED SERVICE

Bob Howard's automatic rifle barked angrily as spent brass casings clattered onto the ground around him. With his chopper flared out over the landing zone, he carefully avoided the recon men swarming toward the extraction ship. His shots were placed against NVA soldiers racing forward to annihilate the SOG team.

Howard helped pull both Green Berets and indigenous troopers into the slick, the Hueys used for inserting recon teams, before returning to his covering fire. Following this late 1967 mission, he would be written up for the Air Medal for heroism. Although generally issued to pilots and aircrewmen who flew on combat assault missions, the Air Medal was also awarded to SOG Green Berets for heroism in support of ground troops. In such cases, the recon man was normally praised for offering fire support with an automatic rifle, a helicopter machine gun, or a grenade launcher while helping to extract a besieged team.

Howard would eventually be pinned with four Air Medals for service in Vietnam during the period from fall 1967 through December 1968. His first was issued for a late 1967 mission for which Green Beret medic Luke Nance and First Lieutenant Gary Zukav were also issued Air Medals on the same U.S. Army general orders document. Zukav and others had been sent in to offer fire support to extract a SOG team in Laos that had declared a Prairie Fire emergency near the Ho Chi Minh Trail. (Zukav, a Hatchet Force officer who returned from Vietnam in early 1968, was best known decades later as an American spiritual teacher and inspirational author.)[1]

AIR SUPPORT WAS critical for recon teams, but Howard's first love was being on the ground and across the fence in enemy territory. He had participated in only one mission as a straphanger for Joe Messer. The next man to offer Howard a chance to run recon was Sergeant First Class Robert Sprouse, a buddy of Messer's who had joined FOB-2 at the same time as Messer. Sprouse, whose radio call sign was "Squirrel," had started his recon work at Kontum straphanging with other teams. He was now the one-zero of ST Kentucky. Squirrel was only too happy to let Bob straphang with him, seeing the same desire in Howard's eyes that he himself had felt months prior.

By July 1967, FOB-2 was in a state of change. Soon after Howard arrived, the first commanding officer that he had known, Major Jerry Kilburn, was transferred to Fort Bragg. Major Frank Leach took temporary acting command until July 21, when thirty-six-year-old Major Roxie Ray Hart from Georgia arrived on the scene. Hart would command FOB-2 for the next nine months. At the time of the new CO's arrival, Kontum had a dozen permanently assigned spike teams: Arizona, Colorado, Florida, Hawaii, Illinois, Iowa, Maine, Nevada, New York, Ohio, Texas, and Wyoming. Some teams, like ST Arizona, were just forming and had not run missions. Others had been in service since the first days of the base, and they had been commanded by multiple one-zeros during that time.

The need for straphangers like Howard was constant. Hart's base was still building up to its full complement of sixty Green Berets, which was continually challenged due to personnel losses and injuries. During June and July, there were several casualties, some resulting from a midair collision between two heavily loaded South Vietnamese CH-34 helicopters returning from a cross-border mission on the Fourth of July. Six members of ST New York, including two Green Berets, were killed in that crash. Two weeks later, on July 15, the one-zero of ST Florida was killed in an NVA ambush across the fence.[2]

Howard thus found teams regularly in need of a temporary replacement, a fair excuse to leave his supply room duties behind for several days each time. By late summer of 1967, he was getting into the field on a more regular basis, either with a spike team, with one of the temporary Project Omega B-50 teams, or with a Hatchet Force operation. He did not bother keeping notes on each of his missions. The exact dates of some have been lost over time since many MACV-SOG mission records were destroyed after the Vietnam War.

Howard quickly became known as a solid, dependable, and fearless straphanger for anyone in need. Although he was not a regular at the base club during his first year at FOB-2, the Green Berets sharing drinks there heard plenty about his exploits in enemy territory. His first recon mission with Joe Messer might have been void of enemy contact, but Howard found or created plenty of action on many of his subsequent trips into Laos and Cambodia.

One of the teams that Howard volunteered to join was assigned a nineteen-day mission to explore small east-west valleys near the Laos–North Vietnam border to identify potential escape routes for downed American pilots. Howard and his team located little-known mountain passes through which U.S. aviators evading capture in North Vietnam's panhandle could escape safely into Laos. Gathering such intelligence was vital work conducted by SOG recon men, but Howard preferred to deliver devastating blows to NVA forces.[3]

Howard dreamed up one clever strike while working in his supply room. One of his military specialties was demolition, so he concocted a plan while waiting for his next straphanger opportunity. He took an old footlocker and spent hours painting it bright red. Howard's biggest challenge was convincing his Kontum intelligence officers to allow him to rig it up to be a special booby trap. Inside it, he packed about eighty pounds of aging TNT that was beginning to sweat nitro. He dual-primed the deadly locker with a pair of five-minute time-delay detonators.

As the team was airlifted into Laos the next day, Howard maintained a hand on the bright red locker to keep its contents steady. His Montagnard comrades eyed the strange box with nervous looks but said nothing. At the LZ, the first recon men swarmed out of the chopper as Howard struggled to lift the heavy box. Setting it level in the tall grass, he motioned his final Yards from the bird just before the pilot pulled away. Howard knew that NVA trackers routinely monitored the insert of Green Beret teams, and he had a special surprise in store for them.[4]

The team quickly raced into the jungle, giving the appearance of being in such haste that they had forgotten their supply locker. Howard's team circled back through the foliage and took up station nearby to watch. As expected, several North Vietnamese soldiers soon swarmed the LZ and began prying open the locker, whose time-delay detonator had been set. "That bastard blew a hole in the ground," Howard recalled. "It blew shit for a quarter of a mile. That's how much TNT we had in it."

Howard's reputation grew around the base as stories came back of his exploits across the fence. Also in 1967, his team was assigned to monitor NVA truck traffic at night along Highway 110. Several nights into the assignment, the sound of a rumbling engine soon broke the silence of the dark jungle. Howard crept up alongside the road and lay in wait. As a loaded troop truck rolled past his position, he sprang into action. He ran alongside the truck, clutching a Claymore in his hand. Howard tossed the mine into the truck full of startled NVA soldiers. At a full sprint, he disappeared back into the jungle as the time-fused Claymore exploded seconds later, destroying the vehicle.[5]

Hailing from Arkansas, Staff Sergeant Larry Melton White was about the same age as Howard, and he had arrived at Kontum in early 1967. His first missions were carrying the radio for one-zero Johnny Arvai's ST Maine and on other cross-border operations with one-zero Charles Smith of Project Omega's RT Brace. By the fall, White had assumed command of Arvai's team. His code name was "Six Pack," referring to his preference of running a smaller spike team with three Americans and three indigenous members. He soon befriended Bob Howard and allowed him to straphang with his spike team.

"I never saw him show any fear whatsoever," White recalled of Howard. He had never experienced a soldier like this supply sergeant. "He would do anything you wanted him to do. You couldn't ask for a better guy on a team." White found Howard to be subdued in peaceful situations, not one to make a lot of idle small talk around the compound.[6]

In late 1967, Howard accompanied White's team on five missions. On their first, they made no contact at all. They went in as a "pilot team" assigned to flush out local Montagnards and bring some of them back to Kontum. Upon exiting their chopper, the team ran for a nearby wood line to take cover. There White and Howard discovered many eroding wooden caskets lying on top of the ground in the forest. It seemed odd, but they pushed on in search of the NVA-sympathetic Yards reported in the area. "We spent a number of days in there but never saw a living person," White recalled. "We were going to take the entire bunch and bring them back to Kontum. We were going to deny the NVA of their use. But we guessed they had moved them out of the area."

Soon after this luckless mission, Howard accompanied Six Pack White's team on another trip across the fence. Along with three Yards and a junior man carrying the radio, they were inserted by a Huey and accompanying gunships from Dak To into Laos. All six men on the team dressed in regular green jungle fatigues with soft boonie hats. "We added black spray paint, which made it an even better-style camouflage," said White. Going into the combat zone as one-zero, he always carried a high-power Browning automatic pistol strapped to his waist for easy access, in the event he was forced to ditch his gear in a running firefight.

In Laos, his team moved quietly through the jungle in search of their enemy. During the day, White insisted that his men keep moving at all times. "We would move from daylight to dark," he said. "I didn't take breaks or sit down for lunch. That's where most of the teams got into trouble. If we really needed a rest, we'd lean up against trees for a while."

Howard and his fellow teammates simply munched on dried sardines and indigenous rations. These little bags of rice, dried peppers, and various proteins required a small amount of water poured in from the soldiers' canteens. "You'd just fill it up to the line, and then you could eat your rice as you went along through the jungle," White recalled. "You could also make a rice ball to eat, or take bites of what we called 'donkey-dick' sausage." Those who were becoming drowsy or did not wish to eat could simply pop an amphetamine tablet to keep them alert and curb their appetite.[7]

White and Howard kept their team moving near the Ho Chi Minh Trail the first two days. Unlike other teams, where the junior man carried the team radio, Six Pack White always insisted he would handle that duty. "The only way you're going to get pulled out of there is if you have a radio," he reasoned. "My other stuff was distributed amongst the team." They moved from daylight to dark. Once sunset approached, the jungle became dark very quickly. At that point, White advanced his team near the trail they were shadowing and then employed a fishhook maneuver to double back a short distance.

Settling down near the trail, he had his team stretch out to rest for the night. "We would lay toe to toe in a circle," White related. "We didn't have a guard or any of that stuff. I would get me a stick, because those Montagnards had respiratory problems. They often coughed and hacked and carried on. If someone would act up during the night, I'd hit them or tap them with that stick to get them quiet."

Shortly before daybreak, the team was on the move again. "You'd move your tail gunner back and start another day," he said. During their movement, White and Howard became aware that trail watchers had spotted their team. From time to time, they heard signal shots in the distance as a tracker tried to rally other troops.

"When you're being tracked, you really can't shake them," said White. His team simply kept tabs on where signaling sounds were coming from in order to determine which direction they should move next. "We carried silenced .22s, and sometimes we would pop a guy who was following us too close," White added. "We surprised them instead of them surprising us. You'd just take out a few of them and keep going."

The trackers began to move too close to their team, so White asked Howard to put out toe poppers to slow them down. Similar to hockey pucks in appearance, M-14 antipersonnel mines were one of many special toys utilized by Special Forces men to stop pursuing opponents. Composed largely of plastic, the small,

Bob Howard in the field wearing tiger-stripe camouflage, talking with his one-zero Larry White.

Robert L. Howard Collection, courtesy of Melissa Howard Gentsch

thick devices required only about thirty pounds of pressure to detonate enough explosives to remove a man's foot. As the pursuers gained on the team, Howard ripped off his shirt and tossed it across a bush after quickly planting a few toe poppers in front of it. Minutes later, he heard two explosions after his curious followers approached to examine the shirt. White's team was thereafter free of these trackers.[8]

During their final day across the fence, White's team finally made heavy contact with a large NVA force. A firefight ensued, and he called his Covey Rider for an extraction. Two Hueys moved in, each with four McGuire rigs hanging below them; the canopy was too thick to lower extraction ladders. Invented by Special Forces sergeant major Charles T. McGuire, the

McGuire rig was a hundred-foot rope with a six-foot loop fitted with a padded canvas seat at the end. Each Huey could drop four weighted rigs, or "strings" in recon jargon, two to each side.

As the first bird went into a hover, Howard and White had their indigenous team leader load two of his men and one American into the strings. The first Huey pulled away, leaving White, Howard, and one Yard laying down covering fire as the second bird dropped low. The three slipped into their rope seats and were soon pulled through the heavy canopy, branches slapping at their arms and faces as they were lifted clear.

Although his team had failed to grab a prisoner, as White had hoped, they had at least all been extracted without injury. He appreciated the eagerness of Bob Howard as his volunteer one-one each time they ran together. "He was the only man I'd ever seen whose pulse rate never got up," White recalled. "He was just calm, cool, and collected."

On their fifth mission together in Laos, Howard and White used Claymores with time-delay fuses to destroy a vital NVA fuel pipeline.

White would be transferred to another base in early 1968, but it was not the last time he would run recon with Staff Sergeant Howard.

In September 1967, Bob received a new boss in the S-4 division. Thirty-two-year-old Captain Eugene Crouch McCarley Jr., who hailed from Wilmington, North Carolina, became Kontum's new logistics boss. Like Howard, he was tough as nails and he already had advanced Special Forces training.

Gene McCarley had completed Officer Candidate School in August 1962 at Fort Benning, Georgia. He had commanded a wide variety of SF detachments and graduated from the Army's Special Warfare School. Despite his experience, McCarley still arrived at FOB-2 as an FNG without experience running a Prairie Fire or Daniel Boone mission. "Anybody that went to Kontum had to run one mission with a recon team," McCarley recalled.[9]

Gene's first trip across the fence was with SFC Don Steele's ST Florida. His one-zero was wounded during that insert, and Captain McCarley was tapped to take over Florida when the team's other Green Beret was deemed to be suffering from combat fatigue. Gene had no fear of taking on the toughest assignments. "I always ran with a small team, so it was usually just myself and one American and three or four indig," he remembered. "I was crazy as hell."

He found his supply sergeant to be equally bold in any situation. One day, Howard and his new captain checked out a deuce-and-a-half truck to secure supplies from nearby Kontum City. As they crossed a small stream, the makeshift bridge they were using partially collapsed, preventing them from returning. As McCarley and Howard surveyed the situation, potshots rang out from nearby.

A pair of Viet Cong soldiers had advanced and they were firing on the Green Berets with single-shot rifles. It was McCarley and Howard's first firefight together—but it was never even a contest. Both men were expert shots and they were heavily armed. In less than a minute, they downed both opponents.[10]

After that moment, McCarley occasionally used Howard when he needed a straphanger for ST Florida. Neither man was wounded on their late 1967 missions, and they developed a deep trust in and friendship with each other. "Howard just loved combat," Gene recalled. "He was tough, and he just loved to fight the enemy. He was one hell of a man."

Captain McCarley would later, in early 1968, be assigned to take command of Company B of FOB-2's Hatchet Force, which soon became officially known as the "Exploitation Force." "Politicians didn't like the word 'Hatchet,'" McCarley remembered. "It sounded too sinister. We changed names at the FOB so many times, but the mission never changed." During his time with the Exploitation Force, McCarley would call on Howard to join his company when he needed an extra man he could depend on.

Sergeant First Class Johnnie Gilreath Jr. was another one-zero who was more than happy to let Bob Howard straphang with his team. A youthful-looking twenty-four-year-old Tennessean with dark hair and a thin mustache, Gilreath was fearless in the field. He had arrived in Kontum in April 1967 from the 10th Special Forces Group in Germany, along with Sergeant Larry David Williams. With a year of Vietnam service under his belt already, Gilreath ran a few missions with ST Colorado, one of Kontum's original teams.

By August 1967, Johnnie had taken over Colorado after his one-zero, SFC Jerry "Pinky" Lee, received new orders. Larry Williams, whose SOG code name was "After Shave," became Gilreath's one-one. He carried the PRC-25 radio on at least eight missions that their team ran across the fence, and on in-country patrols. In September 1967, they pulled Bob Howard in to strap for their team for a mission into Laos, where they managed to break contact with an enemy force and be safely extracted.[11]

Howard's toughest mission with Spike Team Colorado came in November 1967. Johnnie Gilreath's team had orders to insert into southeast Laos for a wiretap operation to gather intelligence on NVA operations. Their target area was H-9, or Hotel 9. SOG command used alphanumeric designations to divide up the maps of Laos and Cambodia into six-kilometer-by-six-kilometer target boxes. Target areas approved by both the White House and SOG headquarters in Saigon were then relayed to the forward operating base's S-3 (operations) shop. Together with their S-2 (intelligence) officers, the S-3 team would select a team for each mission and prepare briefing materials for the chosen one-zero.[12]

During their early months of running recon, FOB-2 men were always flown into enemy territory in CH-34 Kingbee choppers operated by the South Vietnamese Air Force's 219th Helicopter Squadron. But as ST Colorado reviewed their mission plan on November 18, Gilreath announced that they would be inserted by American pilots this time.

In October, the 57th Assault Helicopter Company (AHC) began setting up camp near FOB-2 at the new Kontum Army Airfield. They had two platoons of UH-1H model Huey helicopters and eight UH-1C Huey gunships. The slicks were lightly armed, while the more heavily armed gunship division 1C choppers went by the call name "Cougars." The 57th pilots nicknamed their slicks "Gladiators," and used radio call signs such as "Gladiator 167."[13]

On the morning of November 19, Gilreath, Williams, and their Yards were inserted into Hotel 9. Low on water after two days in denied territory, ST Colorado consulted its maps and moved toward a stream located in their area. Gilreath and his men assumed position on a hill while Williams took a Montagnard down the hill to stock up on water. While doing so, Williams noticed massive bags of rice stacked by the hundreds along with large quantities of ammunition. Upon reporting this find of NVA supplies to Gilreath, the team relayed a message back to base via their circling Covey Rider.

Major Hart ordered a Hatchet Team platoon to be flown into the area immediately to destroy the enemy supply dump. This Exploitation Force would have its hands full with the NVA goods, so Bob Howard volunteered to lead a small recon team in as well. He would guide the Hatchet men to the dump area and then scout for approaching NVA to prevent any loss of men while the supplies were destroyed.[14]

Howard's recon unit and the large Hatchet Force platoon were flown in by 57th AHC slicks. On the ground, one-one Larry Williams helped prepare a large LZ by using a Claymore to blow down a tree. He then took one of his Yards down to inspect the NVA rice cache. Gilreath and the remainder of ST Colorado remained in their hillside position as the Kontum Hueys began settling down on the oversized landing zone.

His rucksack loaded with provisions and weapons, Howard was ready to leap off the chopper. Clutching his M16, he anxiously pressed his boots on the skids, watching the waving grass below as his Huey flared out. A short distance away, Williams tripped an ambush as the Hatchet Force men began pouring out of their UH-1Hs. He and his Yard ran up on an NVA soldier near the stockpile and exchanged fire with him.

The instant Williams and his Montagnard teammate commenced shooting, the calm jungle all around the LZ erupted into violent explosions of small-arms and machine-gun fire. "All hell broke loose," recalled Williams. "We had stirred up a hornet's nest!"[15]

Unseen machine-gun nests unleashed volleys of bullets into the choppers. The last of the Hatchet Force men raced for nearby cover. By the time the slicks cleared the LZ, three had been badly shot up by ground fire. Howard and his men now had a hot mission—and they needed to take out enemy resistance. Howard swiftly guided the Kontum platoon around the dangerous ambush zone and made contact with one-zero Gilreath's team. The group had gone in with a new first lieutenant as a straphanger, an officer who had hoped to earn his Combat Infantryman Badge.

Gilreath left this officer in charge of some of his Yards. He pushed forward with Williams, Howard, and the small security element that Howard had brought in. The Hatchet Force Green Berets and their Montagnards quickly set to work, slashing open the hundreds of bags of rice and salt and setting fire to the NVA goods. But this process would take some time, due to the enormous stockpile in front of them. Howard would have to keep the NVA men at bay if the mission was to succeed.

Spike Team Colorado and the Kontum Exploitation Force faced heavier enemy opposition than they had expected. The firefight Williams had triggered during the relief team's insert soon brought plenty more action. Enemy gunners moved in close enough to man machine-gun bunkers near the bivouac area that the American recon forces were in the process of destroying. Bob Howard, leading a small group of Yards in search of the enemy gun nests, suddenly encountered four North Vietnamese soldiers charging toward him.

With a single magazine, Howard gunned down all four NVA with his M16. No sooner had he eliminated this threat than his team faced an even greater challenge. A short distance away, a camouflaged machine-gun bunker roared to life. Howard, Gilreath, Williams, and others hit the deck and tried to take cover. Bullets pierced the ground all around them. Although Williams and others had their jackets ripped by slugs, none of them were directly hit.[16]

In the meantime, the Hatchet Force men continued to destroy the NVA battalion's food cache. During this work, they uncovered a thousand rounds of recoilless rifle ammunition and seven hundred rounds of AK-47 ammunition. The Kontum men utilized mortars to detonate all of this ammunition, but the massive volumes of explosions only further riled up the nearby NVA. Enemy soldiers raced forward to man other pillboxes in the vicinity. Their growing volume of firepower would play hell on Howard and his comrades.

One-zero Gilreath was still learning just how brave Robert Howard was. "He ran *toward* the enemy at all times," he later related. Machine-gun bullets continued to stitch the ground all about the small team of Green Berets and Montagnards. Oblivious to his own safety, Howard began crawling forward toward the machine-gun bunker. In the process, he became aware of a lone North Vietnamese soldier firing shots at him with a rifle.

Taking careful aim, Howard put a lethal round into the sniper, then resumed his crawling toward the bunker. Steeling his nerve, Bob stood and charged. Racing to point-blank range, he used his automatic weapon to mow down all the gunners within the nest. Before he could retreat, NVA manning another nest nearby opened fire on him.

Howard hit the jungle floor and crawled quickly for cover. Sergeant Williams stood and opened fire on the second pillbox, providing cover for Howard's retreat. His barrage suppressed fire from the nest long enough for Howard to reach safety and pull his men to a covered position. Bob then opened up on the radio, calling to the Covey Rider circling above the action. Air strikes were called in to destroy this bunker.

Sergeant First Class Bob Howard with Sergeant Larry Williams (right) *of Spike Team Colorado. Howard accompanied Williams and ST Colorado as a straphanger on multiple missions in late 1967.* Jason Hardy

The NVA machine-gun nest fell silent as the aircraft pulled clear of the area. Howard inched forward to assess the bomb damage. Some of the NVA had either survived or had been quickly replaced by other soldiers. The machine gun came to life again, firing bursts of bullets at Howard. Bullets and frags from explosions began to take a toll on Howard's body. His right clavicle was fractured by shrapnel, and minutes later another fragment or bullet ripped through his right cheek.[17]

Howard cheated death once again when he was hit in the face by a bullet for the second time in three years. Like his 1965 facial wound, this bullet was another ricochet that struck him in the head above his left eye. The bullet failed to penetrate his skull, but the concussion knocked him to the ground, rendering him briefly unconscious.[18]

Howard was in an unenviable position as he regained his senses. He was pinned to the ground as bullets sprayed out just six inches above his head. His shoulder was separated, and blood gushed from his face. But he was far from giving up. He knew his life and those of others nearby were on the line if the enemy bunker could not be knocked out. Howard removed a fragmentation grenade from his gear, pulled the pin, and tossed the grenade into the aperture of the emplacement.

A brilliant orange burst of flame erupted in the pillbox, and the explosion killed the remaining enemy gunners. With the bunker silenced once more, Howard dashed across the clearing to where his comrades were taking cover. Within minutes, fresh NVA troops manned the machine-gun nest and pinned down the SOG men.

This time Howard grabbed an anti-tank rocket launcher

from one of the Yard grenadiers. A withering hail of bullets poured from the nest.

"Cover me!" Howard shouted.

Larry Williams opened fire with his automatic weapon as Howard rose to his feet and moved forward. Machine-gun bullets swept the area, but the NVA gunners were obviously frightened. Their aim was off. Howard carefully put the launcher against his left shoulder and took aim. He fired from close range and winced as the recoil jarred his broken clavicle. The rocket screamed into the bunker and exploded, tossing shrapnel, jungle foliage, and body parts in all directions. Howard's one-man assaults, covered well by Williams and others, had eliminated two machine-gun teams in a matter of minutes.

The SOG force was now able to ease back in. As they moved up a road toward the NVA cache area, more machine-gun nests opened fire on them. Williams fired grenades at an enemy bunker, then stood to charge. He fired his M16 as he ran, wiping out the entire gun crew on his own.

Along with Howard and Gilreath, Williams continued to assault any NVA that threatened their movements. Gilreath soon deemed the area too hot to handle. Ample numbers of North Vietnamese from the battalion remained, and their return fire increased. By this point, the Hatchet Force had succeeded in destroying all of the enemy's ammo pile and a good portion of the food cache.

Gilreath radioed in extraction choppers and began moving the large force back through the jungle hundreds of yards toward their original LZ. One by one, Huey slicks dropped in to begin pulling out the dozens of Montagnards and Americans.

By the time the last chopper lifted free, the entire Kontum force was safely extracted, with only Staff Sergeant Howard wounded. Heavy air strikes were called in to plaster the NVA platoon and any surviving supplies.

Howard's wounds were not life-threatening, and he was quickly patched up by Army medics. Although it was the second time he had been wounded in the Vietnam War, November 21, 1967, would mark the first date on which he was officially written up for a Purple Heart for his injuries. For his heroism in the assault on the NVA platoon, Larry Williams would later be pinned with a Silver Star.

Soon after the FOB-2 men were returned to their base, one-zero Johnnie Gilreath and Howard received a summons. Chief SOG Jack Singlaub had them flown to Saigon on a C-130 Blackbird to brief his boss, General William Westmoreland, who was clearly impressed with the SOG mission. Gilreath and Howard detailed their individual actions and those of their accompanying Hatchet Force. The four-star general paused, then asked if there was anything he could do for them.

"Sir, I'd like to go to flight school and become an aviator," said Gilreath.[19]

Westmoreland promised the ST Colorado team leader a commission and the chance to enter flight training. Gilreath was the second one-zero from FOB-2 to receive a battlefield commission to become an officer. The first had been Dick Meadows, whose recon team had captured a number of enemy prisoners during the early months of Kontum's history. Weeks after the meeting with Westmoreland, Gilreath was sent to Command and Control North (CCN) in Da Nang for a special mission on December 10. Operating with the 1st Cavalry Division in the A Shau Valley, Second Lieutenant Gilreath earned a Bronze Star for this mission before returning to FOB-2 to command a Hatchet Force platoon. He would eventually retire as a lieutenant colonel after nearly twenty-eight years of military service.[20]

As for himself, Bob Howard merely asked that he be allowed to continue active combat duty from Kontum. Westmoreland and Singlaub were only too happy to oblige their eager Green Beret. His base commander, Major Hart, had Howard written up for the Medal of Honor for his selfless assaults against the NVA machine-gun nests on November 21. In the end, the paperwork stalled out, and the FOB-2 supply sergeant was instead issued the nation's second-highest award for valor, the Distinguished Service Cross.

Such awards were generally not swift in being processed. In Howard's case, his DSC was not formalized until May 2, 1968, nearly six months after the action. It cited his "extraordinary heroism" while being subjected to "a withering hail of bullets." It further praised his "fearless and determined action in close combat" while allowing his patrol to destroy the enemy cache.[21]

Staff Sergeant Howard was little concerned with what medal was eventually pinned to his chest. His tour of duty in Vietnam was far from over, and it would not be the last time his superiors considered him worthy enough to be written up for the Medal of Honor.

★ EIGHT ★

PURPLE HEARTS

Bob Howard returned to his supply sergeant duties at FOB-2, allowing his wounds sustained in the late November mission a few days to recover. As team leaders dropped in to check out various weapons and gear for their next mission, he spent time learning as much as he could from them on their techniques.

Among the one-zeros he greatly respected was Fred Zabitosky, a twenty-five-year-old staff sergeant who had gone through Special Forces training four years earlier. Like Howard, his early family life had been tough, and he had dropped out of high school. But Fred found his calling in the U.S. Army. When he reached Kontum in September 1967, he was already on his third tour of duty in Vietnam. Zabitosky, known as "Zab" to his buddies, had quickly moved up into the one-zero role with ST Maine. In early November, his spike team was narrowly pulled out on McGuire rigs from target area India 9 in Laos after a bloody firefight in which three of his Yards had been wounded.[1]

Howard particularly respected Zab's desire never to leave a fellow Green Beret behind. On November 27, Zabitosky's ST Maine was called upon to perform a Bright Light mission, a special insert made to retrieve either the bodies or any surviving members of a team that had been overrun by the enemy. In this case, Master Sergeant Samuel Theriault's platoon had fought a nasty gun battle with Viet Cong forces. Before he succumbed to his own wounds, Theriault had directed his team's firefight with great valor, earning the Distinguished Service Cross.

Zab's team was inserted to retrieve the bodies of three Green Berets and three of the indigenous members of Theriault's team. Using three of the bodies as bait, VC forces lured Zab's Bright Light team into a hellacious ambush. Despite a twenty-minute fight against superior forces, ST Maine managed to recover all of their comrades' bodies without loss to their own team. The example shown by Zab's team in risking all to retrieve fallen soldiers was one that would not be forgotten by Howard.

By the second week of December, Bob was feeling well enough to run another mission. His facial wounds had no effect on his mobility, and his broken clavicle was more of a nuisance than something that was going to keep him grounded in a supply room.

Spike Team Colorado's one-zero, Johnnie Gilreath, had been temporarily shipped over to CCN in Da Nang to run a special mission. In his place, former one-one Larry Williams had assumed command of the recon team. When base command handed out his next target assignment, Williams was not at all surprised that Howard offered to strap with him.

The target grid was a familiar one: Hotel 9. SOG command wanted a team to go in and conduct a reconnaissance mission near the NVA battalion headquarters and supply area that Howard and Williams had assaulted less than three weeks prior. They expected enemy encounters, and they prepared for the worst.

Spike Team Colorado had added another Green Beret, Staff Sergeant Paul Poole, to handle the one-one position for one-zero Williams. While the twenty-five-year-old from Horatio, Arkansas, was relatively new to Kontum, he appeared solid. But Williams wanted the added security of Bob Howard along as a third Green Beret to help manage their Yards. He knew this ground and how hot their reception might be.

On the morning of December 7, the anniversary of the Pearl Harbor attack that had pulled America into World War II, slicks from the 57th Assault Helicopter Company dropped the team at an LZ in Hotel 9. Williams kept his team on a steady pace on the first day through rugged mountainous terrain. On December 8, they spotted a dozen NVA troops and engaged them in a firefight. Williams had Poole contact their Covey Rider to call in air strikes to help blast back their opponents. During the ensuing bomb explosions and gunfire, Bob Howard was hit.

A bullet pierced his right shoulder. Another bullet or a chunk of shrapnel ripped his left forearm open. Although painful, neither wound was considered severe enough by Howard to warrant his extraction. He would simply not be the cause of ending a mission if his body felt strong enough to endure. He was later written up for his second official Purple Heart. Efforts by one-zero Williams to call for medical help were refused. Once the firefight was subdued, Howard simply allowed his fellow Green Berets to patch up his lacerations so the mission could continue.[2]

The air strikes killed enough NVA that the remaining troops scattered into the jungle. Spike Team Colorado pushed forward for another two days. They covered plenty of ground in their long-range reconnaissance, and they carefully chose RON locations each night. On the morning of December 10, they finally located another significant NVA staging area. It was a battalion-sized camp from which more than five hundred North Vietnamese soldiers operated. Williams counted at least twenty-one bamboo structures and an estimated twenty tons of stockpiled rice. It was beginning to feel like November 21 all over again.

Williams again contacted his Covey Rider to bring in air strikes. His team took cover from a vantage point with a good view of the camp. Fighter planes and bombers soon moved in and began raining devastation down on the NVA base. The ground rumbled with explosions, and black smoke drifted up above the jungle canopy. Based on the number of men seen scurrying about the area, Williams decided his recon men had discovered not one but two NVA battalions.

His ten men had unwittingly stumbled onto a major bivouac area containing upward of a thousand opponents.

Spike Team Colorado waited until their air support had finished before easing forward to conduct a bomb-damage assessment (BDA). Howard quickly noticed that some of the bamboo huts and cache points remained intact.

He led several Montagnards in slashing and burning rice bags and in pillaging through the huts in search of ammunition and other supplies. During the next half hour, Howard and his men destroyed a ton of medical supplies and tons of rice bags, in addition to burning down the remnant bamboo structures. They used Claymores to explode thousands of pounds of ammunition and NVA weapons they also uncovered. One-zero Williams then ordered his team to clear the area before the North Vietnamese decided that it was safe enough to assault them.

They had moved only a short distance before they found themselves facing a perilously steep ridgeline. Spike Team Colorado paused, allowing Howard and the point men to recon the immediate vicinity for a more suitable path to use to bypass the jagged bluffs. But the men had been tracked. Moments later, a heavy NVA assault opened up on them. Machine-gun bullets shredded nearby greenery, and mortar rounds began erupting around the team.

As the NVA massed forward in a human-wave assault, several of the Yards became spooked and lost their composure. Howard moved about, angrily shouting to rally his indig to assume proper defensive positions to help fight off the surging North Vietnamese soldiers. They fired back heavily, mowing down opponents with bursts of their automatic weapons. Larry Williams grabbed the radio from Paul Poole and made a Prairie Fire emergency call.

His ten men hunkered down as A-1 Skyraiders and Huey gunships tore up the enemy's position. Howard estimated that they had run afoul of somewhere between thirty and fifty opponents. He and his men continued to fire back at any NVA brave enough to advance among the air strikes. At the same time, team leader Williams directed inbound choppers toward a suitable landing zone. He and Poole began moving their seven Yards toward the extraction point, leaving Howard behind to cover their retreat with heavy defensive fire.

Conspicuously exposed at times, Howard bravely held off the surviving NVA as the first chopper pulled out Poole and several Yards. In short order, a second bird hovered low, allowing the remainder of the team to scramble on board. Williams finally ordered Howard onto the Huey, and because he was the one-zero, his boots were the last to jump into the hovering slick. Aside from Howard's bullet and shrapnel wounds from two days prior, the team was extracted without further injury. For the second time in three weeks, they had created major devastation at an important NVA outpost, resulting in the destruction of thousands of tons of ammunition and supplies and large numbers of enemy soldiers.

Howard would later be written up for the Bronze Star Medal for valor, added to his second Purple Heart.

By YEAR'S END 1967, Colonel Jack Singlaub had authorized additional forward operating bases in South Vietnam to help support the growing number of Operation Daniel Boone missions into Cambodia, as well as the ongoing Prairie Fire missions into

Laos. FOB-4 opened for business in November on the beach at Da Nang, adjacent to Marble Mountain. Two other forward recon bases—FOB-5 at Ban Me Thuot and FOB-6 at Ho Ngoc Tao—were soon housing SF troops for missions.

MACV-SOG brass estimated by the end of December that the North Vietnamese were reducing the amount of supplies and the number of personnel on the Ho Chi Minh Trail. The use of mechanized equipment was increasing as the NVA prepared for a major offensive in early 1968 that would become known as the Tet Offensive. Singlaub's staff later estimated that some forty-four thousand NVA troops had been infiltrated through the trail system between October 1967 and January 1968 to take part in Tet.[3]

SOG intelligence also showed that their NVA opposition was getting wise to their covert operations, which had played hell with some battalions. Special counter-recon units had been created to specifically address the American spike teams. Sergeant First Class Paul Villarosa's ST Python, based out of the new FOB-4, was overpowered by one such NVA specialist team on January 4, 1968. One Green Beret escaped through the jungle, but the balance of the team was captured alive. Python's young one-two was allowed to survive to witness the horror that followed. The Vietnamese counter-recon team slit one-zero Villarosa's belly open, inserted a flamethrower, and burned him alive. The team's Montagnards were then incinerated, one by one, as the lone American was made to watch.[4]

The Green Beret was allowed to escape, radio for help, and be extracted. From Kontum, Fred Zabitosky's ST Maine was called in to perform the Bright Light recovery mission. Shot out of their LZ that afternoon, they returned the next day from Dak To. Zab's team, including Sergeant Bill Boyle, recovered the SOG team's bodies despite heavy enemy resistance. Boyle and Zab, both friends of Bob Howard, related the gruesome details of their mission to him soon after their return. He could scarcely think at the time that he might one day run a mission in which he would face being burned alive by a Vietnamese flamethrower.

In January, Howard continued his supply sergeant duties and managed to slip out as a straphanger when he could. During these trips across the fence, he did not suffer any additional wounds or get into any deadly firefights, but others from his base did. On January 21, Master Sergeant Steve Comerford became the fifth FOB-2 man to have paperwork submitted for the Distinguished Service Cross. He and two other Green Berets of his Hatchet Force platoon had been seriously wounded in a lengthy battle with an NVA force of about two companies.

By January 31, the date celebrated as Vietnamese New Year, the Tet Offensive raged throughout South Vietnam. More than 80,000 Communist troops began assaults against military and civilian command and control centers throughout the country. Among the bases attacked was Kontum's FOB-2, which endured a rocket attack and sniper fire. Communist forces would take control of several cities during the lengthy campaign, during which more than 9,500 U.S. and South Vietnamese soldiers were killed, another 1,500 went missing, and more than 35,000 were wounded. In return, an estimated 17,000 NVA were killed and another 20,000 were wounded during the Tet Offensive.[5]

Bob Howard wasn't present at the base to participate in the

skirmishes that some of his comrades fought against NVA riflemen on the night of January 31. Once again, he had volunteered to straphang with his buddies of ST Colorado as their acting one-one. In company with one-zero Larry Williams, one-two Paul Poole, and their Montagnards, Howard had been flown into a very familiar Laos target area, Hotel 9. Team Colorado had drawn a long-range reconnaissance mission to help determine if the North Vietnamese were grouping for a massive thrust into the Central Highlands or Dak To.

Williams and his team operated for several days without incident. On their final day within Hotel 9, the team was shadowed by trackers. As ST Colorado advanced along their recon route, they were suddenly assaulted by a large force of NVA soldiers and pinned down by heavy automatic weapons fire. Staff Sergeant Howard was on the move almost instantly.

He crawled about the team's position, carefully placing his Yards into effective firing positions. In that process, he continually exposed himself to enemy gunfire. Howard returned their fire, killing some of his opponents as he moved about. Commo man Poole used his radio to alert his Covey Rider of their Prairie Fire emergency. From Dak To, slicks from the 57th AHC were soon on their way, but their arrival could not be quick enough.

Howard and Poole continued to lay down covering fire as Williams directed his team to move toward the relative safety of a nearby large bomb crater in the jungle. In between firing back at the NVA troops, they surveyed the area for advantageous positions that could be used for air strike reference. When the air cover finally arrived, Howard was still moving about the crater, picking off opponents as the opportunities presented themselves. Poole coolly eased about the perimeter, calling in bombing runs and strafing attacks from the aircraft above against specific target zones.

The team's collective efforts paid off. The air strikes subdued the NVA sufficiently to allow Hueys to swoop in and collect the entire team uninjured. They could have just as easily been eliminated had it not been for swift thinking and steady fighting to ward off the surging enemy soldiers. For the heroic actions displayed in saving their team on February 1, Howard and Poole would each be submitted for the Army Commendation Medal for Valor.

UPON RETURNING FROM this mission, Larry Williams began training to serve as a Covey Rider. Other former team leaders operating from Cessna O-1 Bird Dog planes had helped save his life. Williams found it only fitting that he was able to return the favor during the next several months for his fellow FOB-2 recon teams that were in trouble.

The morning of February 19 proved to be so hot that every Bird Dog, strike plane, and Huey team in the area would be called into service to save three of SOG's teams. They had been inserted into a particularly intense operation area on the Dak Xou River in Laos known as "the Bra." Double bends of the river that resembled a woman's brassiere from the air were skirted by Highway 110, which snaked through the Central Highlands of South Vietnam near Cambodia's northern half.

This road split northeastward from the Ho Chi Minh Trail's major north-south route, Highway 96, at one of the bends of the Bra. Heavily defended by the NVA, this area contained some of FOB-2's deadliest target areas—Hotel 9, India 9, Juliett 9, November 9, and Quebec 1.[6]

Staff Sergeant Howard, on duty in the Kontum compound, listened as chaos played out over the radio in the tactical operation center. His buddy Joe Messer, the first one-zero to take Howard across the fence in May 1967, was among those in trouble. Inserted near the radio relay station known as Heavy Drop, Messer's ST Wyoming came under enemy assault right away. A pair of H-34s soon pulled out his men, but Messer was left alone on the ground for desperate minutes until another chase ship, a lightly crewed chopper that hung back to hastily extract men in peril, could be directed in to get him. North Vietnamese troops were surging toward his ridgeline by the time Messer was finally extracted. Howard was greatly relieved to hear that his comrade was safely en route back to the Dak To staging area.

But two other Kontum teams, Spike Teams Maine and Florida, were still heavily engaged with NVA forces. Fred Zabitosky had already handed command of his team over to his former one-one, Staff Sergeant Doug Glover, another good friend of Howard's. The night before the mission, Glover had told Zabitosky that he'd had a dream that he would be killed. Zab reassured his comrade that things would be all right, and he offered to go in on February 19 as his assistant team leader just to prove it.[7]

Soon after being inserted by choppers into the Bra region, ST Maine was taken under fire by NVA forces. Zab then accepted Glover's offer to take control of the team for the duration of the mission. Using Claymore mines, grenades, and his CAR-15, Zabitosky fought off surging NVA forces racing through the bamboo to get to his team. He called in air strikes and remained in the rear, fighting the enemy, while he sent Glover and the balance of ST Maine racing for an LZ. There the team was told that they would have to hold their ground for a while. All available slicks were in the process of extracting Messer's ST Wyoming and ST Florida. When slicks from the 57th AHC finally arrived, Zab sent his one-two and three of his Nungs out on the first bird.

Zabitosky, Glover, and their remaining indig fought off multiple NVA charges near the LZ as they waited for the next extraction chopper. A fifth enemy assault commenced as First Lieutenant Rick Griffith settled his UH-1 Gladiator chopper down on the short elephant grass in the LZ's center. Zab and the chopper's door gunners mowed down NVA soldiers as they swarmed toward the chopper. Once the remainder of ST Maine was on board, Griffith lifted off.

His Huey made it only seventy-five feet into the sky before it was slammed by a North Vietnamese RPG. The force of the rocket explosion blew Zabitosky out of the open door and clear of the UH-1. The blazing helicopter slammed into the ground twenty feet from Zab. Blazing fuel and exploding ammunition added to the chaos. The impact crushed vertebrae in Zabitosky's back, broke his ribs, ripped his body with shrapnel, and splashed fuel caused his fatigues to burst into flames. Inside the downed Gladiator chopper, eight men were still alive, all badly injured and being cooked by the inferno.

The screams of his comrades were too much to bear. Zabitosky rushed to the burning chopper, extracting both pilot Griffith and his copilot, Warrant Officer John Cook. By the time he raced back to the UH-1 for the third time, there was nothing to do. Doug Glover and five other men had died from their wounds and the horrific fire. Turning his attention to saving the two downed airmen, Zabitosky fired at approaching NVA and threw grenades.

Back at FOB-2, Bob Howard and others listened in shock as the horrible drama played out over the radio. He and some other men, like Hatchet Force captain Gene McCarley, volunteered to go in and join the fight. Long before they could be mobilized, a third Gladiator slick settled onto the LZ. Its crewmen helped Zab shoot down surging NVA as he worked to get his rescue pilots into the UH-1. Pilot Rick Griffith would survive his wounds, but Cook perished that day. Fred Zabitosky collapsed on the floor of the Huey as it pulled clear.

His body was horribly burned, his back was broken, some of his ribs were shattered, and he was bloodied from numerous shrapnel hits. Zabitosky would spend six weeks recovering in hospitals before he defiantly returned to FOB-2 to continue his tour of duty. The brave Green Beret was written up for the Medal of Honor, the second man from Kontum's small recon company to be recognized in little more than one year's time.

Supply Sergeant Howard kept busy during March 1968, writing up requisitions and outfitting teams that were scheduled to run recon missions. By this time, FOB-2's recon company had expanded to its largest size. Sixteen spike teams, each named after a state, were in various stages of running missions, training, or re-forming: Arizona, Arkansas, California, Colorado, Delaware, Florida, Hawaii, Illinois, Iowa, Kentucky, Maine, Nevada, New York, Ohio, Texas, and Wyoming. During that time, SOG brass revamped the naming system for spike teams, and they became known from that point forward as "recon teams."

Old-timers like Howard would alternately refer to the teams as either spike teams (STs) or recon teams (RTs). Either way, their deadly work remained the same. In March, a number of new Green Berets reported for duty at Major Roxie Hart's forward operating base. Personnel losses on the teams made it fairly easy for the new guys to begin working their way onto the recon teams.

Howard did not record the exact dates of some of his spring 1968 trips across the fence, but he later offered details of two of his Daniel Boone missions. For one of his Cambodian inserts, the team with which he was straphanging had orders to seek out information on a large artillery piece that had been spotted by other forces. Howard's team was called on to perform wiretap operations on enemy communication lines to confirm what units were operating the artillery piece. They learned that the heavy gun was moved on a rail system. Before returning to base with this intel, Howard pulled a stunt that left base commander Major Hart scratching his head.[8]

The team was moving through Cambodia overnight to locate an acceptable extraction area. At one point, they silently slipped through a large cemetery near a Cambodian village. Howard was easing through a tiny monastery in the cemetery when he bumped right into a large brass bell in the darkness. Although it was extremely heavy, he worked with another team member to lug it back for extraction. "I brought it back just to prove that I'd got it out of a pagoda in a cemetery in Cambodia," he said. "Politically, it had to go to our command authority."[9]

Back at FOB-2, Howard's team reported on their artillery-piece wiretap intelligence. Once the tapes were reviewed, MACV command sent orders for the team to return to Cambodia to destroy it. Howard and his comrades were inserted for a jungle reconnaissance mission on which they discovered and cautiously traced a rail system that led them to a cave entrance up in the hills. "They would pull it [the artillery piece] out of the cave, fire it at certain times, and then pull it back inside," said Howard. His team crept to within point-blank range of the cavern before using heavy explosives to destroy the rails and the artillery piece's hiding spot.

In late March, Howard made another mission as assistant team leader for RT Colorado. He had pulled so many missions with the team, he was almost a regular member by this point. With former one-zero Larry Williams now operating as a Covey Rider from Kontum, SSG Paul Poole had taken command of Colorado. Their new one-two was Specialist Fifth Class Charles Dunlap, who was tasked with carrying the team radio.

After four days of moving without contact, on March 30 Poole's small team came upon a trail that showed signs of heavy use. As RT Colorado investigated the surrounding area, Howard suddenly observed five NVA soldiers advancing in their direction. He and Poole hastily moved into an ambush position.

When the enemy soldiers were within ten yards, Specialist Dunlap opened fire to initiate the ambush.[10]

Howard, Poole, Dunlap, and their Yards blazed away with deadly accuracy. The NVA fought back, but in short order the team had annihilated the North Vietnamese soldiers without any injury to themselves. Recon Team Colorado moved forward to check the enemy bodies and equipment for any valuable intelligence before clearing out of the area quickly. Poole had the men climb a nearby hill to form a defensive perimeter, as other forces could be heard moving nearby.

A short time later, a much larger NVA force took the team under fire. Commo man Dunlap used his PRC-25 radio to establish contact with the nearby radio relay site. In between firing his CAR-15, he requested an immediate extract, a Prairie Fire emergency. During that time, one-zero Poole braved enemy fire to ease forward and plant a Claymore mine in the path of the aggressors, should they choose to storm the hill. Poole was shot through the hand in the process, but he still managed to plant the mine. He waited until advancing soldiers were almost on his position before he detonated it. The NVA were forced to pull back and seek cover, but Poole estimated that the explosion had killed eight of them.[11]

Howard directed the actions of his Montagnards and maintained heavy fire on any troops who dared to advance. Dunlap's radio calls soon secured a Covey Rider and air support. Dunlap eased about the perimeter, calmly directing in air strikes with deadly accuracy.

Team leader Poole was shot a second time during the firefight as automatic fire and rifle grenades rained down on his recon team. At one point, a rifle grenade landed between two of his team members. Poole bravely pushed them away from it, and only had his life spared when the device failed to explode. During the enemy attack, Bob Howard suffered his own injuries. Shrapnel from North Vietnamese RPGs ripped through the men, and Howard was wounded in one ear and in the back of his neck.[12]

The team's rifle fire, and M79 grenades fired by Poole, added devastation to the hell being handed to the NVA by the aerial fighters and gunships. When the NVA appeared to be effectively suppressed, Dunlap called in the waiting Hueys for a hasty extract. Poole continued to work his grenade launcher as the first UH-1 pulled out half of his team via harness. Meanwhile, Dunlap called in air strikes until a second chopper hovered low to drop harnesses for the final four men.

Dunlap, Howard, and their leading Yard strapped in. Only after they were safely rigged did the wounded one-zero secure himself in the final harness for extraction. Poole would be out of action for some time, but he was written up for his first Silver Star for his valor on March 30. Charles Dunlap would receive the Army Commendation Medal for Heroism. Bob Howard was later awarded another Oak Leaf Cluster to his original Purple Heart award, for the fragment wounds he sustained on this mission. In a span of four months, he had been wounded three times on SOG recon missions.

Bob Howard's part in this mission went without any other official awards, but the recognition was not something he sought. His team had escaped with their lives after handing out severe losses to an NVA battalion, and that was good enough for him.

By early April 1968, a familiar old face had returned to Kontum. It was Staff Sergeant Fred Zabitosky, who had spent six weeks in hospitals recovering from his broken back, broken ribs, severe burns, and shrapnel wounds. Howard was pleased to see his buddy, and he spent time listening to the details of Zab's February mission.

With the Medal of Honor award pending for many months, base commander Roxie Hart forbade Zab from running any further recon missions. During that time, he made himself useful by assisting one of FOB-2's recently arrived Green Berets, SFC George Wilson Hunt, with taking over his former RT Maine team. Hunt, who had run missions with RT California before Kontum master sergeant Lionel Pinn assigned him to take over Maine, appreciated the expert steering advice offered by Zabitosky. When Zab's sleeves were rolled up, Wilson Hunt could clearly see the nasty burn scars on his upper arms.[13]

Another relatively new Green Beret on base was Sergeant Lou DeSeta, a young man from Delaware already on his second tour in Vietnam. Since arriving at FOB-2, Lou had made several missions with RT Nevada. When Specialist Fifth Class John Kedenburg joined the team later that month, DeSeta was happy to let the newbie take over running the radio. The two became close. At one point, Lou became impressed with an M1 carbine bayonet that Kedenburg used as a combat knife during missions. Together they headed for the supply shed to see if Staff Sergeant Howard might have another one.[14]

When they arrived, DeSeta and Kedenburg found Howard shooting the breeze with his buddy Zabitosky.

"Whatcha need, soldier?" Howard asked.

"I want an M1 carbine bayonet like my buddy John uses," said DeSeta. "I've got a Gerber Mk II combat dagger. It's only good for killing people. I want something in the field that will also be a good utility knife."

Howard disappeared back into his supply room for a few minutes and then returned with a stout knife with a purplish-hued seven-inch blade. Although it contained no branding, it was an official SOG weapon, stamped "No. 2704." It had been designed by Conrad "Ben" Baker, who headed a special counter-insurgency support office whose mission was to help design weapons, uniforms, and equipment for use by Special Forces.

"Will this do?" Howard asked.

DeSeta was more than impressed with the Special Forces knife. He later wondered if Zab and Howard had set him up by pretending not to have a carbine bayonet so he would have to "settle" for a rugged SOG knife. Either way, he was well pleased with his new weapon and was more than ready for his next mission with Kedenburg and RT Nevada. Years later, Lou would reflect on the irony of that moment. "Here I am in the supply room, asking questions about gear and being tended to by three guys who would earn the Medal of Honor!"[15]

DeSeta was impressed that Howard was not short with him. If the young Green Beret had questions on any piece of SF equipment, Howard calmly answered them. Lou had also heard stories of some instances of the supply sergeant's bravery while he was running recon as a straphanger. "He had a rucksack with his rifle right at the end of the counter when you went into the supply room," DeSeta remembered. "He was ready, so at a moment's notice, he could be on a chopper. For us new guys, that meant a lot."

John Kedenburg was soon in command of RT Nevada, but he and DeSeta were not running targets together for long. In early May, DeSeta was sent to Khe Sanh on temporary duty for several months. For his part, Bob Howard tried to keep his rifle and rucksack out of the supply room as often as possible. During the second week of April, he joined a Hatchet Force team sent in to attack NVA forces.

The officer leading the mission, Captain Gene McCarley, was an old friend. In 1967, McCarley had been one of the one-zeros who had given Howard his shot at running recon as a straphanger. McCarley's team was inserted into a hot target area, with Howard serving as the assistant team leader. Their insert went as well as it could, and the captain kept his recon team moving steadily toward their objective area on April 16.

At midday, McCarley allowed his company to slow their advance just long enough to have lunch. They finished their rations and began moving out toward their objective area. McCarley and Howard's platoon was suddenly ambushed from the rear by a sizable NVA force. The amount of automatic gunfire and RPGs unleashed by the North Vietnamese was staggering. Many of the team's Yards, both new and inexperienced, panicked and fled, splitting the team in the process. "I had a lot of young Montagnards and they turned and ran up on top of a hill and left me up there by myself," McCarley recalled.[16]

Bob Howard immediately began placing the remaining

troops in a defensive perimeter. McCarley was so angry with the Yards who had fled that he began shooting his way through NVA troops to go up the hill after them. Howard, seeing the captain could not scale the mountain without support, exposed himself to NVA fire to help McCarley reach his objective. McCarley chewed out the frightened Yards and motivated them to move back down the mountain with him to the safety of their team's perimeter.[17]

McCarley was just easing back down the mountain with his indig when the NVA made a serious assault. A barrage of mortars exploded all around the team's perimeter. Howard stood and exposed himself to enemy bullets to fire numerous rounds from his grenade launcher. Bullets and RPG shrapnel filled the air. His own grenade work soon knocked out the NVA mortar position.[18]

Howard continued to shoot at the advancing North Vietnamese while Captain McCarley worked to keep his indigenous troops from fleeing again. Throughout the night, he kept his Yards at the most crucial areas of the Hatchet team's perimeter. McCarley's words of encouragement helped maintain order.

Dawn of the following morning, April 17, found another former FOB-2 recon man, First Lieutenant Ken Etheredge, flying forward air controller (FAC) duty as a Covey Rider. Etheredge called in air support to help knock out the nearby NVA platoon until extraction choppers could reach the area. As the last man to board a slick that day, Captain McCarley would later receive the Silver Star for this mission.

Sergeant Howard would later receive an Army Commendation Medal for Heroism for directing his subordinates and for knocking out the NVA mortar position. "His actions on that day were responsible for saving the lives of many of his men," Howard's citation reads.

In between such missions, Howard worked to keep the base supplies flowing and the mess hall well stocked. His forward operating base had gone months without losing a Green Beret, but that streak ended on April 29.

On April 26, Captain Gene McCarley's Company B of Hatchet Force had been inserted into eastern Laos for a road-interdiction mission in target area Tango 7 along Highway 110. The team made heavy contact and was finally extracted by McGuire rigs on April 28 while under fire.[19]

The following day, McCarley's Hatchet Force company was reinserted to mine the road. The large force dug themselves in defensively near the road, and a demolition team led by platoon leader Lieutenant Joseph L. Shreve was sent down to plant explosives. But the team was ambushed. Shreve and three indigenous Hatchet Force men were killed, and multiple Green Berets were wounded. McCarley's force succeeded in blasting a large hole in the road, but the extraction choppers were loaded with the injured by the time the company was finally pulled. At least seven Americans would receive the Purple Heart for their injuries.

Fortunately for FOB-2's recon company, new personnel arrived over the next two weeks to offset these losses. Among them, arriving on May 10, was Sergeant Joe Parnar, who had dropped out of the University of Massachusetts during his junior year to become a Special Forces medic. When Parnar checked into base that day, he was told to see Staff Sergeant

Howard to draw his weapons and other gear. Although Parnar expressed his eagerness to join a spike team, he was told his services were more immediately needed at the base dispensary. His superior, Staff Sergeant John Probart, was still treating the wounded from the road-interdiction mission. Howard assured the young medic that he would find plenty of action and chances to go across the field in the months ahead. It was not an idle promise.

Parnar learned quickly enough that the Kontum supply sergeant had already established quite a reputation on the base. Soon after his arrival, Parnar witnessed a heated exchange in the FOB-2 club between Howard and SFC Clarence Webb, the one-zero of RT Texas. At the age of forty, Webb was commonly known to the younger Green Berets as "Pappy." Like Howard, he was fearless in combat, and he had already accumulated a string of commendations for valor. But Pappy had a short fuse, and he routinely dismissed junior recon team members who did not meet his high standards across the fence.

After a few drinks, Webb exchanged some words with Howard, and things quickly grew tense. "Bob Howard and Pappy Webb got nose to nose," Parnar recalled. "Many of us felt that one of them was going to die." Other SF men intervened and the two were separated without bloodshed. For young medic Parnar, FOB-2 was a world far removed from normal Army regulations. He could scarcely imagine after that tense confrontation between two fiery Green Berets that he would soon find himself running missions with both Howard and Webb.[20]

Just days later, on May 14, Howard would make what would prove to be his last mission as a straphanger during his second tour of Vietnam. Based on the description from the third Army Commendation Medal he would later receive, he was inserted into enemy territory with either a Hatchet Force detachment or a standard recon team. Exact details of this mission no longer exist due to mass destruction of MACV-SOG's classified records after the Vietnam War. Newspaper stories printed months after this action state that Sergeant First Class Howard risked his life to save his team from being overrun by NVA forces.[21]

Based on the information that still exists, Howard's team was moving through the jungle on a recon mission across the fence. A large enemy force assaulted the FOB-2 team and soon had them pinned down with heavy automatic weapons fire. Howard volunteered to fight off the surging NVA while the balance of his team moved hastily toward a nearby bomb crater. During his fight, Bob was shot and hit multiple times by shrapnel that seriously injured his right leg. Pulling himself to the bomb crater, Howard continued to fight off North Vietnamese attackers while his team's one-two called in air support.[22]

Air strikes were able to successfully keep the NVA at bay long enough for extraction choppers to pull the team. That time, Howard's combat wounds were too severe for base medics like John Probart and Joe Parnar to handle. When the helicopters reached Dak To, he was rushed into surgery at a local field hospital. Howard would remain there until he was stabilized, but the doctors had limits to their treatments near the front lines. Howard would need specialized care at a hospital outside Vietnam.

In an interview given decades later, Howard briefly mentioned his wounds. "I got shot up real bad, and they had to send me back," he said. "I went to Japan to the hospital." Howard's medical records for this period reflect that he had taken a gunshot wound to the left shoulder, another bullet to his right leg, and other fragment wounds.[23]

The NVA had set Howard back, knocking him out of action in the prime of his SOG career. His return to combat would take a little longer this time.

★ NINE ★

THIRD TRIP TO VIETNAM

Hospitalization capabilities in Vietnam were limited, and long flights back to America were often too traumatic for seriously wounded soldiers. By 1968, Japan was an obvious choice for treating men like Howard, as it was a routine fuel stop for aircraft flying between the States and Vietnam.

Howard spent weeks at the U.S. Army 106th General Hospital at Kishine Barracks in Yokohama, Japan. Specializing in burn victim treatment, the hospital also handled numerous soldiers who had sustained serious bullet or shrapnel wounds. The staff tending to him was first-rate, and he was soon pronounced stable enough for the long flight required to transfer him back to his homeland. Howard's military records show that his second trip to Vietnam ended on June 3, 1968.

The Army decided Staff Sergeant Howard could rehabilitate at Fort Bragg, North Carolina, as part of the Special Forces Group (Airborne). From Temple, Texas, his wife, Tina, shuffled over to the East Coast so that daughters Denicia and Melissa could see their daddy again. Howard was able to secure temporary housing near the base in the town of Spring Lake. Despite his shrapnel and gunshot wounds, he was never one to be down and out. His latest injuries were simply physical challenges to overcome with physical therapy. Running and calisthenics had always been part of Bob's routine, but they were even more important to him now.

During his rehab at Fort Bragg in the summer of 1968, Howard received notice of his promotion from staff sergeant to sergeant first class (pay grade E-7). He was eager to return to his service at FOB-2, and by early October, he was medically cleared for full active duty. By this time, U.S. Army awards board notices had arrived with valor awards for the recovering sergeant. He was notified by the commanding general of the Special Warfare Center and School, Brigadier General Edward M. Flanagan Jr., that he would be honored before his return to Vietnam.

On the morning of October 4, Howard was called to Kennedy Hall, part of the JFK Special Warfare Center at Fort Bragg. Accompanying him were his wife, Tina; their seven-year-old daughter, Denicia; and four-year-old Melissa. Howard had merely mentioned to his wife that he was getting an award or two. But Tina Howard was surprised by the amount of time General Flanagan stood before her husband.

Wearing his SFC khakis, Bob stood stiffly at attention, his face expressionless, as the general's aide, Captain Walter Mayew, read each citation aloud. Those viewing this stout warrior had little idea how badly his body had been ravaged by enemy bullets and shrapnel. A crowd of high-ranking officers and senior noncoms was on hand to help congratulate the Vietnam hero as he received not one but eight different awards for valor. They included three Purple Hearts for wounds sustained on November 21, 1967; December 8, 1967; and March 29, 1968. The second and third Purple Hearts were in the form of Oak Leaf Clusters. At the time of the ceremony, an award for his most recent May 14 mission had not yet been processed.

Captain Mayew also read the citations for three Army Commendation Medals (ACMs), two awarded for Howard's valor during specific actions on February 1 and April 16, 1968. The third ACM was given for his "diligence and determination, unrelenting loyalty, initiative and perseverance" for FOB-2 combat missions spanning a full year—from May 15, 1967, through May 14, 1968. In addition, Howard was decorated with the Bronze Star with "V" device for his "exceptionally valorous actions on 10 December 1967." Finally, Captain Mayew presented Howard with the U.S. Army's highest award and the nation's second highest, the Distinguished Service Cross.[1]

Although this medal had been earned in November 1967, the Army paperwork to issue it had not been approved until late May 1968. Because Howard was a member of MACV-SOG, the precise details of his covert missions were classified. His DSC mission had been conducted across the fence in Laos, but the citation could detail only that he had been involved in "conflict with an armed force in [the] Republic of Vietnam."[2]

Tina Howard listened in awe to the details, learning for the first time that Howard had led a team to destroy NVA supplies, but they were pinned down by enemy machine-gun nests.

Multiple times he had assaulted the bunkers, wiping out soldiers with his rifle, a grenade, and even an anti-tank weapon. In conclusion, the citation said that "Sergeant First Class Howard's extraordinary heroism and devotion to duty were in keeping with the highest traditions of the military service."

A humble man, Tina's husband had offered no details on any of this. But his family was rightfully proud of him that day. In addition to seven other commendations, Howard had just received the highest military award for valor that the U.S. Army could issue on its own.

Immediately following the ceremony, Robert Howard said his goodbyes to his family. After three months at Fort Bragg, Howard was deemed to be in good physical condition again by the military. His personal fitness routine and constant running had helped strengthen his body. "They sent me back to Vietnam again," he recalled. "I was sent back to Kontum because I was familiar with the target areas we went into."[3]

Howard's family moved to Rogers, Texas, southeast of Temple, where Tina was again assisted by her aunt, Annie, and other family members. Clearly her husband was heading back for dangerous duty, but there was no stopping him. He had found his calling, and he felt he needed to be back with his comrades to continue his tour of duty.

Bob Howard made his return to the Central Highlands area of South Vietnam on October 28, 1968. He saw some familiar faces whom he respected, like Captain Gene McCarley, when he reached FOB-2. There were also plenty of fresh faces among the young Green Berets running missions. Command of the Kontum base was now under Lieutenant Colonel Donald Smith, a veteran paratrooper who was well educated in both international business and special warfare. He was a first-rate soldier and an intellectual. But some of his recon men called him "Whiskey" Smith behind his back for his love of that libation and the severe stance he could take against any soldier who had screwed up.

The officer now serving as the recon company commander was Captain Edward Lesesne. He had served at FOB-2 in its early days and helped to organize the Montagnard camp, but he departed in February 1967 after suffering serious wounds on a recon mission. Ed Lesesne, like Howard, loved to run missions, and he had already fallen back into that routine when he was not assisting Colonel Smith with the new guys arriving on base. Lesesne had gone out as a straphanger with one-zero Wilson Hunt's RT Maine in September. They had wounded an NVA soldier and brought him back; he was the first prisoner captured by SOG men in nine months, and an officer to boot. Wilson Hunt and Lesesne were sent right back into the same hot zone with a Hatchet Force company three day later. Wilson Hunt and his one-one, Bill Janc, wounded and subdued yet another NVA officer, who was hauled back to Saigon for interrogation.

Howard also learned that a third man from FOB-2 had earned the Medal of Honor during his absence. On June 13, John Kedenburg's RT Nevada was pinned down by a battalion-sized NVA force. Kedenburg gave up his life in the fight, allowing the last of his team to be extracted on McGuire rigs while he fought to his death. The Bright Light team inserted to extract his body very nearly ended up in body bags as well. Several indigenous team members were killed, and all of the Green Berets were wounded in the process.

The return of Sergeant Howard was a reason to celebrate. Word had had already circulated that he had been pinned with the Distinguished Service Cross back at Fort Bragg. In his honor, a party was thrown for him at the Kontum base club. Normally, Bob was not big on downing drinks at the club, but he was coerced into joining his comrades. "The Vietnamese had a party for him, and he got drunk," Gene McCarley recalled. The base commander finally asked McCarley and the bar manager, Big Bobby Barnes, to put Howard to bed.

"Howard didn't drink much, but when he did, he was hard to handle," McCarley recalled. McCarley weighed around two hundred pounds and Barnes was more than two hundred fifty. Even though they were big, strong men, they could not drag Howard to his room. Howard grabbed each of them under one arm and carried them along more than they carried him. "He was all man!" McCarley said.[4]

Barnes had recently served as the one-one for Recon Team California. His one-zero, Joe Walker, often joked about the enormous size of Barnes and how hard it might be to extract him from a firefight due to his weight. When that joke became reality after a late-summer mission, Barnes was moved off RT California and became the manager of the FOB-2 base club for the balance of his service period.

In addition to Barnes, Bob Howard became close friends with Sergeant Walker, who had taken over RT California during the time Howard was back home at Fort Bragg recovering. Walker did not look the part of a typical one-zero. Tall and gangly, with horn-rimmed glasses, he appeared more like a schoolteacher than a fearless killer. Joe Johnnie Walker was born in 1943 in West Virginia; his name was partially derived from his father's favorite brand of whiskey. Walker was an aggressive combatant, and he found friendship with Howard immediately.[5]

Howard greatly appreciated his friend's burning desire to destroy the enemy. Joe's code name was "Gladiator," and some of the missions he had run while Howard was recovering at Bragg were outstanding. Before reaching FOB-2, Walker had been promoted for capturing Vietnamese prisoners of war with his Project Delta team. Assigned to FOB-2's RT California in July 1968, he had made heavy contact with the enemy on each mission, but he always managed to bring his team back to base. Gladiator had already earned a Bronze Star for one mission.

Walker was also the first Kontum one-zero to keep a pet python, which he nicknamed "Georgia." He kept her in a pit just outside his team's hooch area, and fed her a live chicken or some other animal once a week. In terms of recon missions, Walker's greatest desire was to snatch an NVA soldier and return him to base alive for the intelligence boys to interrogate. During one of his recent October missions, RT California had made such an attempt. But Walker's indigenous team members had panicked, and they had killed both NVA whom Walker had hoped to bring back alive. Walker straightened out his Yards, and he made plans to attempt another POW grab on his next mission.

Bob Howard got to know Big Bobby Barnes and Joe "Gladiator" Walker well during his first two weeks back on base. And on November 10, he learned that Walker's team had gotten into serious trouble across the fence trying to pull another prisoner-snatch operation. They needed emergency assistance to survive, and Bob was more than willing to help his friend.

RECON TEAM CALIFORNIA had been inserted by helicopter on November 8 into Laos target area Juliett 9, located near the Bra region of the Dak Xou River. This area was densely populated with NVA, and it was known to be dangerous. The Hanoi high command was using route-protection battalions and rear-security units along the Ho Chi Minh Trail to specifically work against SOG forces. Members of the NVA's elite 305th Airborne Brigade had been converted into "sappers," or night infiltrators who raided U.S. camps. Others were put to work on special counter-recon units assigned to hunt down and kill SOG teams. These killer groups communicated efficiently via phones and radios. LZ watch forces alerted them whenever an American SOG team was inserted.[6]

Joe Walker hoped to grab an enemy prisoner on this mission to make up for the mistakes made by his Yards weeks prior. He was "running heavy" on this insert, with nine men on RT California. He had six Montagnards and two newer Green Berets: Sergeant Terry Brents as his one-one, and Staff Sergeant Rudolph "Mike" Machata as his one-two and commo man. After two days in Laos, Walker's team was ready.

Around 0900 on November 10, four NVA soldiers walked into the kill zone of Walker's carefully prepared ambush site. Gladiator's team had no inkling that they were about to assault a highly skilled, heavily armed North Vietnamese counter-recon patrol well prepared to fight SOG operatives. Everything went awry for Walker from the start.

Terry Brents attempted to initiate the ambush, but his CAR-15 malfunctioned as he pulled the trigger. The four NVA soldiers immediately dropped to kneeling positions. Two of them unleashed continuous rounds of machine-gun fire. The other two lobbed a dozen grenades into RT California's ambush area. Walker realized he was dealing with experts. In minutes, the four NVA disappeared into the jungle, leaving the SOG team with one seriously wounded Green Beret.

Sergeant Brents had taken grenade shrapnel to his head and chest. A bullet had sliced his head open like a melon, leaving his brain exposed. The slug had not penetrated his brain; it was a clean, open wound. "A surgeon couldn't have done any better," Walker recalled. "Every time his heart beat, you could watch his brain pulse."[7]

"Hang in there, Brents," Walker assured him. "We're going to get you some help."

Mike Machata called on his PRC-25 radio for an emergency extraction. In addition to Brents, three of the team's Yards had been wounded in the firefight. Kontum sent back word that all available air support was tied up and that RT California would have to sweat it out for a few hours. At Dak To, a response team was already on standby. Knowing that Walker's team had gone in hoping to pull a prisoner, First Lieutenant Lee Swain had been waiting with his Hatchet Force platoon for just such an emergency.

With other air emergencies cleared by midafternoon on

November 10, Swain's platoon (thirty-three Montagnards and three Green Berets) was inserted. Medevac choppers pulled Brents and Walker's three wounded Montagnards and returned them to the 4th Division medical facility at Dak To for treatment. Reinforced now by Lieutenant Swain's platoon, Walker's RT California was ordered to remain on the ground in search of enemy targets.[8]

The large SOG force remained on the move the following day. They operated in an offensive fashion, hoping to engage any enemy forces encountered. On the morning of November 12, Swain's force contacted more NVA troops. In the aftermath, Hueys were called in to extract two members of the group, a wounded Montagnard and one of Swain's sergeants who had sprained his knee during the operation. In their place, two replacement NCOs from Kontum's Hatchet Force company were added to Lieutenant Swain's ground forces: Sergeants Bill Kendall and Floyd Bryant.

The following evening, November 13, Swain and Walker's force made their RON site near a river. During the early-morning hours of November 14, the American recon force was assaulted by another skilled NVA force. The platoon was hit with mortars, grenades, and automatic weapons. Swain, lying side by side with Walker during the assault, put in an emergency radio call to Leghorn, the mountaintop radio relay site that had been established by Ken Sisler's team in early 1967.[9]

Mortar explosions wounded several men from Lee Swain's Hatchet Force platoon, and Joe Walker was badly hit. Shrapnel from one grenade ripped Gladiator Walker's flesh in four places. The worst hit ripped through his eyebrow, shattered his glasses, and left a flap of skin hanging into his field of vision. Then a bullet hit Walker's left leg and remained embedded. During this firefight, another half dozen men were wounded.

As darkness covered the area, the Kontum force was on its own. Their air cover was worried about bombing or strafing the wrong men in the dark. Swain told them to dive and shoot anyway. They would hope for the best. As their perimeter started to collapse, Lieutenant Swain's Montagnards began retreating toward a tree line. With his own force beginning to splinter, Swain decided to move the remainder of his men across the river. Walker, who had been immobile for some time, regained his senses enough to move across the water. Swain and Bill Kendall helped move one of their badly wounded Green Berets, SFC Richard Girard, through the current and up the other bank.

The NVA forces were still attacking intensely as the bulk of Swain's platoon retreated across the river. During the battle, one of Swain's men, Sergeant Floyd Bryant, became separated. Bryant was in company with five wounded Yards; his group took shelter in foxholes they located up on a nearby hillside. Once across the river, Swain grouped his most seriously wounded men together within a tight perimeter. They had no choice but to ride out enemy attacks and hope that a rescue force would reach them by first light.

The desperate radio calls received at FOB-2 put the base in motion like a kicked-over anthill. Bob Howard, having only returned to Vietnam two weeks prior, was eager to get into this battle. His buddy Joe Walker and other men needed all the help they could get.

★ TEN ★

SLAM SEVEN

November 14, 1968

Sergeant First Class Howard was pleased that his force was going in heavy. Joe Walker's team had been hit twice within a matter of days. He knew they were not dealing with run-of-the-mill NVA soldiers. These were likely NVA counter-recon units tracking his SOG comrades.

Lieutenant Colonel Whiskey Smith shared the same view. Both RT California and Lee Swain's exploitation platoon sent in to help them remained under siege during the overnight hours. Prior to dawn on November 14, Smith prepared a company-sized unit at FOB-2 Kontum. Including indigenous troopers and a dozen U.S. Army Green Berets, his force numbered about 115 soldiers. Officially, it was code-named SLAM VII.

Small-team units performed specific missions, as assigned by MACV leadership. But SLAM work was not centered on stealth operations. The first such SLAM (search, locate, annihilate, monitor) operation run from Kontum had taken place during the second week of October 1966. It was a coordinated assault along Route 110, near the tri-border region where Cambodia's, Laos's, and South Vietnam's borders meet. The results were impressive enough to MACV-SOG leadership that a platoon-sized force was inserted to conduct SLAM II just days later in Laos. Several months passed before SLAM III was conducted on January 30, 1967, against another target complex near Highway 110.[1]

Between February and August 1967, three more Hatchet Force SLAM missions had been conducted. In many cases, these mass operations inserted bomb-damage assessment (BDA) teams into particularly hot areas in the immediate wake of Air Force B-52 bombing missions against key NVA targets. Most had been carried out successfully without significant casualties.

One-zero Joe Walker later recapped the use of SOG SLAM operations. "The purpose of the mission was to go out in the operational area, to make contact with a larger military force, and to hold that target until such time as a Hatchet Force or an air strike could destroy it," he stated. "We wanted to make a major effort to take control of the Ho Chi Minh Trail."[2]

More than a year had passed since SOG had conducted SLAM VI. The low rate of injuries incurred on these sizable operations had been fortunate. That record would be sorely tested by the SLAM team that Whiskey Smith was preparing to send into Juliett 9 on a mission.

SLAM SEVEN

Bob Howard wanted to hit back against the NVA who had hit Walker's team.

The senior officer in command of the planned SLAM operation was First Lieutenant Thomas Wayne Jaeger, a Missouri native making his first Vietnam tour of duty. He had arrived at FOB-2 in late April 1968, and he had run several missions with recon teams as a straphanger. By July, Lieutenant Jaeger had been put in command of the Reaction Company, which was part of the Exploitation Force, also known as the Hatchet Force.[3]

Jaeger's platoon was staffed with three additional lieutenants—Walt Huczko, Bill Groves, and Robert Price—and several NCOs, all of whom had trained together for several months. Specialist Fifth Class Steve Roche, a Connecticut native who had taken part in the John Kedenburg Bright Light mission in early 1968, was added to the company at the last minute. Jaeger's indigenous troops were combat seasoned and had performed well under fire on previous missions.

Jaeger had not worked with SFC Bob Howard, and was unfamiliar with his valorous reputation as a straphanger on many RT missions at FOB-2. When Lieutenant Colonel Smith told Jaeger that he was being assigned a former supply sergeant as his first sergeant, he was surprised but happy to have a senior NCO. As the company's first sergeant, Howard became the ranking noncommissioned officer on the mission. Four Hatchet Force platoons would comprise the Exploitation Force.[4]

As the large group was being sorted out for movement from

base to the Dak To staging area, Lieutenant Jaeger was surprised by a decision made by Whiskey Smith. The lieutenant colonel decided not to follow the established SOG practice of putting experience over rank, but instead chose a new arrival at FOB-2 who had no SOG or cross-border experience. He put thirty-one-year-old Captain Lolly Sciriaev in command of the company and assigned Jaeger as the executive officer.[5]

The 115-man force required two trips of eight helicopters, an equal mix of Hueys and Kingbees, to ferry the entire Reaction Company to Dak To. The second half of the group landed at Dak To almost an hour after the first half had arrived. At that point, the first slicks lifted off for Juliett 9, under escort of four Huey gunships. The H-34 Kingbees carried about fifty men for Captain Sciriaev's Bright Light mission to recover Swain and Walker's platoon. These transport choppers would then return to ferry in the second half of the SLAM company.

Meanwhile, the besieged men on the ground prepared for the arrival of the first SLAM group. Lieutenant Swain, using his survival radio shortly after dawn, spoke with a Bird Dog pilot who was flying his Cessna O-1 above the Juliett 9 area to assess enemy activity. Swain, Joe Walker, and the bulk of their platoon were still across the river from the RON position where they had been overrun the previous evening.

Swain hoped to cross back over the river and search for Sergeant Floyd Bryant and his five Montagnards. They had not been seen since the overnight firefight when they had been separated. In preparation for this move, Swain called the Covey Rider to use air support to soften up the other side of the river. The Cessna's rear-seat recon man dropped a smoke canister where Swain had indicated via radio. But screams rang out as a Huey gunship prepared to chew up that area with bullets.

Joe Walker spotted two of his RT California Montagnards racing toward the river to escape. The pair of indig had gotten separated from his team during the previous night's firefight. Walker ran into the middle of the river to meet them and help them to his new perimeter, while the Cessna Bird Dog continued to swoop low over the team's previous RON site. Lieutenant Swain called his Covey to ask that no gunfire be placed between the river and the top of the hill, just in case others from his group were alive.

The first H-34 Kingbees carrying Bob Howard, Captain Sciriaev, and a SLAM platoon were ready to arrive. Once Sergeant Walker had moved his two Yards up the hill to their new defensive area, a big chopper landed on a twenty-yard-wide sandbar in the middle of the river. Captain Sciriaev and members of his platoon poured out of one chopper. From the second Kingbee, Howard and more than a dozen Hatchet Force men were preparing to jump into the river when their aircraft began taking heavy enemy fire from both 37mm antiaircraft (AA) weapons and .50-caliber machine guns. Before the chopper touched down, Howard jumped to the ground fifteen feet below and began returning the NVA fire.[6]

While the balance of his platoon dismounted the Kingbee, Howard provided protection until all had moved safely off the landing zone. For the moment, Lieutenant Jaeger remained on board Howard's chopper as it lifted off to make a quick tour of the battlefield. Taking the point position, Howard led his platoon toward nearby woods without any of his men sustaining injuries. As his men neared the trees, Howard spotted two enemy soldiers. Alone, he charged their position with his M16 and gunned down both men.

Jaeger's Kingbee flew to another LZ a half mile away to link up with the remaining contingent of the company. Based on his recon, he was able to conclude that the enemy's AA guns were not in a position to impair the landing of the remainder of the company at the second LZ. They could be dealt with later.

Captain Sciriaev, SFC Howard, and their platoon were on the move to assist. Howard was pleased to see his one-zero buddy Walker alive, but he was a mess. Joe's glasses were shattered, he had been ripped by shrapnel in multiple places, and he had a bullet in his leg. But Gladiator was a fighter, and he was not ready to be medically evacuated from the scene. Some of his men were still missing. Green Beret combat medic Joe Parnar, who had jumped from one of the chase slicks into the riverbed, was already treating the wounded. He put stitches in the loose flap of skin hanging over Walker's eye, helping him to see.[7]

Parnar then began treating Sergeant Girard and other wounded men. A second Huey chase slick nestled onto the river sandbar and another SOG medic, SSG Tony Dorff, jumped out to help. At the same time, Howard was moving wounded Montagnards toward the rescue choppers to have them lifted out for medical attention.

Howard and Walker helped push three of RT California's wounded Yards into the helicopter. The balance of the SLAM company would take some time to be inserted at the second LZ a half mile away. One-zero Walker insisted on finding the five other Montagnards and Sergeant Bryant, who were still unaccounted for.

While Parnar was dressing Walker's eye wound, Gladiator expressed concern about his missing men.

"If any of them are still alive up there at your RON site, they're going to need medical attention ASAP," Parnar said.[8]

"I'm going up there!" Walker suddenly announced.

Medic Dorff was stunned to see Walker's wounded Montagnards jump back off their evacuation helicopter with weapons in hand. If their wounded one-zero was going back in, they were going right with him until the bitter end. "It was the damnedest thing I've ever seen in my life," Dorff recalled.[9]

"I'm going with you," Bob Howard said.

Walker explained his plans to the newly arrived Hatchet Force commander, Captain Sciriaev. He was intent on leading a small team back across the river in hopes of recovering the balance of his lost men. The captain agreed, and the group set out: Walker, Howard, SFC Lloyd O'Daniel, Sergeant Alan Farrell, medic Joe Parnar, and several Montagnards.

Although the river contained a large sandbar, it reached depths of nearly six feet in places. Walker was amused to see powerfully built SFC Howard having to hold the heads of the smaller Montagnards above the water in places. Heavily loaded with gear, he bounced up and down off the bottom until he could deposit them in shallower water.

Walker's team then eased up the hillside to his team's former RON site. They soon found the foxholes where Sergeant Bryant and the five other Montagnards had taken cover. It was the chilling scene of a massacre. Enemy soldiers had moved from foxhole to foxhole during the night, shooting in the head at close range each recon team member they encountered and leaving them for dead.

Howard cautiously probed each body as he moved through the foxholes. As he moved past Sergeant Bryant's body, something caught his attention. Howard stared intently at the Green Beret's face and noticed one of Bryant's eyes moving. The eye was tracking his movement.[10]

"Damn!" shouted Howard. "This one's alive."

Lloyd O'Daniel and Alan Farrell joined Howard to examine Bryant. He had been shot in multiple places, including the crotch. By some miracle, the executioner's bullet to his head had failed to do the job. Bryant was lying in a pool of coagulated blood, clinging to life.[11]

Medic Parnar opened Bryant's shirt to start an IV, and soon found that the young man had at least nineteen wounds over his body. Howard and the rescue team were shocked and angered to hear the young SOG man tell his survival tale. Shortly after sunrise, as a heavy fog lingered near the river, NVA troops had moved through their RON site. Bryant said that they shot each Montagnard to make sure he was dead. When they approached him, Bryant said the NVA soldiers shot him in the crotch and then in the head. But the kill shot did not penetrate his skull, instead bouncing off his skull and exiting from the side of his face.[12]

Howard and the others rigged a makeshift stretcher to move Bryant. Parnar ran alongside, holding his IV bottle, as the Green Berets hauled their severely wounded comrade down toward the river sandbar for extraction. When the medevac choppers arrived, they loaded Bryant, the dead indigenous soldiers, the wounded Joe Walker, his three wounded Montagnards, and another wounded Green Beret, Bill Kendall, onto the chopper. "I think we took a hell of a beating on this operation," Kendall noted that night in an illegal diary he kept. By his count, Walker's mission and SLAM VII had already recorded four men killed, eight missing in action, and twenty-three wounded.[13]

The final insult to Walker's RT California came as the extraction Hueys were pulling the group of wounded men out from the riverbank. The NVA antiaircraft guns that had been firing at the insert choppers all morning finally made their rounds count. The Huey containing Mike Machata and some of Walker's Yards was hit and was forced to make an emergency crash landing. Machata was injured and briefly pinned in the wreckage. After extracting himself, he helped the chopper crew blow up their downed aircraft and fight off NVA attacks until another Huey was able to extract them.

Bob Howard assumed the SLAM force had done its work. The dead and wounded had been pulled. Lieutenant Lee Swain's troops were still on the ground, now under the direction of SLAM VII's commander, Captain Sciriaev. But MACV-SOG's senior leadership had other ideas. Always ready for a fight, Howard was pleased with the new orders that were issued. Sciriaev had more than a hundred SF soldiers at his disposal. From Saigon, word was passed down that the company would remain on the ground. They were to proceed in the direction of the 37mm guns that had been shooting up their choppers. Once properly located, these batteries could be destroyed by air strikes.

As the assault force's first sergeant, Howard helped direct

the movements of indigenous troops as the SLAM company moved south through rugged terrain. The men followed the river for half a mile as it snaked through a couple of turns. Where they chose to recross it, they found the water was as deep as chest high. Again, Howard helped the smaller Yards avoid being swept away by the strong currents. Captain Sciriaev then moved his element a few hundred yards to where the largest contingent of the company, including Lieutenant Jaeger, had landed and then set up their RON position.

Howard knew the enemy was close by. An SF unit that large could not move through the jungle unnoticed without the enemy tracking them. Although there were no attacks on the SLAM company that night, the unit heard the whining of truck engines along nearby Highway 96 as NVA troops and supplies traveled on the dirt road to their west.

The following morning, November 15, Howard munched on some rations for his breakfast. The SLAM company was on the move for its second day through target area Juliett 9. For Lee Swain's platoon, it was already their sixth day on the ground and his men felt the effects of the extended mission. After a full day of advancing along the riverside, the unit still had not located the 37mm AA batteries. As darkness approached, Sciriaev directed the company to prepare its next RON site atop a small hill overlooking the nearby river.

Lieutenant Bill Groves, one of the platoon leaders, was not happy with the RON site selection and he had let Captain Sciriaev know it. But Sciriaev said he was following direct orders. Irritated, Groves and Sergeant Bob Van Hall ordered their Yards to dig foxholes for their platoon.[14]

Howard and most of the Green Berets chose to simply stretch out on the open ground. He selected a location close to a large rotten log. Medic Joe Parnar, who had not expected the SLAM mission to continue beyond the extraction of Walker's men, was ill prepared. He was happy to accept a can of C rations from Specialist Fifth Class Steve Roche and share a poncho liner with him for the night to keep warm.

Parnar had selfish reasons for sleeping near Roche and Howard. He knew of Howard's impeccable reputation and the fact that he had recently been awarded the DSC for his valor under fire. "I figured if anyone would know what to do if we got hit, it was Howard," Parnar recalled. "I felt more secure being near his area."[15]

Parnar's worries were realized about 0400 on November 16. North Vietnamese troops assaulted the SLAM company's RON site. Mortar shells and rifle grenades rained down in the darkness. In the initial chaos, the Yards from Bill Groves's platoon started firing back. Groves and Van Hall raced about their perimeter, shouting at the Montagnards to cease fire, as their muzzle flashes were only further pinpointing the location of the recon company. In the process, both Van Hall and Groves were painfully wounded by shrapnel. Red-hot shards of ferrous metal slashed through rucksacks, fatigues, and flesh alike. Two other American recon men, Jon Davidson and Staff Sergeant Fred Hubel, were also injured during this predawn barrage.

Near Bob Howard, the explosions shook the soil, startling the resting Green Berets to their senses.

"We're getting hit!" Parnar hollered.

Howard and those sleeping nearest him began crawling

toward the nearby fallen log and a rotten tree stump. Explosions blew soil, shrapnel, and vegetation in every direction. As he moved, Howard winced as a searing sliver of rifle grenade shrapnel sliced through his fatigues and embedded itself in his back. "Howard and I were the last to get to the stump and were on top of the pile," recalled Parnar. "We both got a single small frag wound in our backs."[16]

Howard had no time to fret about his injury. He crawled from position to position within the company's large RON area. He admonished the Montagnards still firing their weapons on full automatic. Howard instead ordered them to fire only their M79 grenade launchers in the darkness.

As RPGs and bullets swept their perimeter, Lieutenant Jaeger was in search of his radio. Both Jaeger and Captain Sciriaev had an indigenous soldier assigned to carry their radio gear, but Jaeger found that his radioman had run for cover when the shooting began. After finding his indig, Jaeger took control of his radio and decided he would carry it from that point on. "I was not going to get caught again where I was unable to call in air support because I couldn't find my radio operator," he recalled.[17]

Jaeger used his radio to contact the Leghorn radio relay site and inform the operations center (Ops Ctr) at Kontum that they were experiencing a ground attack. He asked that a forward air controller (FAC) and air support be launched. The NVA assault persisted off and on for the next hour. During that time, medics Parnar and Dorff worked to treat the wounded. Howard and the platoon leaders continued moving about the perimeter to direct their unit's defensive efforts to the most threatened areas.

Shortly after dawn on November 16, the welcome sound of an A-1 Skyraider could be heard. The single-prop U.S. Air Force attack aircraft pounded the NVA positions with its guns, rockets, and cluster bomb units (CBU). The enemy's assault was temporarily stopped. Using his call sign, "Dungeon," Lieutenant Jaeger called the overhead Covey to request a medevac for the badly wounded, and provided a status report to the FOB-2 Ops Ctr at Kontum. Jaeger assumed that the Ops Ctr was updating Lieutenant Colonel Smith and SOG headquarters in Saigon.

By this time, several of the lieutenants had gathered in conversation with Tom Jaeger to assess the situation and to plan a course of action going forward. Captain Sciriaev, whom Jaeger had not been in contact with during the attack, asked the group, "What do you think we should do?"[18]

"The enemy is testing our position for vulnerabilities and harassing us at this point," Jaeger responded. "They know our location and will know it for the duration because of our large size. If they have large forces in the area, they will likely amass them and attack, as they did two nights ago. If we are a threat to their forces or their weapons and ammo caches, they will obviously attack."

At this point, Whiskey Smith at the Kontum Ops Ctr came back with directions regarding Dungeon's prior situation report.

"Dungeon, your unit is to break out of the enemy encirclement and continue your mission."[19]

Lieutenant Jaeger had not been briefed on the unit's mission by the Ops Ctr or by Captain Sciriaev prior to the operation's launch, and he was surprised by this response. He now realized that it was SOG headquarters, not Lieutenant Colonel Smith, directing the operation and that their intent was for the company to conduct a search-and-destroy operation.

After several minutes of the lieutenants discussing the unit's options, including extraction, Jaeger asked Sciriaev, "What do you want to do?"

The captain said, "Call them back and recommend extraction."

"It sounds like the orders are coming from SOG HQ," replied Jaeger. "Are you sure you want to do that?"

"Yes," Sciriaev said.

Jaeger then placed the call. "Ops Ctr, this is Dungeon." He further stated that his captain recommended their unit be extracted.

After a long silence, the next response was from Smith.

"Dungeon, you are to take command." The Kontum Ops Ctr further detailed that Sciriaev was to return to base on the medevac chopper.

The captain was relieved of command, leaving Lieutenant Jaeger in charge of the SLAM VII operation. Sciriaev and his most seriously wounded men were soon loaded onto a 57th AHC Huey. Among those departing was platoon leader Bill Groves, whose back had been penetrated by mortar shrapnel. First Lieutenant Craig Collier's UH-1H was so overloaded with injured men that he could barely clear the mountain passes on the flight back to Dak To. Another man departing with this flight was medic Tony Dorff. He had wished to stay, despite his minor wounds, but he had been ordered to evacuate.

Bob Howard, also lightly wounded by shrapnel, made no

mention of his own injury. He had no intention of being ordered out of the fight. In seven days of action, Kontum recon forces had suffered eighteen Americans and three dozen indigenous personnel wounded. Another six indig were missing and at least that many had perished.

Howard would continue the mission as first sergeant. Lieutenant Jaeger's new XO, or second officer in command, was a close friend, Lieutenant Lee Swain.

The early-morning firefight and chopper extract were taxing on the men remaining behind to continue the offensive. November 16 was memorable to Swain for another reason.

What a hell of a way to spend my twenty-sixth birthday, he thought.[20]

★ ELEVEN ★

"LET'S JUST SPRING THE AMBUSH"

Although his back throbbed from a deep laceration, Bob Howard complained to no one. Medic Joe Parnar patched him up quickly.

Down to only about a hundred men, the SLAM operation had orders to continue. The prior commander had been pulled out, along with the wounded. Howard and his company were to continue marching their large force near Laos Highway 96. Their directive was to locate the NVA's 37mm antiaircraft guns that had assaulted their choppers days before. With Lieutenant Tom Jaeger now in charge, the recon force moved as swiftly as possible through the hostile jungle.

There's no hiding a group this big, Howard thought. *The NVA know we're here. They've already hit us, and it's just a matter of time before we get hit again.*

The RON site selected by Jaeger that evening was on extremely rocky ground. Entrenching tools could barely scrape out depressions deep enough for men to partially protect themselves. On the morning of November 17, a resupply plane flew in low over the SLAM team's position. Jaeger had called for food and ammunition supplies, as the team was running low after days in enemy territory. He radioed in an appropriate drop zone, an open area in the jungle that covered about one hundred yards by fifty yards.

The first supply drop, a crate swinging below a parachute, missed the mark and drifted far beyond the SLAM company's position. With heavy NVA presence in the area, Jaeger decided it was too far away to recover safely. Fortunately, the second parachute supply bundle landed only a hundred yards away. Howard sent a group of indig out to retrieve the wooden case. Instead of ammunition, it was found to contain numerous cartons of cigarettes and other goods.[1]

Jaeger ordered the team to move another quarter mile to a different clearing. There he was able to call in another chopper to make a drop of food and plastic water bladders for his men. Squads of men were tasked with moving the fresh supplies from the open area to a nearby RON position located on a gentle slope, where the company would stay until morning.

Sergeant Howard soon heard over his radio that one of the Yards had been hit by sniper fire. First Lieutenant Walt Huczko's platoon was sent to guard the troops moving the supplies. Howard raced back downhill with them, accompanied by medic Parnar. As the wounded Montagnard spotted them, he scurried toward Howard. He and Parnar both opened fire with their automatic rifles until the wounded man had cleared the LZ.[2]

Howard helped assist the wounded Yard to a safe position

where Parnar could work on the bullet wound he had sustained in his elbow. Small-arms fire continued for some time until the NVA squads were eliminated or chased from the area.

Once Jaeger's SLAM company established its RON that evening, Howard made the rounds. He positioned Montagnards around their perimeter and then checked on the Yard who had been wounded while recovering the food supplies. The poor man's arm was shattered, and medic Parnar had to apply morphine during the night to keep his moaning from drawing more NVA attacks on the company.

Soon after daybreak on November 18, Lieutenant Jaeger was able to call in a medevac Huey to have the wounded Montagnard extracted. His force resumed the push forward, walking carefully a short distance from the river and the nearby road that followed it. The terrain was thick with heavy undergrowth. Jaeger split his large force into two columns, each about sixteen yards apart. If attacked, they would be better able to return fire from either flank.

During the midafternoon, the SLAM company eased out of the thick jungle and headed toward a crucial clearing. They had reached a point near Highway 96 with a large open area where a well-worn secondary road intersected with the larger highway. The area directly ahead was filled with small shrubs and low-lying brush. A couple hundred yards farther, the low brush gave way to an open field of knee-high green grass. Just beyond the start of the secondary road, there were numerous bomb craters, many half filled with water from tropical showers.

The wide-open area gave Lieutenant Jaeger cause for concern. *Taking a company-sized unit into such a clearing is not a good blueprint for success*, he thought. *We are likely to get into contact pretty quickly here.*[3]

Jaeger radioed Leghorn to give notice of his company's situation. He asked for an FAC to be sent out, with a rear seat Covey Rider to provide support for what appeared to be inevitable enemy contact. Jaeger also requested that air support at Dak To stand by for deployment. "We are in a situation where we may require air support very soon," he advised.

The lieutenant halted his company for a quarter hour, allowing time for an FAC plane to approach their area. Sensing that things were not right, Jaeger asked Lieutenant Swain to have a seasoned Green Beret take the point position.[4]

Swain turned to Bob Howard and repeated the request from the company commander.

"I'll go with you," Howard volunteered.

Jaeger was unaware that Swain and Howard had decided to perform the point role themselves. Had he known that two of his most senior Americans were pushing forward on point, he would have halted that move in favor of another NCO taking the assignment.

Swain and Howard walked forward slowly as they clutched their Colt M16 automatic rifles. If conditions appeared safe, they would then motion or radio for other troops to follow them. Side by side, the two passed from the scrub brush into the knee-high green jungle grass. Their advance was slow. Each man carefully scanned the distant tree lines, looking for any signs of a trap. Their M16s were raised and ready to fire. If something caught Howard's eye, his muzzle would already be pointing in that direction.

One hundred yards ahead, Howard could see another pocket of trees beyond the roadbed. To each side of the field, other thickets afforded cover for any enemy soldiers who might have been hidden. "To the left of us, the clearing went down through a little valley," recalled Swain. "Howard and I were in advance of everyone, walking point." Slightly behind them, their leading Montagnards followed, each spread out abreast a few steps back from the two Americans. There was no single-file movement here, but rather a small group carefully spread, ready for the worst.[5]

Three-quarters of the way across the opening, Howard sensed something was wrong.

He stopped, staring straight ahead. Silently motioning to the lieutenant, he pointed toward the trouble.

"There's NVA up ahead," Howard whispered. "I saw movement up in that tree line. What should we do?"

The lieutenant's answer was the one Howard fully expected. It was an aggressive move that he completely respected.

"Well, they know we're here," Swain said. "Let's just spring the ambush first. We're starting it now, because we don't want the rest of the company in it."

Sometimes the best defense is hitting an opponent with a strong offense first. Swain and Howard realized that a superior force of NVA soldiers was just seconds away from opening up on the SLAM company. The Kontum recon men had nearly walked right into the kill zone of a well-situated North Vietnamese Army ambush.

Without hesitation, Howard and Swain opened fire with

their M16s. The deadly torrent of bullets erupting from their barrels began shredding the thicket in which Howard had caught a fleeting glimpse of the concealed enemy soldiers.

The response was immediate. Heavy automatic fire answered from the tree line. The scream of rifle grenades filled the air, and mortar explosions erupted all about the point team. Thirty yards ahead of their SLAM company, Howard and Swain were in a hell of a fix. They were the most exposed, and NVA forces were intent on taking them out.

Behind them, the SLAM company was startled by the violent eruption of gunfire. Green Berets and Montagnards alike opened fire, emptying magazines toward the distant trees. Tom Jaeger was immediately disappointed that his men were having an undisciplined "mad minute," with everyone simply firing at no particular target and wasting ammunition. The lieutenant hurried to calm his men, and ordered them to start forming a defensive perimeter.

Howard hit the ground near a small bush. Swain was just feet away from him as both men fired into the tree line. Explosions shook the earth all about them. Shortly into the fight, one of the RPG rounds erupted alarmingly close. Howard felt the heat and concussion, and he was peppered with rocks, soil, and tiny slivers of metal. Lieutenant Swain screamed out in pain.

Looking back down the length of his body, Swain was stunned by the sight of his left foot. It was twisted at an odd angle, one that defied any normal position. He reached over and jabbed Sergeant Howard.[6]

"I'm wounded!"

Howard paused from firing and shot a quick glance at his lieutenant. To him, the lieutenant's face and upper torso seemed intact.

"You're okay," Howard assured him. He swung his M16 back toward the trees and continued firing.

Swain was insistent. "Look again! It's my foot!"

Glancing down at the lieutenant's legs, Howard saw Swain's peril. The tail end of the NVA rocket had sheared off the lieutenant's right calf all the way down to the ankle. His lower leg bone was snapped, and his right foot was hanging on only by the Achilles tendon.

"I can't move," Swain cried. "If you have to leave me, kill me first."

"I'm not leaving you here," Howard promised as he continued to fire at the distant NVA.

Some thirty yards behind them, Tom Jaeger knew that his point men had triggered an enemy attack. He called his overhead FAC and asked that air support be moved in immediately. They were overhead within ten minutes, by which time Jaeger and the main body of his SLAM company were taking heavy rifle, machine-gun, and RPG fire from their west and south flanks.[7]

Jaeger heard Sergeant Howard scream above the chaos, "The lieutenant is wounded!"

Jaeger had already dodged through a hail of fire to provide first aid to an indigenous member of his SLAM company. Hearing Howard's shout, he now raced forward, unaware of exactly which lieutenant had been hit.

Dropping onto the ground beside Howard and Swain, he

looked over his friend's legs. Swain's right leg was hanging by a tendon. His left leg was ripped by shrapnel, bleeding profusely. Removing his belt, Jaeger made a tourniquet around Swain's left thigh while Howard offered covering fire for the lifesaving work. Jaeger then administered a syrette of morphine and called for a medic.

While waiting for trained help, Howard removed his own belt and fashioned a second tourniquet around Swain's right leg to control the bleeding.

SOG medic Joe Parnar soon arrived in company with his Green Beret buddy Steve Roche. Howard and Jaeger had just finished tying on their tourniquets. Parnar was shocked by the sight of exposed white bones protruding from Swain's right leg. But he was impressed by the cool demeanor the lieutenant was attempting to maintain. Lying on his stomach, Swain had his chin propped on his crossed wrists while he spoke to Sergeant Howard.[8]

"Well, Bob, I guess this will put an end to my pheasant hunting when I get back home," he said while grimacing through the pain.

Young medic Parnar tried to keep a positive demeanor for his patient. "Don't worry, sir," he said. "You're going to do a lot of pheasant hunting."

Swain immediately fired back, "What do you mean? My foot's blown off!"

Parnar administered morphine to Swain, then pinned the empty syrette to the lieutenant's collar. In the heat of the action, he was unaware that Jaeger had already given another syrette to Swain. After calling for an immediate medevac chopper from Dak To, Jaeger crawled over close to Howard. "Then I saw the enemy coming off the southwest hill," Jaeger remembered. "They were coming out of the forest, and I knew if we didn't get a strike in there quickly, we were going to get overrun."[9]

Together with Howard, Jaeger called in air strikes against enemy troops that were now massing on their company's eastern, western, and southern positions. Jaeger asked his FAC to have the planes drop CBUs in hopes of eliminating the advancing ground forces. He radioed back to one of his NCOs to throw a smoke grenade to mark the far boundary of the main company's perimeter.

A-1E Skyraiders were soon working over the NVA troops as they received directions from Jaeger. The enemy appeared to be most heavily concentrated on the SLAM company's southern perimeter, so Jaeger asked the aviators to lay their ordnance extremely close. Howard and Jaeger were pleased when the next passes of the Skyraiders rained hell upon the NVA who were heavily concentrated in that area.

Bomb cluster fragments knocked branches from some trees and tore into the flesh of personnel from both sides of the conflict. Parnar and Howard were both hit by fragments as they continued to work on Swain. One red-hot piece of metal burned into the muscle on Parnar's calf, but he had no time to extract it. As he worked to put combat dressings around the lieutenant's legs, a wounded Montagnard from Lloyd O'Daniel's platoon was hustled over to him. The man's jaw had been partially shot away from his head, leaving Parnar to do his best to pull it back together with combat dressings.[10]

Jaeger was anxious for medevac choppers as the casualties

continued to grow. He and Parnar both hurried over to help tend to Sergeant Lee Dickerson, who had suffered a bad chest wound. Jaeger could see that the sergeant was also in dire need of being medically evacuated. Another half hour would pass while the SLAM company remained pinned under murderous fire. Meanwhile, Sergeant O'Daniel charged an NVA machine-gun bunker and wiped out the four gunners with a light anti-tank rocket.

As the air-cover strikes subsided, Bob Howard became aware of another strange sound in the jungle, but the source of that sound was hidden behind the heavy cover of woods. It appeared to Howard to be the engine of a tank or a half-track armored vehicle.

Tom Jaeger remained in contact with his Covey Rider, former RT Colorado one-zero Mike Bingo, who was flying rear seat in a Cessna O-2 Skymaster. Bingo went by the call sign "Cheetah."[11]

"Dungeon, this is Cheetah," Bingo radioed. "We have slicks inbound now."

"Roger that, Cheetah."

Four Huey slicks from the 57th AHC were soon overhead, circling as their Bird Dog spotter communicated with Jaeger on the best extraction point. But each time the choppers moved in, the NVA unleashed hellacious ground fire toward them. "Attempts to just recon the area drew such intense fire that you couldn't hear the radio's talk," recalled First Lieutenant Craig Collier, pilot of one of the four extraction choppers.[12]

Bingo called for the Hueys to circle at high altitude while he sorted out the mess with the SLAM company leader below. As

A SOG recon team scrambles to board a 57th Assault Helicopter Company Huey during an extract in Laos. EDWARD WOLCOFF

time passed, desperation for the survival of Lee Swain rose. It was finally decided that the 57th AHC choppers would make one fast pass and attempt to pick up some wounded while they still had ample fuel for the return flight. The first chopper to move in low for a landing was Gladiator 167, a slick flown by Warrant Officer Carl M. Hoeck. Among the crew flying with him was chase medic Tony Dorff, who had been extracted from the SLAM mission two days prior due to shrapnel wounds.

Hoeck's UH-1 took small-arms fire on its approach, but

things took a turn for the worse as the chopper went into a hover. A previously unseen quad-mount .51-caliber (12.7mm) heavy antiaircraft machine gun on tracks opened fire. It was the half-track armored vehicle Howard had heard moving in the distance.

Gladiator 167 staggered under direct hits from the powerful NVA tracked gun. Rounds slammed into its engine, through the passenger compartment, and into all vital hydraulic gear. Pilot Hoeck struggled to control his crippled bird as it staggered directly above Sergeant Howard and his besieged SLAM company. Hoeck had only a split second to select a thin patch of grass in the large clearing into which his helicopter would crash.

Howard was mortified to see that the would-be extraction chopper was now just another casualty. Hoeck's Huey slammed hard into the jungle greenery, its blades chopping through all sorts of vegetation. The UH-1 bounced off the ground and went about ten feet into the air before it crashed back into soft jungle soil, flinging dirt, debris, and grass in all directions. Red-orange flames erupted from the Huey's shattered tanks as the injured occupants tried to collect their senses.[13]

Oh, no, thought medic Joe Parnar. *I don't need any more wounded!*[14]

Bob Howard and Tom Jaeger had other thoughts. The downed medevac Huey had no sooner crashed down than NVA troops began emerging from the nearby jungle thicket to finish off the wounded occupants. The burning Huey was about 150 yards away. Shouting to others to cover them, Howard and Jaeger jumped to their feet and sprinted toward the disaster scene.

Jaeger had one hand on his pants to keep them from falling down, as he had used his belt as a tourniquet.

En route to the chopper, Jaeger shot down two enemy soldiers emerging from the thicket to the south. Howard cut down a couple others running in from north of the crash scene. Pilot Carl Hoeck was stunned and still fumbling with his shoulder harness. Howard pried open the door and reached in to help pull the Huey pilot out onto the jungle floor. Jaeger and Howard were joined by another platoon first lieutenant, Bob Price. All three had been wounded by shrapnel already, but they worked quickly to save lives and shoot down other NVA soldiers charging toward the downed chopper.

Pilot Hoeck, his copilot, Lieutenant Fred Ledfors, and their crew chief, Specialist Fifth Class Jerry Huffman, scurried away from their burning chopper. Their door gunner, Specialist Fourth Class Wayne Gilmore, remained pinned in the chopper, screaming with pain. His right hip and upper leg had been ripped open by the antiaircraft gun's fire. As Howard worked to free him from the wreckage, he spotted a North Vietnamese soldier attempting to climb into the back of the downed Huey.

A quick burst from Howard's M16 ended that threat. Jaeger gunned down another NVA who tried to reach the chopper's open door. Once Gilmore was free of the blazing chopper, Jaeger and pilot Hoeck tried to help him run for safety. But Gilmore collapsed in pain, screaming because of his severe leg wounds. Sergeant Howard ignored the heavy enemy fire and fired vigorously toward the surging NVA.

During these minutes of fighting side by side, Jaeger noticed the actions of his first sergeant. "It was the first time I'd seen him in a combat situation," he recalled. "I was impressed by how it didn't bother him, and that's rare." To the lieutenant, it seemed as if Howard simply operated as if he were invincible.[15]

Howard's covering fire allowed Hoeck and Jaeger to drag the wounded door gunner back to a safer position within the SLAM company's perimeter. Tony Dorff, now on the ground with the Kontum force, rushed to help fellow medic Parnar tend to the wounded. A short distance away, the blazing Gladiator 167 created such intense heat that its ammunition began cooking off.

For the moment, all hopes of rescue faded away.

Covey Rider Mike Bingo tried to offer encouragement to SLAM leader Tom Jaeger. The three remaining 57th AHC choppers needed to return to Dak To in order to refuel. Too much time had been wasted trying to get through the NVA's heavy fire. But Bingo assured Jaeger their tactical air support (TAC air) would work to suppress the numerous enemy troops for the time being.

Bob Howard carefully deployed his indigenous troops, while other men dug in with their entrenching tools to try to cover themselves. He low-crawled over to confer with Lieutenant Jaeger, who was still directing the bombing and strafing efforts of A-1 Skyraider pilots. Enemy ordnance was working over the Americans.

As Jaeger conferred with Cheetah, he suddenly saw Howard begin flailing about. His first sergeant was making violent contortions as if in a seizure.[16]

"What the hell's going on, Howard?" Jaeger shouted.

"Shrapnel!" Howard said.

A North Vietnamese RPG had exploded so close to Howard's position that pieces of red-hot steel shrapnel had struck his body. Small pieces of metal had lodged in his thigh and butt cheeks, where they continued to sear his flesh. Enjoying a moment of dark humor, Jaeger could not suppress a chuckle as Howard jumped around in pain. "Once it cooled off, he was okay," Jaeger recalled. "But he probably didn't appreciate me chuckling at him."[17]

Within a minute, both were again prone on the ground, defending their perimeter. To their surprise, Howard and Jaeger now found that one of the three remaining Gladiator slicks from the 57th AHC had not headed back to Dak To. As the A-1 attack planes completed their last runs, pilot Craig Collier, flying the Huey nicknamed Gladiator 26, decided to take a shot at pulling some of the wounded recon men from the jungle LZ.

Dusk was now approaching in the late afternoon of November 18. As Collier brought his slick into a hover, medics Parnar and Dorff raced forward with their two most critically wounded patients, Lieutenant Swain and Sergeant Dickerson.

Howard and Parnar carried Swain, trying to protect his mangled legs as best as they could. They gingerly lifted him up into the chopper, where his body was laid across the laps of Montagnards. As the Huey began to lift off, Swain's body shifted, and his dangling leg flopped over the side. Hanging only by a tendon, his foot twisted about in the wind stream as Lee screamed in agony.

Minutes later, one of Collier's fellow 57th AHC pilots followed him in to make another hasty extract. This time the five men from the downed Huey were recovered, including freshly wounded chase medic Tony Dorff. For the second time in three days, Dorff would be written up for a Purple Heart, both earned while he was working on the same SLAM mission.

Howard, now on his fifth day on the ground, was racking up his own injuries on this mission. But collecting another Purple Heart was never a thought for him. The mission at hand and keeping his men safe were all that mattered to him. His team had effectively laid down covering fire to allow the more seriously wounded men to be pulled out. His men had saved the lives of all five Americans after their Huey had been shot down.

Darkness swallowed up the jungle floor as the thumping sounds of chopper blades faded away. Lieutenant Jaeger's SLAM company would have to ride out at least one more night before having any chance of being extracted.

"Sergeant, get a status on ammunition," he ordered.

Howard moved about the perimeter, checking with each Green Beret and indigenous soldier. Some had been a little more conservative, but all had been forced to shoot for their lives throughout the afternoon. Jaeger was not surprised by Howard's report.

"They've got about one magazine left per man, sir, plus some grenades."

Howard also reported that he and many of the hundred SF men remaining were wounded to varying degrees. His own body had been pierced by shrapnel in several places. Alan Farrell had shrapnel in his right shoulder, and Lieutenant Bob Price had been wounded four times by shrapnel and bullets. Lieutenant Jaeger had shrapnel in his back, and the one remaining combat medic, Joe Parnar, had collected his own steel souvenirs. Parnar was one of the few with a full supply of M16 magazines, as he had spent most of his time saving lives. Howard put the least wounded Montagnards to work digging foxholes about the perimeter.

During this time, the wounded men still on the ground did their best to patch themselves up. Parnar cleaned up his own leg wound while Howard struggled with the shrapnel lacerations in his buttocks. For the moment, he simply fashioned a makeshift "field diaper" from his rain poncho around his rear and upper legs to cover his ripped and bloodied fatigues.[18]

Jaeger received word from Kontum that his men would have to fight through the night before an extraction was possible. He felt that an ammo resupply was imperative if his recon force was to have a prayer of making it through the night. This request was granted, and a resupply chopper arrived within the hour.

As the Huey settled into the nearby meadow to off-load ammunition, Howard suddenly heard the ominous engine sounds that had spelled disaster for another Huey hours before.

"The track is heading back!" Howard shouted.

At the last second, Jaeger, fearful of losing another chopper and more lives, made the gut-wrenching decision to call off the resupply bird. The NVA half-track was rumbling closer with its deadly AA gun. As the Huey lifted away in the darkness, many were left to wonder if they would see another dawn. In the hours that followed, some Green Berets lay on their backs on the rear edges of their foxholes. Should the NVA surge toward them, they would be in position to fire back.

With shrapnel in his hip, back, and buttocks, Howard could find no position that offered him any comfort. He instead spent the overnight hours assisting Lieutenant Jaeger in calling in strikes against the NVA. From Saigon, MACV-SOG command was committed to saving their SLAM force. Jets worked the vicinity as long as their fuel would allow, and then they were replaced by other fast movers (A-4 Skyhawks) as they cleared the area.

The rain of bullets and ordnance helped Howard and his comrades conserve their remaining magazines through the evening. A short time later, the SLAM men were pleased to hear that a powerful gunship was en route. Nicknamed "Puff, the Magic Dragon" by SF men, the Douglas AC-47 Spooky gunship was particularly deadly. Its three 7.62mm miniguns could be set to fire either fifty or a hundred rounds per second.

Jaeger and Howard had their men outline the company's perimeter with strobe lights before the Spooky gunship arrived around ten p.m. Its gunfire ripped through the darkened jungle like a hailstorm, knocking down trees, branches, and leaves. When the AC-47 finally moved out, other jets picked up the effort to suppress the NVA attacks against the SLAM company.[19]

Sometime around midnight, the napalm and bombing strikes hit what must have been a major North Vietnamese ammunition dump. Located on a ridgeline where the NVA's 37mm guns had been located, the dump exploded in spectacular fashion. The ridge glowed throughout the night as secondary explosions of ammunition continued to cook off from the cache. "I was later told the explosions that night and morning had destroyed the largest in-theater NVA ammo dump in all of 1968," Jaeger remembered.[20]

The exploding ammo dump and repeated air strikes apparently unnerved the nearby NVA soldiers to a great degree. A heavy white fog rolled through the green jungle around daybreak. Mixed with the smoke from the cache explosions, it made for an eerie scene until the sun rose enough to burn through it all hours later.

Expecting a heavy enemy assault shortly after daybreak on November 19, Lieutenant Jaeger had his men set their Claymores around their perimeter. His wounds still throbbing, Sergeant Howard had not slept a wink through the night. He listened as Jaeger worked with Leghorn to arrange an extraction of the company as soon as the heavy fog burned off.

What happened next was a complete shock to Howard. Two North Vietnamese soldiers suddenly materialized from the mist, moving toward the SLAM company's perimeter. Each soldier had his hands above his head, yelling, *"Chu hoi!"* Their rifles were held high above their heads. They were intent on surrendering.

Jaeger and Howard began yelling, "Don't fire! Don't fire!"

But their shouts were in vain. Specialist Fourth Class Bob Gron, a Hatchet Force Green Beret who was positioned near Howard, watched several of his indigenous team members raise their M16s to fire. "Before we could stop them, the Montagnards ripped them," Gron recalled.[21]

Howard was irate. Although the two NVA could have been

booby-trapped, he wanted them alive. Their intelligence could have proven to be vital. He and other Green Berets shouted at the Yards to cease firing.

A short while later, a third North Vietnamese soldier appeared, walking slowly toward the American perimeter. This soldier had no rifle, and advanced with his hands held high. Howard and Jaeger again screamed at their men not to shoot. "We had a hell of a time keeping our Montagnards from opening fire," Steve Roche recalled.[22]

Although this NVA soldier had no visible weapon, many members of the company were still concerned. This time Bob Howard sprang forward. He was not about to let the overzealous Yards gun down another potential POW. He raced forward, gun in hand. The NVA soldier made no attempt to resist as the muscular first sergeant overpowered him and knocked him to the ground. "SFC Howard was like a one-man Army," Roche later testified.[23]

Howard quickly checked his opponent for guns and knives. He had no zip-tie restraints, so Howard simply slung the man over his shoulder in a fireman's carry and began racing back toward his company's perimeter. If the soldier was hiding some kind of explosive pack, or if he was able to snatch away one of Howard's grenades, he might manage to kill or maim many within the American perimeter.

Howard charged through his defensive lines and dropped the POW like a sack of potatoes on the ground. Lieutenant Jaeger, busy calling in air strikes, quickly separated himself from the potential hazard and yelled for an interpreter. Howard and others searched the prisoner again and zip-tied his hands for safety. One of the company's indigenous interpreters, who spoke both fluent Montagnard and Vietnamese, began quizzing Howard's prisoner.

"He told us that we were currently facing two companies surrounding us, and that another regiment was in the immediate area," Jaeger recalled. The NVA soldier also related that many of his comrades had been killed or wounded, thus compelling some of them to attempt to surrender.[24]

No further NVA attempted to surrender. It was just as well. The company was exhausted, short on ammunition, and weary from lack of sleep over the past two days. Howard was greatly relieved to hear the rhythmic thumping of chopper blades approaching. About an hour after he had captured his prisoner, the first extraction choppers were on scene from Dak To. The extract team was once again the Gladiators from the 57th Assault Helicopter Company.

To keep the enemy suppressed, Jaeger ordered his men to detonate at least one Claymore as the chopper flared out to land. Air support was overhead as well, and the Skyraider pilots continued to blast the areas where NVA troops had been pointed out. It worked. This time the half-track AA gun was silent, perhaps because it had been destroyed, and the Hueys were not subjected to any heavy gunfire.

Bob Howard remained on the ground until the end, in company with Tom Jaeger, medic Joe Parnar, and three other Americans. In small groups, the balance of the SLAM company was lifted out and flown back to Dak To. Howard later heard from command that base intelligence officers who quizzed his prisoner found that the heavy air cover was the only reason the

Portrait of Robert Lewis Howard, the U.S. Army's most decorated Green Beret. He is seen in 1971 wearing his Medal of Honor. CONGRESSIONAL MEDAL OF HONOR SOCIETY, COURTESY OF MELISSA HOWARD GENTSCH

(*Above*) This caricature of Robert Howard graced the October 1969 cover of *The Green Beret* magazine. (*Left*) Sergeant First Class Howard in 1968 at FOB-2 in Vietnam. ROBERT L. HOWARD COLLECTION, COURTESY OF MELISSA HOWARD GENTSCH

An aerial view of Forward Operating Base 2 (FOB-2) at Kontum, where Robert Howard was assigned. Highway 14 divided the former Army of the Republic of Vietnam (ARVN) truck park, which was converted into a SOG base. JOE PARNAR

During 1967, Kontum recon teams were inserted into target areas by H-34 "Kingbee" helicopters. Here a Kingbee from the South Vietnamese 219th Helicopter Squadron lands atop the Leghorn radio relay site. ALAN KELLER

Staff Sergeant Paul Poole, wearing glasses at far right, seated with indigenous members of his recon team, Spike Team (ST) Colorado, where they have established an RON position.

Robert L. Howard Collection, courtesy of Melissa Howard Gentsch

Bob Howard and SSG Paul Poole breaking down their RON site while on a recon patrol in late 1967. Poole was then the one-one, or assistant team leader, of ST Colorado, which he later took over after one-zero Larry Williams was reassigned.

Robert L. Howard Collection, courtesy of Melissa Howard Gentsch

Captain Gene McCarley was a Kontum team leader who took Howard on multiple missions. Seen around January 1968 are, left to right: SSG Bill Boyle (killed in 1970), Gene McCarley, SFC Howard, and Sergeant Doug Glover, who was killed weeks after this photo.

ROBERT L. HOWARD COLLECTION, COURTESY OF MELISSA HOWARD GENTSCH

Robert Howard's photo of RT Wyoming during a training exercise in the fall of 1967. The team's one-one, SFC Guy Albregio (*second from left*), is taking a break with his indigenous squad.

ROBERT L. HOWARD COLLECTION, COURTESY OF MELISSA HOWARD GENTSCH

One-zero Larry White, whose SOG code name was "Six Pack." Robert Howard ran missions as a straphanger with White's recon team in 1967 and 1968. JASON HARDY

This Robert Howard photo was taken while his FOB-2 reaction force platoon is taking a break along an NVA trail, likely in Laos. Their larger size force allowed such an exposed break from marching, as opposed to a small recon team's more stealthy movement. Robert L. Howard Collection, courtesy of Melissa Howard Gentsch

Bob Howard collected dozens of valor medals during Vietnam. This awards ceremony took place at FOB-2, with Colonel Roy Bahr presenting to him.

Howard practicing with an M14 with a forward grip that fired duplex ammo at FOB-2 in 1969. The photo was taken by one-zero Edward Wolcoff.

Howard seen inspecting a Russian light machine gun in 1969 mounted at a Fort Bragg base firing range.

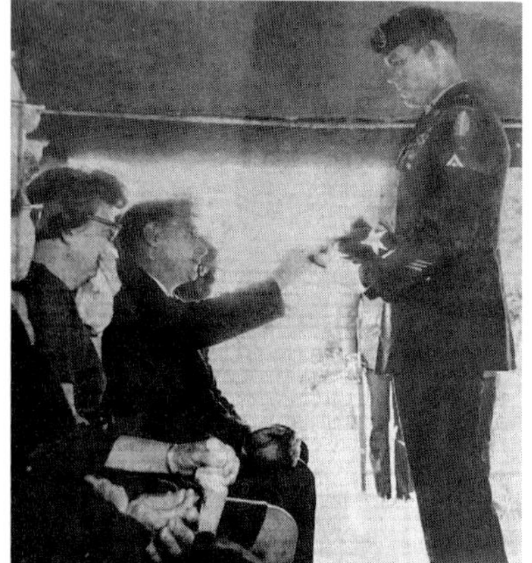

In late August 1968, SFC Howard returned to the US. Before seeing his family, he flew to Minnesota with the body of a fellow Kontum Green Beret, SSG Ken Worthley. Howard, wearing a black arm band, holds the U.S. flag that covered the casket of his Special Forces friend. John Worthley is reaching out to touch his son's flag.

SLAM VII MISSION: NOVEMBER 1968

First Lieutenant Lee Swain (*right*), seen with one of his platoon's Montagnards, lost one of his legs due to this mission. Lee Swain via Jason Hardy

Mission commander First Lieutenant Tom Jaeger earned the Distinguished Service Cross. Tom Jaeger via Jason Hardy

Staff Sergeant Joe "Gladiator" Walker, the one-zero of RT California, on patrol across the fence in face paint, with his CAR-15. Joe Walker

Sergeant Joe Parnar, SOG medic who worked to save lives.

Byron Loucks via Joe Parnar

(*Top*) Bob Howard, his bloodied midsection swaddled with a pancho, is seen with his NVA prisoner after SLAM VII upon returning to FOB-2 on November 19, 1968. Wounded in numerous places, he is holding a post-mission "welcome home" beer. (*Right*) Howard carries his POW to interrogators.

Robert L. Howard Collection, courtesy of Melissa Howard Gentsch

Private First Class Robert Scherdin (*left*) was the missing Green Beret that Howard's Bright Light team was sent to retrieve. To his right is First Lieutenant James Jerson, who was mortally wounded on December 30, 1968.

CRAIG DAVIS VIA JOE PARNAR

Staff Sergeant Bob Gron earned a Bronze Star for valor during this December 30 mission. ROBERT GRON

An armed A-1 Skyraider, called "fast movers" by SOG Green Berets. Howard asked his A-1 support aircraft to drop ordnance so close to his team that he was wounded by shrapnel. DON ENGEBRETSEN

A 57th Assault Helicopter Company Huey landing to pick up a SOG recon team in Laos. Howard and Gron were finally extracted by a slick like this on December 30. EDWARD WOLCOFF

SFC Howard is pinned with the 1st Oak Leaf Cluster to his Distinguished Service Cross by Lieutenant General Frank T. Mildren in 1969. The scars from his 1965 bullet wound are still visible on Howard's right cheek.

Bob Howard with team leader Floyd Ambrose, one-zero of RT Kentucky, in early 1969 at CCC.

Supply sergeant Howard on base with an M60 machine gun at Kontum.

Howard is awarded a special firearm by Colonel Billy Gibson in 1969.

Robert L. Howard Collection, courtesy of Melissa Howard Gentsch

First Lieutenant Bob Howard carries a handcuffed wounded POW, captured by one-zero David Gilmer's RT Texas, from a chopper through the Kontum compound in July 1969. Joe Parnar

Nervous and almost faint, Captain Howard is draped with the Medal of Honor on March 2, 1971, by President Richard Nixon.

Howard remains serious beside a beaming president.

President Nixon congratulates Howard and his young daughters.

Medal of Honor Presentation
by
Richard Nixon
President of the United States of America

AT THE WHITE HOUSE
ON
2 MARCH 1971
AT
1130 HOURS

The ceremony program.

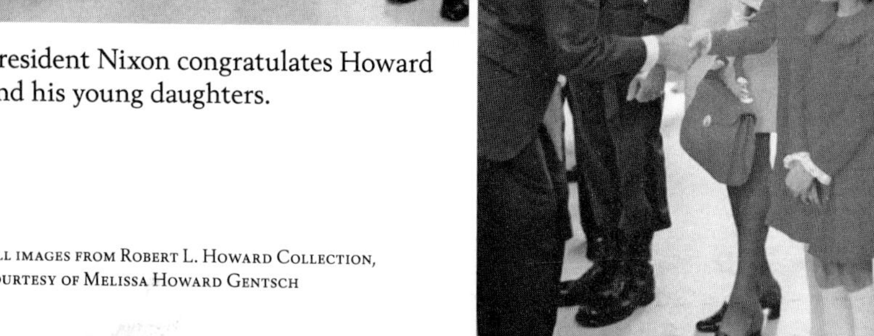

All images from Robert L. Howard Collection, courtesy of Melissa Howard Gentsch

Howard and family following the 1971 White House ceremony. Left to right, front row: General William Westmoreland, Bob Howard, Tina Howard, Melissa Howard, Denicia Howard, Annie Punchard, and other officials.

Howard poses before a shot-up helicopter while serving in Vietnam.

Colonel Howard seen during his service in Korea. From July 1989 to June 1990, he was the commander of Special Operations Korea, located at Camp Humphreys near Seoul.

Bob Howard is pinned with his first lieutenant's bars by his wife Tina and Brigadier General Edward M. Flanagan Jr., commander of the JFK Center. During the ceremony, Howard was also given the Bronze Star.

Tina and Robert Howard, with their daughters Melissa (*front, left*) and Denicia.

Howard with his third wife, Sun Young, at home in Texas in 1993.

Colonel Howard congratulates his son, Robert Howard Jr., during his 2006 graduation ceremony from U.S. Army Infantry School.

Bob's father, Charlie Howard, and his younger brother, Charlie "Bo" Howard Jr.

Family life. Howard seen in Texas with (*left to right*): his daughter Missy, granddaughter Holley, son Robert Jr., granddaughter Victoria, and daughter Rosslyn.

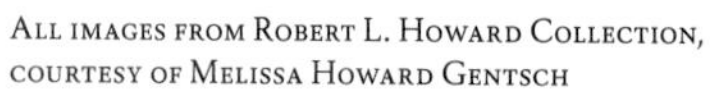

All images from Robert L. Howard Collection, courtesy of Melissa Howard Gentsch

Colonel Bob Howard, seen wearing his Medal of Honor, continued to greet troops overseas even as he was secretly fighting cancer.

Robert L. Howard Collection, courtesy of Melissa Howard Gentsch

During April 2009, Medal of Honor recipients Bob Howard and Gary Littrell (*far right*) greet soldiers and sign copies of their MOH citations in southwest Asia.

US Navy photo, 090412-N-0636S-007

Colonel Howard's coffin is drawn toward his snow-covered plot in the Arlington National Cemetery on February 22, 2010.

Vietnam Medal of Honor recipient Sammy Lee Davis salutes the casket of Robert Howard.

The headstone of Colonel Howard in Section 7A of the Arlington National Cemetery.

Military officials offer their condolences to Melissa Howard Gentsch, holding the flag, and her husband, Frank Gentsch.

Melissa Gentsch accepts the Bull Simons Award in 2014 on behalf of her father, from Admiral William H. McRaven of the U.S. Special Operations Command.

All images from Robert L. Howard Collection, courtesy of Melissa Howard Gentsch

NVA had not tried to finish off the American recon men overnight.

Howard detonated the last Claymore before his men jumped onto the final waiting Huey. He was the second to last to leave the Laotian soil, with leader Lieutenant Jaeger being the final one. All of the men were physically and mentally spent.

Medic Parnar sat on the edge of the doorframe of this last Huey. Tears involuntarily began streaming down his face. He had not slept in two days, and his remaining energy was now gone. Parnar stuck his face into the wind stream to help hide his tears. His greatest fear was that Bob Howard or the lieutenant might see him. "I wanted them to think the wind was just making my eyes water, and I wasn't a candy-ass," he recalled.[25]

SLAM VII WAS a record mission for MACV-SOG.

The entire operation had involved thirteen different recon teams, plus four platoons and four companies, over a multiweek period that ended in early December. Forty-two helicopter gunships sorties and 112 tactical air strikes had been launched to support the anti-NVA mission. More than forty-five men had been wounded during this operation, but only five indigenous personnel had perished on November 14.[26]

Even the most severely wounded men would survive. Lieutenant Lee Swain was operated on in Dak To through the night. The following day, he was flown to Pleiku. SOG command was impressed with the work accomplished by SLAM VII, and the valor displayed by many to keep their comrades alive. Recon Team California one-zero Joe Walker was written up for a

Silver Star, but it was later downgraded to an Army Commendation Medal. Disgusted by this move, he told others that what really mattered was what his team had accomplished in the field. He had no further use for Army awards.[27]

Colonel Smith and recon company commander Ed Lesesne kept their staff busy writing up plenty of other awards for members of SLAM mission. Numerous men, including Bob Howard, would receive Purple Hearts. Mission commander Tom Jaeger was written up for a Silver Star, but this was upgraded to the Distinguished Service Cross, making him the seventh Kontum recon man to earn this distinction. Silver Stars went to Lee Swain, Bob Price, and Lloyd O'Daniel. Bronze Stars were later pinned on Joe Parnar, Steve Roche, and Terry Brents. Air Medals went to Bill Kendall and Bill De Lima, while Army Commendation Medals were soon bestowed upon Walker, Mike Machata, Walt Huczko, and Tony Dorff.

Upon his return to FOB-2, Howard—still wearing his makeshift field diaper to protect his rear-side wounds—happily accepted a cold beer as he stood guard over his NVA prisoner. Prior to landing at the base, he and Jaeger had covered the enemy soldier's head with a black bag. Howard downed his beer, slung the POW over his shoulder in a fireman's carry, and marched toward the tactical operations center to deposit his captured man.

Mission commander Jaeger wrote Sergeant First Class Howard up for a Silver Star, but base commander Whiskey Smith and recon company commander Lesesne went a step further. The NVA prisoner captured by Howard, an officer, proved quite valuable to the intelligence teams who interrogated him. They learned plenty about North Vietnamese operations, and his testimony eventually led to nine successful Arc Light bombing missions in the Juliett 9 region of Laos.[28]

For the second time in his tenure at FOB-2 Kontum, Robert Howard was submitted for the Medal of Honor. His first write-up for the medal in late 1967 had later been downgraded to a Distinguished Service Cross. This time the recommendation would be downgraded to a Silver Star during the months ahead.

Howard was praised for his repeated attacks on enemy forces on an operation deep into enemy-held territory that lasted from November 12 to November 20, 1968. The Silver Star citation noted that although wounded twice during the operation, Howard had also rescued a pilot from a burning helicopter and single-handedly captured an important enemy soldier. While he was quick to shrug off such awards, he would in time be recognized before his peers for his "exceptionally valorous actions."[29]

★ TWELVE ★

SIX PACK'S RETURN

His latest shrapnel wounds kept Bob Howard out of recon missions for a few days. The slices in his buttocks were a nuisance, but they did not keep him from his duties as recon company training sergeant, nor from checking up on his comrades.

Just two days after returning to Kontum, he hopped a flight with chase medic Joe Parnar to return to the 71st Evacuation Hospital at Pleiku. They visited Sergeant Dickerson and Lieutenant Lee Swain, both of whom were making progress with their recoveries. Like Swain, Dickerson had been treated initially at Dak To before being medevaced to Pleiku.[1]

Both men would survive. Doctors had already pinned Swain's foot back on, and he told Howard that he had hopes that he would walk again one day. Swain would soon be shifted to a more advanced hospital, the 106th General Hospital in Japan. Over the next two years, doctors performed multiple surgeries on Swain's shattered legs, but he ultimately agreed to have his right leg amputated. A born fighter, Swain would not be held back by any such loss. Following his U.S. Army service, he later learned to ski in snow with special crutches and eventually earned his commercial pilot's license.

During late November, Howard continued to work training the newer Green Berets coming into Kontum. "Lessons learned" was an important part of Special Forces training, and the most recent SLAM operation from FOB-2 was filled with examples, both good and bad, on how to conduct various aspects of recon work across the fence.

Howard's capture of the NVA officer during the SLAM mission was significant. Such feats were generally rewarded by SOG with bonus pay and special R & R. "We got a flight down to the Chongqing Air Base at Taiwan, and Bob Howard was along with us on that one," Bob Gron recalled. "It was like a freebie ride, because we had taken a prisoner on the SLAM mission, and Howard had been instrumental in that. They were operating Special Operations C-130s from there, and we were given a couple days of downtime."[2]

Upon returning to base, Sergeant First Class Howard was all business as he worked to help train the newest Green Berets. One of the faces reporting to Howard in November was a familiar one. It was Staff Sergeant Larry "Six Pack" White, with whom he had run recon missions in late 1967. In early 1968, White had been shifted to SOG's southern Ban Me Thuot base to command an Omega team. As a well-seasoned one-zero, White was quick to pull together a composite team to run a Prairie Fire mission into Laos in late November.

Although his scabs from shrapnel wounds were still healing, Bob Howard could not be held back. He jumped at the chance to run another mission as one-one for his old buddy. For their commo man, or one-two, Howard suggested a new guy at the Kontum base, Sergeant Robert E. Clough. Assigned the call name "Buckwheat," Clough was a seasoned Army man, although new to small-team recon missions.

Maintaining his team size preference of a half dozen, Six Pack White went in with three Americans and three Yards. Choppers inserted the team into an active grid zone near Laotian Highway 110. The next day, White's team stealthily shadowed an NVA battalion near the roadway, then watched from a hilltop as their enemy set up a night encampment. With the element of surprise in their favor, the Command and Control Center (CCC) team discussed what a great target this would make for a tactical air strike. Unfortunately, low-hanging clouds negated the opportunity.[3]

As Howard and White whispered carefully, they noticed Buckwheat Clough digging in his rucksack. He produced a pair of Nightingale devices—relatively new CIA-produced diversionary tools. These air-dropped firefight simulators were mounted on four-foot-by-three-foot screens, each containing powder trails leading to clusters of cherry bombs and firecrackers. With an acid-delay pencil to ignite its fuse, the Nightingale could be set to erupt for several hours or even days after it was emplaced near an enemy's position. The Nightingales had been designed primarily for false inserts, but White's team now had a different idea.

Clough whispered that he and one of his Montagnards could

creep up on the NVA position after dark. They would hide the two Nightingales after setting a two-hour delay, and then sneak back. Although Howard considered it to be an "unbelievable" proposition, he and White were not about to undermine Clough's enthusiasm.[4]

Over the next seven hours, Clough and a Yard moved very slowly, creeping up on the camp where hundreds of North Vietnamese soldiers lay resting. Clough activated the two-hour fuses, and the pair eased back to the nearby hilltop where Howard and the others lay prone, watching. Not long after Clough and his companion returned, the Nightingales began erupting in a series of bangs and pops.

The badly startled NVA began firing wildly. To Howard, it was "the biggest firefight" he had yet witnessed. Between the periodic eruptions of fireworks, gunshots rang out in all directions as their enemy tried to determine who was firing. "This son of a bitch goes on for at least an hour and a half," Howard later related. Daylight was beginning to break by the time NVA officers managed to stop their men from wildly firing into one another.[5]

The North Vietnamese battalion cleared the area hastily, apparently figuring an American air strike was imminent. When White's team crept up on the empty bivouac area to inspect it, they were shocked. "We found dead bodies everywhere," said Howard.

On December 1, command of FOB-2 passed to a new man, thirty-eight-year-old Lieutenant Colonel Roy Bahr. A Florida native, Bahr had been an infantry platoon leader during the Korean War. In the Vietnam War, he had already commanded two other MACV-SOG forward operating bases.

As Bahr took over FOB-2, his recon teams continued to run Prairie Fire missions into Laos and Daniel Boone recon operations as deep as eighteen miles into Cambodia. He was already aware of the outstanding work of his company training NCO, Bob Howard, who had captured one of only three NVA prisoners taken alive in 1968 by SOG men. Bahr had no opposition to Howard's desire to run missions as often as possible.

The exact number of recon missions run by Howard will probably never be known. His earliest dated back to his 1966 long-range reconnaissance missions with Project Omega's B-50 detachment. Since May 1967, during his second and third tours in Vietnam, Howard had pulled more than two dozen missions. Even with a five-month break in 1968 due to wounds, he had still racked up more time in enemy territory than many Green Berets regularly assigned to recon teams. "I would say he probably ran twenty-five or thirty missions, more than the average recon man would have run," Howard's friend Billy Greenwood later estimated.[6]

Howard did not keep personal notes or such, and following the Vietnam War, the U.S. government destroyed a large portion of SOG's covert mission reports. Not all dates of his missions can be precisely given, except for the instances when Howard or others received the Purple Heart or various valor awards.

Some trips across the fence lasted more than a week. But Howard's final mission with one-zero Six Pack White didn't even last a day.

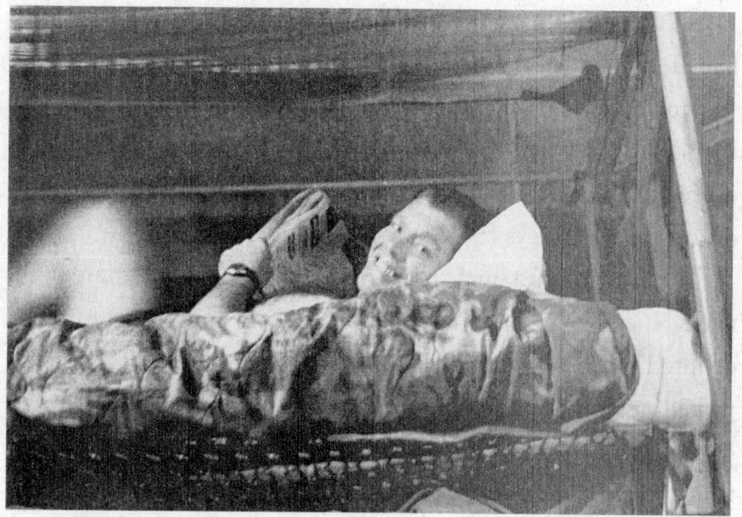

A grinning Bob Howard catches up on his reading in his bunk at FOB-2. Robert L. Howard Collection, courtesy of Melissa Howard Gentsch

On December 8, 1968, Howard geared up to go in with the composite team. White and Clough had plans to attempt a prisoner-snatch operation in the Bra region of Laos in target area November 9. Six Pack had turned to his old friend, checking to see if he was willing to join him across the fence in hopes of nabbing an NVA soldier. He had had no doubts about what Howard's answer would be. "He was ready to go all the time," White recalled.

This time there would be no six-pack team. It would consist of the three Americans and an ARVN officer to assist with interrogating any soldier they could subdue. White also tapped six of his Montagnards. He knew extra firepower might be needed to cover those who attempted to manhandle a live enemy soldier for rapid extraction.[7]

As was customary prior to such a key mission, the one-zero had flown an aerial reconnaissance over the Bra region, where they planned to insert. White selected three acceptable LZs, returned to Dak To, and completed his mission planning that evening. The following morning, December 8, his team loaded onto a pair of Hueys for the flight into Laos.

The insert was a bust from the start. As the pilots flared out their Hueys to hover above the first landing zone, NVA gunfire erupted from all sides of the heavy cover below. The pilots pulled away and flew a short distance to the second LZ that White had selected. Once again, enemy gunfire was so intense that the pilots refused to stick around.

White's recon team was then flown about a mile to the third and final LZ that he had picked out. Although the insert site was not his preferred one, Six Pack decided it would have to do. He and Howard were eager to pull off a prisoner snatch. Clutching their assault rifles, with their feet on the skids, they watched the tall grass dancing below as the prop wash stirred up dust and debris. All looked good at first, but then hellfire erupted for the third time.

The team's insert birds were so low this time that the NVA simply could not miss. Small-arms fire and machine-gun bullets ripped through the thin-skinned Hueys as if they were tin cans. In one bird, the ARVN officer was hit and killed by several rounds.

As one-zero, Larry White was always the first man on the ground. He had jumped from the skid just as the chopper flared out above the grass on the LZ. Almost immediately, White was struck in the leg by a bullet that knocked him down. Still on board the chopper, Howard saw him drop. In the same instant, other bullets pierced the chopper's windshield, winging both the pilot and the copilot. Other rounds hit the Huey door gunner, splattering blood throughout the interior and leaving his limp body swinging from his gun strap.

One-two Buckwheat Clough and one of the team's Yards were just leaping from the chopper when their bodies were also hit. The concussion of slugs thumping into Clough's arm and side knocked him back into the Huey. Ignoring his pain, he immediately dragged the bloodied door gunner back into the chopper and dropped him on the floor. Clough seized the M60 and began blazing away into the nearby tree line. His return fire was vicious enough to force an advancing NVA company to temporarily halt.[8]

Somehow, Howard was not struck. As his Huey was violently laced with bullets, the wounded pilot lost control. The chopper plunged down the last three feet and slammed heavily into the ground. Howard jumped from the Huey and began to lay down a heavy volume of suppressive firepower as an estimated hundred NVA climbed from their bunkers and raced toward the downed American aircraft.

Howard suddenly spotted the reason why the area was so hotly contested. About a hundred yards away, partially covered by the jungle canopy, was a pair of Soviet-made Mi-4 helicopters beneath camouflage nets. Reports had circulated about enemy choppers moving around Laos at night, but the intelligence had largely been dismissed as fantasy. The enemy soldiers racing forward now clearly had no intentions of letting the Americans get off a radio report of this vital discovery.[9]

Clough blazed away with the Huey's M60. Howard and White also sprayed liberal doses of lead from their CAR-15s, dropping many of the surging soldiers. The dazed chopper pilot tried to lift off, but he gained only a few feet of altitude before his power failed and he had to set her back down. The North Vietnamese shouted and pressed forward again, their guns blazing. Howard, his two fellow Green Berets, and their uninjured Yards cut down NVA soldiers, even as some ran as close as fifteen yards from the chopper.

Their efforts forced the NVA to retreat slightly. White shouted at his team to move. Those still on the ground began jumping through the Huey's open side door. White was just scrambling on board when another enemy round ripped through his arm. The one-zero spun around and unleashed a burst that was seen to kill three NVA and wound a fourth. As the final North Vietnamese fell toward the ground, he squeezed off another round. The bullet slammed into the trigger housing of White's CAR-15. It went through his hand before lodging in his chest.

Bloodied by three bullets, White still triggered another burst that finished off his opponent. He then collapsed to the ground near the chopper. All the other team members were on board, save Bob Howard. He opened up again with another tremendous burst of fire to force the NVA back. Howard then raced to his fallen comrade and dragged White back onto the chopper.

In the process, Howard collected a bullet wound to his right shoulder. Clough continued blasting the enemy soldiers with his M60 as the pilot finally built up enough rpms to lift his riddled bird from the LZ. In that moment, White was struck a fourth time by a bullet that sliced through the Huey's underside and went through the back of his right leg. The chopper was able to maintain enough power to pull away, with warning lights flashing on the instrument panel and a shattered windscreen that made vision challenging at best.[10]

Once the aircraft had cleared the canopy, Howard moved about swiftly. He administered lifesaving first aid to several seriously wounded comrades, ignoring his own latest bullet wound. One-zero White regained consciousness during the flight, but he waved off any help from Howard until everyone else had been tended to first.

The recon men called in heavy air strikes to pound the remaining NVA and the two camouflaged helicopters that they had discovered. Medics from the 4th Division medical facility were standing by when the shattered Huey reached its staging base at Dak To. For this mission, Larry "Six Pack" White, shot four different times, would be pinned with a Bronze Star and a Purple Heart. Teammates Clough and Howard would each receive the Air Medal for heroism and a Purple Heart.

Buckwheat Clough recovered and would continue in service. Staff Sergeant White would spend months recovering in military hospitals in Vietnam, Japan, and at Fort Bragg. But the resilient SOG warrior demanded to be returned to service. His wishes were granted, and in 1970, he would be back at Kontum, heading RT Hawaii as its one-zero.

Howard and Clough were detained briefly at Pleiku for treatment. There Howard encountered Sergeant Billy Greenwood, a man he would later serve with at Kontum. Greenwood noted that Howard was still dressed in his hospital pajamas and had gone AWOL from his ward. Howard had decided that he felt good enough to slip out of the hospital in search of better food. He was standing in line with other soldiers, waiting to be served his meal, when two Vietnamese men raced up the road on a motorcycle. The man riding on the back suddenly lobbed a grenade.

"Everyone ducks for cover except Howard," Greenwood later related. "He grabs a rifle from a startled MP guard, gets in a kneeling position, aims, and shoots and kills the passenger on the bike." According to Greenwood, the shooting of the passenger caused the motorcycle's driver to crash. The Vietnamese man jumped up and sprinted away down the road.[11]

Greenwood watched in awe as Howard, clad only in his hospital pajamas, took off in pursuit. A half mile down the road, he stopped and shot the fleeing driver dead. "Bob Howard comes back, returns the rifle to the MP, gets back into the chow line, and got his chow," Greenwood later related.

Howard thought nothing of the incident and never reported it. His only concern was to get back to his FOB as soon as possible.

★ THIRTEEN ★

THE SCHERDIN BRIGHT LIGHT

Nineteen-year-old John Plaster first met Bob Howard on Christmas Eve 1968. The young Green Beret from Minnesota was among three new SOG men flown into the Kontum airport that day. Hauled down Highway 14 to the FOB-2 compound, Plaster and the other newbies would be ordered to join recon teams in need of replacement men.

Spec-4 Plaster was soon assigned by Sergeant First Class Howard to join RT New Mexico as its new one-two, or commo man. During training exercises held each day on base, he learned more about the husky NCO who spoke with a smooth Alabama drawl.

Plaster later wrote that Howard was "the most impressive man I ever met in Special Forces." He recalled him to be "physically imposing. Every ounce of his 170 pounds was solid muscle, backed up by an attitude that didn't take much lightly." The Green Beret was stunned to hear that his new training sergeant had already been written up twice for the Medal of Honor, only to have the award twice downgraded to lesser medals.[1]

In his current role as the recon company training NCO, Howard reviewed the day's training plans with each one-zero. Some of the one-zeros planned range firing drills for their teams. When he found others merely planning for tactical exercises in the jungle, he worried little about whether they were looking for a chance to take it easy.

"Oh, if y'all screw off, don't worry 'bout Bob Howard catchin' you," he told one team. "No, sir, the NVA's gonna kill you. Then you'll know you shoulda trained harder."

As Plaster watched Howard utter this warning, he noted the sergeant's facial squint and tough grin. He felt his training sergeant looked "much like Clint Eastwood playing Dirty Harry. But Howard wasn't playing."[2]

On the afternoon of December 29, just days after the newest Green Berets had reached Kontum, they gathered at the base helipad as a flight of Hueys approached to land. As the dust settled, nine men from Recon Team Vermont climbed out, dirty, unshaven, and some wearing bloodstained fatigues. The one-zero, Staff Sergeant Gerald Apperson, was handed a beer and Bob Howard put an arm around his shoulder to comfort him. John Plaster quickly heard the reason for the concern and commotion: One of Apperson's Green Berets was missing.

Apperson's team had been inserted four miles inside Cambodia, west of the Dak To launch site.[3] The ten-man group included only one other American, a new one-one named Private First Class (PFC) Robert Francis Scherdin, a twenty-one-year-old who hailed from Somerville, New Jersey. Having only recently arrived at FOB-2, Scherdin was carrying the team radio on December 29 when the rear section of RT Vermont was assaulted by NVA forces. Apperson and three of his Vietnamese team members became separated in the firefight. Apperson used his UHF emergency radio to raise his Covey pilot, First Lieutenant Donald Long, and Covey Rider Terry Hamric, a first lieutenant and former Kontum recon man who had run a Hatchet Force platoon from FOB-2 Kontum during the spring of 1968.[4]

Around four p.m., one-zero Apperson and his teammates, unable to reunite with their rear element, were guided by Long and Hamric to an extraction point. About fifteen minutes later, the Covey team spotted the recognition panels being flashed by the rear element of RT Vermont. Five more indigenous team members were extracted, bringing the total to nine. The only man missing was the new one-one, Bob Scherdin. Montagnard team interpreter Nguang had seen Scherdin fall wounded from a gunshot. Nguang tried to pick him up, but Scherdin was lying in a pool of blood, too injured to move. After Nguang was wounded in the face, he had been forced to flee for his life, leaving Scherdin to his fate.[5]

The Covey team continued to fly over the area, calling to Scherdin to no avail. After departing long enough to refuel their O-1 Bird Dog aircraft, Long and Hamric returned to the battle scene to call for Scherdin until darkness. He did not respond to either the FM frequency radio or his emergency UHF responder. Hours later, an Air Force FAC plane overflying the battle zone detected Scherdin's emergency beeper. There was no way to know if he was alive and too badly injured to respond or if the NVA were attempting to use his body as bait for a deadly Bright Light trap.[6]

That evening, Lieutenant Colonel Bahr called a meeting of

his senior officers and noncoms to discuss the Scherdin situation. Bob Howard spoke up, expressing his regrets that the young soldier was missing. Howard had been on duty at the Dak To staging area that day when Scherdin's team went in. Scherdin had related to Bob that he had just recovered from the effects of malaria.

"You don't have to go on this one," Howard had advised him.

But Scherdin insisted he was now physically fit. He had missed enough with his malaria bout, and he wanted to go out with his team this time.

When Bahr said he was sending in a Hatchet Force platoon to perform a Bright Light mission, he could not have found a more willing volunteer.

"I'll go," said Howard.[7]

"Bob, I want you to get our man back," said Bahr. "I'm going to send Lieutenant Jerson in as commander of the platoon, but I want you to give him your assistance and bring that American back."[8]

The Bright Light team's mission was straightforward: Bring Scherdin back for medical attention if he was found to still be living. If he had succumbed to his wounds, they were to recover his body. From his Hatchet Force company, Bahr tapped the blond, youthful-looking First Lieutenant Jim Jerson to command. A twenty-one-year-old married man from New Orleans, Jerson would lead his full Platoon C.

The team included two other Green Berets, Spec-4 Bob Gron and Sergeant Jerome Griffin. SFC Howard would be second-in-command. Their thirty-four-man group also included an ARVN officer and twenty-nine Montagnards.

"It was not my platoon, but they needed me," Gron recalled. He knew Howard well, having fought alongside him during the recent SLAM VII mission. "I didn't really volunteer. I was told, 'You're going with this platoon.'" Gron was also familiar with Sergeant Griffin, as he had worked with Lieutenant Jerson's platoon previously. Jerson's platoon was down a man, as First Lieutenant Walt Huczko had been wounded shortly after the recent SLAM mission by stepping on a toe popper mine during another recon mission. "In this platoon, we had Montagnard platoon leaders, Montagnard platoon sergeants, and squad leaders," said Gron.[9]

For such a mission, time was critical. Jerson's team would be on the move at first light. "We didn't have time to really prepare for the mission or go through immediate action drills," Howard recalled. "We had to go in immediately."

December 30, 1968

The next morning, several big Vietnamese Kingbee choppers roared to life. Lieutenant Jerson's thirty-four-man unit was heavily armed as they boarded the helicopters. Howard, standing a foot taller than the team's Yards, wore combat fatigues and a floppy jungle hat; he clutched his CAR-15 as he climbed into a waiting chopper.

Supported by 170th Assault Helicopter Company gunships, the CH-34s hauled the platoon to Dak To. Last-minute planning between the Kontum SF men and the aviation support that would be required for them consumed the next few hours. The Bright Light Kingbees lifted off before three p.m. and flew four miles deep into Laos to the area where Scherdin's team had been attacked the previous day.

It was immediately obvious that the NVA were waiting for this rescue group, as small-arms fire clawed up from the jungle toward the big helicopters. The jungle canopy had sufficient openings for Jerson's team to be deposited, but the terrain was unforgiving. Rocky and mountainous, it was heavily layered with dense vines, bushes, and bamboo thickets. Decades of dried, decaying vegetation created an earthy aroma and made silent movement all but impossible.

The time was three fifteen p.m. as Lieutenant Jerson's men exited their choppers and took cover. "We started receiving a lot of ground fire because we were on six helicopters on the insert," Howard later recalled. "A couple of the helicopters got shot up pretty bad and had to land quickly." Based on the reception received during this insert, Howard knew this was going to be a particularly rough mission at best.[10]

Once the Kingbees pulled clear, Howard made a quick assessment of their situation with his senior officer, Jerson.

"Bob, we need to secure the LZ," said the lieutenant. "Get a couple of men and secure the exterior. We need to organize, get off this LZ, and move toward our target area."

Howard took three of his Montagnards and pushed back toward the rear of the landing zone to ward off any enemy assault. During the next ten minutes, Howard's men encountered soldiers firing from multiple points. His team engaged in brief firefights before he made his way back to Jerson.

"There's no way we're going to secure this LZ," Howard announced. "We're surrounded, so we're just going to have to fight our way through it."[11]

Lieutenant Jerson took the lead, pushing the platoon forward around four p.m. toward the last known position of Private First Class Scherdin. Howard was responsible for bringing up rear security as the platoon moved forward. As his rear guard advanced, they continued to receive sporadic enemy gunfire.

Squad leader Bob Gron, in charge of the platoon's second squad, was located in the center of the formation as it advanced through the jungle undergrowth. He was certain NVA troops were in the area, based on the amount of slashed vegetation he could see nearby. "After moving approximately fifty meters, we stopped to listen," Gron recalled. He could hear enemy troops moving through the thicket around them. Although unseen, they appeared to be easing along with the recon force, keeping a distance of about seventy-five to a hundred yards away. Gron worried that the North Vietnamese were carefully converging, preparing to hit the Bright Light platoon from both flanks.[12]

With darkness approaching in a couple hours, Jerson decided it was best to move his platoon toward a safe RON position. If they could avoid detection overnight by shaking their trackers, he hoped his team could continue their Bright Light mission at first light. With Howard monitoring the rear of the large group, Jerson advanced his men another 160 yards from their original landing zone.

"We crossed a trail that had been recently used by the enemy," recalled Sergeant Jerome Griffin, who was leading the rear security of the platoon near Howard. "Once my squad was across the trail and a few meters into the brush, we stopped for a security halt."[13]

Howard and his fellow teammates could clearly hear that NVA trackers were close at hand. The unseen enemy warriors sounded to be little more than fifty yards away from them. "We heard banging, like people slapping two sticks together or knocking sticks against tree trunks," Gron remembered.[14]

The banging and rustling of brush and the occasional crunch of careless footsteps warned the Bright Light team that their opponents were on both sides of the platoon. It was a classic hammer-and-anvil tactic: beating the brush to hasten prey into a blocking force. Jerson signaled to his men. He wanted them to continue toward higher ground. There they could form a perimeter and settle in for the night before darkness swallowed them in the dense green jungle. As a platoon, they did not have the option to run and hide like a smaller recon team. It was looking more like a stand-and-fight scenario.

Just ahead of the team, the rugged terrain leveled out somewhat as they neared the crest of a hill. A small depression lay in the side of the slope. Just beyond this trough, the ground began to rise steeply. Lieutenant Jerson and the squad of Yards walking point with him were about thirty yards ahead of the company. They began easing up the slope, moving about fifty yards farther ahead. Specialist Fourth Class Gron's squad was in the center of the formation, while Sergeant Griffin's rear guard trailed slightly behind them.

Jerson carried one of the team's PRC-25 radios with the point and Griffin carried the other radio with the rear guard.

Apprehensive that his comrades might be walking into an NVA trap, Bob Howard became concerned.

Hoping to put a more cohesive plan together, Howard jogged up ahead to the point position as they climbed the hill. He eased his way up toward the front of the platoon. Reaching Jerson, he recommended that the lieutenant should reconsider his advance and instead defensively organize his troops. "The enemy knows where we are," said Howard. "They are following us." It was already too late. "Sure enough, we walked right into an ambush," recalled Howard.[15]

All hell broke loose.

From both sides of the Bright Light force, the jungle exploded in a massive NVA assault with machine-gun and semiautomatic fire. This enemy force was later estimated to comprise roughly two companies, or more than two hundred soldiers. Jerson, Howard, and the forwardmost Montagnards immediately returned fire with their automatic weapons and M79 grenade launchers—the latter a single-shot, shoulder-fired, break-action grenade launcher.

Howard caught sight of four enemy infantrymen. He mowed them down with a swift barrage from his CAR-15 before he hit the ground to take cover. The platoon's Montagnard point man, who had been walking just ahead of Howard, was hit by several bullets in the initial enemy shooting. Three other advance members of Jerson's team were seriously wounded in the first exchange. One indigenous trooper was killed while trying to assist the crippled point man. Howard later estimated that his advance team killed or wounded as many as eight NVA soldiers in this initial exchange of fire.

Lying flat on the jungle floor midway up the steep slope, Howard and Jerson were pinned down close to each other by the enemy fire. Gron's second squad was a good twenty yards behind them, also taking cover and firing back. Jerome Griffin's rearmost squad was fifty to sixty yards back from Howard's position when the ambush commenced.

Howard and Jerson had one slight advantage initially. A large tree near them provided at least some cover as gunfire and grenades shredded foliage and tossed debris all about their position. They fired back as best they could, trying to put forth enough lead to keep their opponents at bay. But several North Vietnamese soldiers raced forward to a point within fifteen yards of their position to throw hand grenades.

The lieutenant shouted to Howard over the deafening barrage.

"Let's make a break for the top of the hill to get some better cover," Jerson yelled.

"All right, let's go!" said Howard.

As the pair of Americans rose to make their bolt for cover, an NVA grenade thumped down in the soil between them. Almost instantaneously, the grenade exploded with a violent red flash and an earthshaking roar.

The concussive effects violently flung Lieutenant Jerson and Sergeant Howard in opposite directions. Howard's body was pitched about ten feet back down the hill and flipped upside down. North Vietnamese soldiers continued to fire steady streams of bullets as Bob slammed into the moist jungle floor.

His body throbbing and his ears ringing, Howard felt his mind fading to black as he collapsed, unconscious.

★ FOURTEEN ★

"GIVE ME YOUR WEAPON!"

Bob Howard's eyes opened to a hazy, chaotic scene.

The smells of smoke and gunpowder were strong. His ears were ringing at first. Slowly, he became aware of a hellish orchestra of battle sounds all about him: chattering machine guns, barking rifles, screams, and deafening grenades blasts.

He tried to focus. But everything was blurry, clouded by a strange red film. Bob said silent prayers, fearful he had been blinded by the terrible blast.

"God, please help me see," he muttered.[1]

If I can see, I can make it, he thought.

His body ached all over. Wiping his eyes, he saw red on his hands, and realized his vision had been obscured by shrapnel wounds to his head. Blood was dripping down his brow into his eyes. He cautiously felt around his body. His legs hurt, and his hands felt as if they were on fire. A quick glance showed nasty lacerations from grenade shrapnel. Two fingers hung limp.

As his vision focused, he saw that part of his web gear had been blown off. His CAR-15 lay nearby, a useless hunk of twisted aluminum and steel. Although his mind was foggy, he knew enough to realize that it would never fire again.

Howard tried moving his legs, but they refused to cooperate. Stabs of pain greeted his efforts. Hot shards of metallic debris from the grenade had sliced into both legs and into his groin. Near his right ankle, a bullet or chunk of shrapnel had torn through his foot. As he put pressure on his right foot to move, he realized that he was unable to walk. Without a rifle and full use of his legs, he was in a terrible position.

And then Howard smelled the most awful aroma he had ever smelled in his life.[2]

It was the scent of burning flesh. As Howard lifted his face above the ground to survey his immediate vicinity, he spotted the unthinkable source of the aroma. A short distance away from him, a North Vietnamese soldier had emerged from the edge of the jungle thicket. He was carrying a flamethrower, and he was liberally dosing downed recon men with liquid flames.

On the enemy soldier's back were tanks filled with diesel fuel and mounted in a canvas backpack-style harness. Connected to the pack was a hose running to the flame gun, which allowed the operator to discharge a twelve-hundred-degree-Fahrenheit stream of burning fuel. Men were screaming as their combat fatigues erupted into flames. Others lay moaning, with smoke billowing from their charred bodies.

The NVA soldier was incinerating the bodies of the forwardmost Montagnards of the point element, those who had been wounded while trying to help one of their comrades. Like the Grim Reaper of Death, the callous soldier moved through the ambush zone, using his flamethrower to eliminate the SOG recon team. Lieutenant Jim Jerson lay wounded, motionless but hollering, just to the left of the soldier with the flamethrower. The nearby tree had absorbed much of the grenade's blast, but Jerson and Howard had taken the rest.

Bullets filled the air from different directions. His body throbbing with pain, Howard now feared the worst. His hands fumbled at his web gear, searching for something with which he could use to defend himself. His fingers were numb, bloody, and clumsy.

I don't want to be burned alive! he thought.

Howard's hands finally came to rest on an M33 hand grenade still dangling from the left side of his shredded web gear. Pulling it free with his left hand, he tried tugging on the pin with two of his lacerated right fingers. Mere seconds seemed an eternity to him as he struggled to activate his grenade. *I may just have to pull the pin with my teeth*, he thought.[3]

As he grappled with the weapon, Howard suddenly saw the NVA soldier turn. His peripheral vision had obviously caught the movements of the bloodied Green Beret lying a short distance from him. SFC Howard's opponent made direct eye contact with him. In that split second, Bob realized the finality of the standoff he faced.

Howard knew in an instant that he was staring into the callous face of a well-trained North Vietnamese soldier. "He had a look of determination and hate on his face. He had an evil look in his eye, like 'I'm going to kill you.'"[4]

Lieutenant Jerson lay a short distance from Howard. He

had not been burned by the flamethrower yet, but he was face down, screaming in pain. The North Vietnamese soldier turned toward Howard, the closest opponent showing any sign of life.

In that horrible instant, Howard contemplated taking his own life. *I'll blow myself up before he can burn me up,* he thought.

Two of his fingers hung limp and useless, but with great effort Howard finally managed to extract the pin. Clutching the live grenade with one hand, he stared down the cold-blooded killer who now faced him. A sly trademark smirk eased across Howard's face.

I've got you! he said to himself. In what appeared to be his own moment of death, Howard realized he now had a fighting chance to take out his opponent. The NVA soldier was smart enough to realize that even if this American killed himself with the grenade, the blast would rip through his body as well. In this macabre scene, Howard was swept by a wave of dark humor. *No matter how bad I'm blown up, I've got you and you know it!*

The North Vietnamese man grinned back at Howard, fully aware of his own peril, perhaps showing a slight nod of respect to the Green Beret who refused to be roasted without a fight. Bullets sprayed the area from an unseen gun beyond Howard. The NVA soldier then lowered his flamethrower and quickly took steps back toward the protection of the jungle forest cover.

For some reason, Howard chose not to lob the grenade and kill this man. He later wondered if the NVA soldier decided not to burn him because of how pitiful he already appeared. Perhaps it was the split-second acknowledgment via eye contact that the two warriors had shared. But this opponent had moved away without finishing him off. So Howard merely tossed the live grenade in the general direction of his fleeing killer. He hoped the blast would hasten the NVA soldier's departure and ward off any other soldier who might be advancing.[5]

Upon lobbing the grenade, Howard began crawling away from the direction of the expected blast. In that instant, he began to realize the full extent of how badly hit his body was. Pain raced through his torn hands, legs, ankle, head, and groin. He was unable to stand, but as soon as his grenade exploded, he was on the move, pulling himself back toward the screaming lieutenant.

Some twenty yards or more behind Howard, Jerson, and the incinerated Montagnards, squad leader Bob Gron had taken cover in the depression near the base of the hill when the initial assault commenced. He had been firing, but he was forced to lie low at times due to heavy volumes of machine-gun fire that ripped the soil above him and filled the air above his head. In the heat of the early moments of the ambush, some of his Montagnard soldiers had panicked.

"I was trying to give covering fire, trying to see past the Montagnards who were running back down the hill trying to get away from the fight," Gron later stated. As in all heated battles, each soldier's perspective was only the scene directly before him. Gron ducked down for cover again as lines of machine-gun bullets spattered into the green vegetation above his depression. Unhit, he paused a few seconds to reload before raising up to fire again.[6]

In that moment, he spotted Lieutenant Jerson and Sergeant Howard down on the ground farther up the hill from him. "I didn't know how badly hurt they were," Gron recalled. He then spotted a wounded Montagnard screaming in his native tongue as the NVA soldier doused his body with the flamethrower. "I immediately open up full auto in that general area," said Gron. "I knew there were no more friendlies up there anymore on their feet."

Dropping back down into the depression, Spec-4 Gron fumbled with his spare magazines, reloading his automatic weapon. Somewhere up the hill, a grenade explosion erupted. When Gron rose up to fire again, he saw that Howard was still alive and was crawling toward his crippled lieutenant.

I've got to offer them support, he thought. *I've got to get to them!*

IN THE MINUTE since tossing his grenade toward the retreating flamethrower man, Bob Howard had painfully dragged his shattered body slightly uphill to reach Jim Jerson. Back beyond his position, he heard the chatter of Gron's automatic rifle, and appreciated the covering fire his comrade was laying down.

The lieutenant was in pitiful shape. The grenade blast had ripped Jerson with shrapnel, leaving him completely immobile. And at least one NVA bullet had since hit his prone body, adding to his agony. With his ankle shattered, Howard knew that he could not lift the officer to carry him. Although he was powerfully built—six feet tall and 170 pounds—Howard was the smaller man in this case. "He was a tall guy, about six feet four, and he weighed about two hundred pounds," Howard remembered.[7]

Jerson, still somewhat coherent, could do little to help Howard move him.

"Hold on, Jim," said Howard. "You're going to make it. I'm going to get you out of here."

His efforts to encourage the lieutenant did little. As Howard struggled to pull his platoon leader down the hill, NVA snipers cracked off more shots at them. Streams of automatic fire sprayed all about the area as well. Howard winced with pain as he struggled to lift and pull the heavy officer. More than once, Jerson screamed out in agony as another enemy bullet tore through his flesh.

Three North Vietnamese soldiers suddenly burst from the thicket and charged forward. They were hell-bent on preventing Howard and Jerson from reaching safety, possibly hoping to take the two senior Americans as prisoners. From the nearby depression in the ground, Bob Gron rose with his automatic weapon and came to their defense. Howard was relieved to see Gron lay down a strong level of base fire that killed the enemy soldiers who were attacking him.[8]

Gron's quick actions saved both Howard and Jerson. The sergeant was able to finish pulling the lieutenant down into the slight depression. Howard immediately began giving first aid to the officer, checking his various shrapnel and bullet wounds. Bob located Jerson's PRC-25 radio and removed it, knowing he would have to take command of any air support that might be available when he had a chance to make a call.

Howard began stripping away Jerson's web gear, working to get to the lieutenant's abdominal wounds, which had stained his fatigues crimson red. As he did, North Vietnamese machine-gun fire ripped through their position. Some of the bullets struck Jerson's belt, detonating ammunition clips stored there. The resulting explosion lifted Howard's body off the ground and tossed him several yards away. Gron dove for cover and was spared any serious injury.

For the second time within minutes, Howard was rendered semiconscious. He felt severe pressure in his stomach that left him gasping for air. Bob regained his senses quicker this time. He was crumpled up on the ground, a short distance from where he had been seconds before. But he was very much exposed, and the chatter of automatic fire motivated him to get moving as soon as he caught his breath.[9]

The ammunition explosion had tossed Lieutenant Jerson a short distance in the other direction. Howard angrily noticed that all of his platoon's Montagnards had retreated from the scene to take cover. Without a weapon, he had only the covering fire of Spec-4 Gron to help protect him for the moment. Howard's mind raced through countless thoughts in split seconds. The childhood steering advice from his Granny Callie had never left his mind. *Run towards your problems, not away!*

His own body had endured plenty of abuse, but Jerson was barely clinging to life.

I've got to do what's right, he thought. *If I don't do it, there's nobody else here to do it. I don't want to go after the lieutenant again, but no one else is going to do it. I guess if I die, people can look back at me and say, "That guy died the way he wanted to die."*[10]

Ignoring bullets thumping into the ground all around him, Howard pulled his torn body forward toward Jerson again.

After he reached the husky lieutenant, Bob began tugging him back down toward the relative safety afforded by the depression. This time he was greatly relieved when Gron crawled forward to assist. Together they lifted and tugged Jerson's bloodied frame back downhill.

Gron donned the PRC-25 radio Howard had removed from the lieutenant moments before. Over the din of enemy fire, he now put in desperate calls for air support to any available Covey plane in the area. Gron operated the radio with one hand and fired his M16 with the other. Howard pulled Jerson along, then paused to take a turn firing Gron's assault rifle. While Howard fired at the nearest enemy soldiers, Gron made his radio calls. He succeeded in raising a Covey pilot in the area, and he outlined their peril.

Handing the radio to Howard, Gron then reloaded his M16 and fired more rounds. Each time the enemy's fire subsided for a few seconds, Howard and Gron moved the lieutenant, and they were finally able to get him back to the edge of the pit and then down into the shallow depression. As Howard began offering emergency aid to Jerson, he became aware of the arrival of another familiar face.

When the firefight had erupted, Sergeant Jerome Griffin was removed from the initial onslaught. In his position of maintaining the platoon's rear guard, he was some sixty yards behind the hill where Howard, Jerson, and their point men were assaulted.

Griffin immediately formed a perimeter with his Montagnards to protect their rear from other attackers. "We started receiving fire from our flanks from approximately four small arms on either side," he later stated. Griffin used his PRC-25 to contact Lieutenant Jerson, but his calls went unanswered. Using his interpreter, Haut, Griffin ordered the Yards in his squad to fire two magazines on full automatic into their flanks.[11]

As soon as their clips were emptied, Griffin shouted at his indigenous troopers to race forward with him. He hoped to link up with the rest of the platoon and assist them in their own firefight. As they surged forward, Griffin was angered to see eight Montagnards from Bob Gron's middle squad racing past them down the hill. Although irritated by their retreat, Griffin shouted to his own Yards to provide covering fire for the panicked men.

The sergeant used those seconds to make a quick assessment of his situation. "At this time, I didn't notice any Americans, so I decided to move forward to see what had happened to them," Griffin recalled. As he and several Yards pressed forward another five yards, he found that the dense vegetation was beginning to thin. Griffin then spotted Sergeant Howard and Specialist Gron about sixteen yards away, to his northeast.[12]

At that moment, the NVA's firing increased again to a very heavy volume. He could see that both Gron and Howard were pinned down as they struggled to retrieve their severely injured platoon leader. After a few seconds, the volume of fire decreased enough for Griffin to crawl forward past his Yards toward their position. By that time, they had managed to deposit Jerson in the depression.

As Howard helped treat the officer, Griffin took note of Howard's serious wounds, including his foot injury. Howard had taken acting command of the survivors, and he was not flinching under the duress.

"I want you two to continue moving the lieutenant on down the hill," Howard ordered. "I'm going to go down the hill ahead of you and try to secure an LZ for extraction."

Bob Howard was in no mood to accept any delays in action. He was angry. His platoon had been ambushed, and his lieutenant was too crippled to move. His whole body ached. To top it off, every indigenous member of the platoon had fled for cover, leaving the four Americans on their own under hellacious fire. Now his ire was raised even further. In the heat of the battle, with bullets and grenades riddling their perimeter, Howard felt that the freshly arrived staff sergeant should have been actively firing back.

After ordering Griffin and Gron to start pulling Jerson down the hill, Howard snapped at Griffin. "Give me your weapon!" he demanded.[13]

Griffin was not wounded, and he was taking cover for the moment as NVA fire filled the air around the men. In fairness to him, Howard had not witnessed any of Griffin's actions since the assault had commenced. At the moment, Howard perceived him to be in a state of shock due to the explosions and heavy automatic fire. Griffin, reluctant to be unarmed while he would be moving the lieutenant, maintained his clutch on his M16. Howard reached for it, but the sergeant declined to hand it over.

"Give me your damn weapon!" Howard shouted.

Griffin kept his automatic rifle but he did hand over his M1911A-1 .45-caliber pistol. Armed for the first time since having his own CAR-15 blown apart, Howard began sliding down the hill ahead of his teammates. He paused at times to watch his two fellow Green Berets struggling with Jerson. Bob could see blood running from the lieutenant's mouth.

"He was a big guy," Gron later recalled of Jerson. "I'm six foot three, and the lieutenant was about the same size." Gron, half on his knees, and Griffin did their best to keep Jerson moving among the flying bullets. Neither could fully stand.[14]

Another wave of anger flashed through Howard as he watched Gron and Griffin struggle and thought of their frightened Yards.

There're at least four or five others who should be helping us, he thought. *They haven't been shot at all.* But his frustration was pointless at the moment. He knew that panic had overcome the others, but with a little motivation, they were excellent fighters. He scanned the nearby jungle thickets as he slid farther along.

But Howard's next sight was not the Yards he hoped to find. He and the other Americans were in a vulnerable position, and the NVA seized this opportunity. Bob suddenly spotted a squad of North Vietnamese soldiers charging toward him. In his right hand, he gripped the pistol and worked one of his slashed fingers up against the trigger.

One of the North Vietnamese was running toward him with the bayonet of his rifle extended. Howard shot that soldier square in the chest, dropping him. Two more were still running toward him. *They're trying to take us alive!* he thought. Howard fired the .45 pistol again, fatally wounding both of the NVA men. One of them stumbled beyond him and fell across the body of Lieutenant Jerson. Howard had downed his opponents without further injury to himself or his comrades.[15]

God is performing miracles for me*!* he thought.

The area was still hot with enemy activity, and Jerson was in no condition to sustain any further bullet wounds.

"You guys hold your position for a little while," Howard instructed. "I'm going to keep moving down the hill and locate a suitable LZ."[16]

Howard said he would signal them once he had determined that the path ahead was safe enough to continue moving the lieutenant. He resumed his painful crawl down the hill, sometimes opting to just slide to avoid putting pressure on his crippled right foot. His progress was slow, and minutes soon turned into a quarter hour as he inched along through the unforgiving vines, brush, and foliage.

Down below the slope, the terrain flattened out a bit. He kept crawling through the brush, looking for a clearing large enough to bring in extraction choppers. Along the way, he found four Montagnards from the Bright Light platoon who had previously fled for cover. He angrily ordered them to join him in making their way toward an exit area. Seeing their badly wounded sergeant pulling himself along as rifle and automatic fire filled the air helped motivate these men. They were uninjured, and there was a Green Beret who should have been seeking medical help.[17]

Now covered by the support of his four indig, Howard continued to crawl. Only a short distance down the hill, they found the ARVN officer, a Vietnamese Special Forces man, who had accompanied the Bright Light team into the field. The ARVN officer had suffered a bullet wound, so Howard crawled to him and provided medical assistance for a short time. The

South Vietnamese officer was in better shape than he was, so Howard ordered the officer to follow his small group toward their original landing zone.[18]

Howard fired the last round from his .45 at another NVA who was firing at his group. He was once again defenseless, as Griffin had failed to give him any extra ammunition for the pistol. Having no recourse but to keep moving, he ordered the five indigenous troopers to cover him. A short distance away, they encountered a downed Montagnard from one of the Hatchet Force squads. The man was groaning from two bullet wounds to his leg. Again, while still under gunfire, Howard paused for a few minutes to help the wounded man.

During this time, Gron and Griffin decided to continue their advance. "We walked crunched over like a duck walk, dragging the lieutenant down the hill," Gron recalled. "You couldn't stand up because of all the gunfire. It was intense." Montagnard interpreter Haut joined them and worked to assist the two Americans move their platoon leader.[19]

They finally caught up to Howard's group. The entire lot now comprised ten men—four Green Berets, one wounded ARVN officer, and five Montagnards, one with bullet-ridden legs. In between moving their wounded, Howard paused to keep the overhead Covey pilot apprised of their situation. About that time, an NVA bullet pierced an M18 smoke grenade strapped to the web gear of one of the Montagnards. The indig screamed in pain as a massive burst of violet smoke began streaming from the heated metal cylinder.[20]

"Where are you in relationship to that purple smoke?" called the pilot.

"That's us!" Howard radioed back.

Howard then ordered his small group to stay put once again and to establish a hasty perimeter to ward off any NVA attack.

"I'm going to keep moving and check out the LZ," he advised.

Sergeant Howard resumed his slow crawl back toward the platoon's original insert point. The nearby North Vietnamese troops, sensing a victory and complete annihilation of the small recon force, were closing in from all sides. The volume of gunfire began to increase again. The nine men remaining behind temporarily did their best to lay down counterfire and to cover Howard as he crawled forward alone through the rain of bullets.

By fate or faith, he was not struck again as he pulled himself yard by yard closer to the LZ. As he approached the area, Howard found the remaining Montagnards from his platoon. Seeing the bravery being displayed by the wounded sergeant, the previously disorganized and frightened troops regained their composure and began laying down covering fire for Howard's advance. Keeping his head low beneath the spray of NVA bullets, Howard led them slowly forward to the edge of the landing zone.

"Let's set up a quick perimeter right here!" he shouted. "We're not moving anymore."

His words were relayed by the platoon's Yard interpreter, Haut, who had caught up to Howard, to those who spoke no English. Howard directed the uninjured Yards to take up various points to protect the group's position. As he worked to establish the perimeter, Sergeant Griffin suddenly raced forward to report in.

Griffin explained that his group was struggling with the three wounded men. A short distance from the landing zone, his group had became totally exhausted and was unable to carry the lieutenant any farther.[21]

Griffin reported to Howard that Spec-4 Gron was tending to Jerson, but they needed help getting him to the LZ. Howard sent two able-bodied Montagnards to return with Griffin to bring the others down to his group. The firing of North Vietnamese troops kept Howard busy directing his small group's counterfire efforts during the next quarter hour until the others were able to join them.

Jerson was only semiconscious by this point, but his fellow Green Berets had managed to start a field IV in his arm. With thirty men at his disposal, Howard had a renewed sense of hope. But he was still furious that so many of his indigenous personnel had failed the platoon earlier in the middle of the firefight.

Turning to Griffin, he said, "I want you to get every living person that we've got that's able to fight. I want to talk to them right now!"

Griffin pulled the Montagnards in tighter for a hasty briefing while Spec-4 Gron moved about, tending to the lieutenant, the wounded ARVN officer, and the wounded Montagnard. Howard encouraged his survivors to assess their remaining ammunition and to distribute their spare magazines to those who were running short on bullets. He then laid down the law, making his intentions crystal clear. His words were relayed by his interpreter.

"We're gonna establish a perimeter right here, and you're gonna fight or die! Or I'm gonna shoot you myself." Pausing for a second to let that statement sink in, Howard then snapped, "I want a weapon!"[22]

To those tending to Jerson, he added, "You keep that lieutenant alive!"

He then called for the PRC-25 radio again and began talking with the O-1 Bird Dog spotter who was circling their position. He outlined his casualties and wounded. Howard's platoon commander was in the worst shape.

"I don't know if he's going to make it or not," Howard radioed. "We need some fire support!"

The Covey Rider assured Howard that air support had been called for, but it might take a little while. He explained that their O-1 was low on fuel, but another Bird Dog had already lifted off from Dak To to replace their aircraft on station.

The platoon's new perimeter was only a short distance from their original landing zone. The flat space surrounding them would have to serve as their defensive position until air support could offer them any further protection. Between them and the approaching NVA troops ran a small tributary to a larger creek. Howard hoped that the small body of water would slow the advance of his enemy, and any men splashing across it would be more easily detected.

Aerial support was en route, so any further movement of the tattered recon group seemed futile. The sun had already dipped below the nearby tree line, and dark shadows were crawling across the tropical battlefield. Darkness would envelop their position soon. Howard silently prayed that proper air support would arrive before the NVA decided to make another organized charge against his men.

With no inbound Hatchet Force troops to support them, he knew it would be a long night, if they were lucky enough to survive it. For the moment, their situation seemed as grim as the one that the Alamo defenders in Texas had faced against an overwhelming Mexican Army in 1836.

★ FIFTEEN ★

"IT SEEMED LIKE A LIFETIME"

Seven p.m., December 30, 1968

Support for the besieged Bright Light platoon was on its way.

The replacement Bird Dog team was solid. The pilot of the Cessna O-1 observation plane was Captain Lyle Hill of the 219th Aviation Company (Recon), which was nicknamed the "Headhunters." His fixed-wing plane was equipped with two AN/ARC-44 FM radios and an AN/ARC-51-Bx UHF radio, with antennas affixed to each wing of the aircraft. At cruising airspeeds of one hundred miles per hour, the O-1 had enough fuel for three and a half hours. But by cutting the airspeed back to sixty miles per hour or less to circle a combat zone, Captain Hill could add an extra hour or two of operational time.

Under each wing, Hill's light plane carried rocket tubes from which he was able to electrically fire a total of four 2.75-inch-diameter rockets armed either with high explosive or white phosphorous (WP) warheads. Sitting in the Cessna's rear seat was First Lieutenant Terry Hamric. Hamric, whose code name was "Peacemaker," had since been trained as one of Kontum's Covey Riders. His job now was to protect and defend fellow Special Forces personnel fighting across the fence.

Far below the approaching second Covey plane of the afternoon, Sergeant First Class Bob Howard was still organizing his men to defend their extraction zone. For hours, he had waved off all attempts by his comrades to treat his own wounds. Having crawled about to position his Montagnards, Howard now worked to properly mark their area and plant devices to ward off any advancing NVA.

He directed his most able men to crawl forward and deploy Claymore mines in the most critical areas surrounding their perimeter. As this took place, Howard was greatly relieved to hear the sound of a Cessna engine approaching their area. It was around seven p.m.—three hours into the battle—when Captain Hill's Bird Dog took up station. Howard was soon on the radio with the rear seat Covey Rider.

"This is Peacemaker. What's your current situation?" Lieutenant Hamric radioed.

Howard then quickly ran through the plight of his team. At least four of his Montagnards had been killed in action. His ARVN officer was wounded, along with several of his Yards. Howard added that he was wounded, but his lieutenant was barely clinging to life, supported by a field IV pack. His men were under fire and needed air support badly.

"It's getting dark," Hamric called. "You're going to have to do something to mark your perimeter. Do you have any strobe lights?"

"Affirmative, Peacemaker," Howard replied.

He promised to have his team's outer perimeter properly marked quickly. Howard sent several of his men crawling to each corner of their defensive area to set up emergency strobe lights. The blinking beacons would serve to outline the specific area where support planes should avoid bombing or strafing. Howard had Sergeant Griffin set one of the strobes near his own feet, where Howard lay propped up with a gun. His right leg was no longer effective for much more than crawling about.

With the blinking strobes effectively positioned, Howard called Hamric, who acknowledged that from his aerial vantage point, the recon platoon was properly located in the gathering dusk.

"I've got your strobe lights," Hamric radioed. "I've called in two helicopter gunships, and I'm also requesting a Moonbeam strike."[1]

Howard knew that the gunships would be Hueys, likely from one of the Dak To–based assault helicopter companies. The mention of the code name "Moonbeam" was even more encouraging. He knew this aircraft to be a Fairchild AC-119G Shadow gunship, a large dual-prop military plane fitted with four six-barrel 7.62mm NATO miniguns that could rain down devastation on ground troops. Daytime versions of such gunships were known as "Hillsborough" by recon men, while the night-version aircraft were dubbed Moonbeam.

Until the arrival of the Moonbeam or any Huey gunships, Captain Hill's little O-1 Bird Dog was the only aircraft available to disrupt the converging NVA troops. Covey Rider Hamric informed Howard that their Cessna was armed with four rockets.

"Sergeant Howard informed us that the enemy were starting to assault his position," Hill recalled. "He requested that I employ them approximately fifty meters on all four sides of his perimeter."[2]

Hill came in low above the darkened jungle canopy, zeroing his sights on the strobe lights that the American platoon had placed about their perimeter. Using them as reference points, he fired his four WP rockets, one by one, over the heads of the recon men below. Each exploded with ground-shaking red bursts of fire, followed by cries of agony. Firing into such a darkened area came with high risk. One of Hill's rockets burst perilously close to Howard's platoon, and two Montagnards were wounded by fragments of white-hot phosphorous.

Splashed with the phosphorous fragments, one of the indig hopped about, shouting in pain. Griffin and Gron raced forward, then used their knives to help scrape out burning pieces of the searing material. "You can't touch that stuff," Gron later explained. "He was screaming and hollering, and we grabbed him. All we could do was knock it off his clothes and dig it out of his skin as fast as we could. We all carried morphine, so Griffin gave him some morphine and calmed him down."[3]

The explosions served to delay the NVA's advance for a few minutes, but heavy firing soon resumed. Mindless of his own pain and life-or-death struggle, Bob Howard let his dark sense of humor prevail.

"Do you have an M16 in that damned plane?" he radioed to Lieutenant Hamric.[4]

"Yeah, we do."

"Throw it out the window!" Howard said. "I need one!"

Captain Hill then banked around and came in low, offering his rear seat Covey Rider a chance to further suppress the NVA forces. Hamric kept tabs on the strobe lights and began tossing grenades from the plane. As Hill made repeated passes over the enemy's positions, Hamric proceeded to fire twenty-eight magazines from his M16. During each pass, Hill observed muzzle flashes. He later estimated that the Kontum platoon was surrounded by at least two full NVA companies.[5]

Having exhausted his ammunition and grenades, Hamric promised Sergeant Howard that TAC air was not far away. As the firing from the circling Bird Dog ceased, the North Vietnamese forces renewed their assault. Howard could hear the splashing of many footsteps as NVA troops advanced through the creek bed near his perimeter. The enemy was only fifty yards away. Shouting to his M79 grenadiers, he ordered them together toward the end of their defensive area nearest to the creek. Their volleys of grenades were effective in knocking down some of the advancing soldiers. For the moment, the remaining NVA troops were heard to retreat down the creek bed.[6]

Howard's success with his grenadiers was uplifting. His spirits soared even higher as he heard the sound of two Huey gunships finally reach station above his landing zone defense area. His prayers answered, Howard returned to his PRC-25 to help direct the gunfire from these choppers.

In advance of the gunships, Howard also picked up a call from another unknown aviator using the call sign "Blind Bat 21."

Spec-4 Gron looked at Howard. Both men were puzzled. "What the hell's a Blind Bat 21?" asked Gron.[7]

"What can you do for us?" Howard called to the pilot.

"I can light it up from here to Saigon" came the reply. "I'm a flare ship."

Howard directed the C-47 flare ship where to go to drop its flares in advance of the approaching Huey gunships. "They flew around dropping these large aircraft flares, out away from us," Gron recalled. "The enemy was lit up good. Then the gunships came in and started working them over. But we were still taking fire the whole time."

Howard called for the Hueys to blast the illuminated creek bed, in which the NVA soldiers were still retreating. Employing a pair of 7.62mm M60 machine guns and a pair of rocket pods, these UH-1s poured heavy volumes of fire into that region.

Howard then coached the gunships to make more firing rounds in a full 360-degree circle all the way around his perimeter. His men conserved ammunition during these runs, and they clutched the ground to avoid any more friendly-fire injuries after the ones that the Covey rockets had caused. When the gunships paused from firing, Howard hoped his situation had improved. But he instead found that the NVA companies his platoon faced were resilient.

The determined North Vietnamese continued pressing toward the American recon company. Howard estimated the troops firing on him were within forty to fifty yards of his position. He began crawling about his large circle, coaching his Montagnards and fellow Green Berets on various directions to place their counterfire. Their high volume of automatic fire and grenade rockets stopped advances from several directions.

Knowing their ammunition supply was perilously low, Howard decided it was time to dampen the enemy's spirits in a new way. Weighing three and a half pounds, each Claymore M18 that the platoon had planted had a convex, rectangular plastic casing that contained a layer of C-4. The explosive force of each mine could project approximately seven hundred steel balls, held together by epoxy resin, at a velocity of 3,937 feet per second.[8]

Howard's recon team began detonating the Claymores by triggering each "clacker," an M57 firing device with a hundred-foot wire attached that had been placed about their perimeter. The effects were lethal. As each M18 erupted, it fired an arrangement of steel balls in a sixty-degree arc to a distance of approximately 110 yards. Surging NVA troops were felled like wheat before a scythe. The deadly roar of Claymores created chaos and mass destruction from all corners of the Bright Light team's perimeter. The surviving NVA troopers recoiled back into the darkened jungle to regroup, affording Howard's men some time to recover from this latest assault.

Minutes after detonating their Claymores, the American team was further uplifted as Howard announced a new defender that had arrived on station. It was their long-awaited Moonbeam gunship, a C-119 armed with powerful quad 7.62mm miniguns and flares. It arrived in company with a fresh pair of Huey gunships. Howard coached the choppers into position, then carefully ordered firing runs. The Huey pilots used the recon team's strobe lights as aiming points that allowed them to place their heavy fire just beyond the pinned-down SOG force.[9]

Throughout this devastating display of firepower, Howard ensured that team members remained with each of their wounded men and continued to provide first aid to keep them alive. "The enemy tried a few ground assaults on us, but we were able to maintain," Howard stated. "It seemed like a lifetime."

At length, the C-119 Moonbeam gunship had exhausted most of its ammunition. The Hueys moved in to continue pouring M60 fire around the perimeter, as the NVA were continuing to fire on the Bright Light team.

Covey Rider Terry Hamric, in communication with the gunships, finally announced over the radio to Howard, "We've gotta pull Moonbeam off because they are running out of ammunition."[10]

"Well, if you pull him off now, we'll all be dead," Howard replied.

"I promise you I'll get another one on station in fifteen minutes," said Hamric. "Can you guys hold on for another fifteen minutes?"

Howard was frustrated, not desiring to hold out another quarter hour on just their scant automatic rifle ammunition.

"Do you have any fast movers on station?" he asked.

Hamric replied that they should be able to get one within five minutes or so. Nicknamed "fast movers" by recon men, McDonnell Douglas F-4 Phantom II twin-engine jet interceptor fighter-bombers were equipped with air-to-air missiles, air-to-ground missiles, and various bombs. True to his word, Hamric had a Phantom on station in short order. Again, Howard worked his PRC-25 to direct the assaults of the fast mover. It was equipped with a 250-pound bomb.

"I want you to drop it right on my position," Howard directed. "I'm going to put out two other strobe lights as a reference point."

Howard pulled himself forward and placed two more of the blinking strobes close to himself. The NVA were surging toward his position, and he was desperate to survive. Crawling back a short distance from his signal lights, he called back to Hamric.

"Have 'em drop his bomb right here on those strobes!"

Seconds later, the F-4 raced in and dropped his two-hundred-fifty-pound bomb perilously close to Sergeant Howard. "I was just saying a prayer," Howard recalled. "I didn't really want it to land on top of me." It missed him, but the bomb impacted the earth only a short distance ahead of him. A mighty explosion broke the latest wave of NVA soldiers, but the blast was so close that Howard winced as several pieces of red-hot shrapnel peppered his tattered body.

Hamric then radioed that the second C-119 Moonbeam was approaching. This good news, coming around ten thirty p.m., was met with a devastating announcement from Sergeant Griffin.

The Green Beret, who had crawled over to check on Lieutenant Jerson, suddenly shouted to Howard, "He's stopped breathing!"

Howard crawled toward them, shouting at Griffin to administer mouth-to-mouth resuscitation and an external heart massage. Griffin set to work, performing CPR on his fallen platoon leader as bullets filled the air around him. But after several minutes of valiant effort, Griffin announced that it was no use. Jim Jerson was gone.

Bob Howard had no time to mourn his fallen comrade. From different corners of his circle, NVA were continuing to advance. He pulled himself about the perimeter, all the while shouting encouragement and firing directions to his men.

At long last, he heard better news from his Covey pilot. Captain Hill announced that Vietnamese-manned extraction choppers from the 219th Squadron were approaching from Dak To. The Kontum recon team had now been in active combat for four and a half hours. Their ammunition was nearly exhausted, and their bodies were nearly spent physically.

Minutes later, the first Sikorsky CH-34 began settling onto the nearby LZ. Although gunfire continued from the remaining NVA troops, Howard coolly directed Gron and Griffin to begin exfiltrating their men. He first had Lieutenant Jerson's body placed in the Kingbee, then ordered the most severely wounded Montagnards to be loaded. Other Yards were helped up into the extract chopper. "We slowly brought our perimeter in as we loaded the wounded and some of the Yards," Gron remembered. "I had to keep them in check, because the Montagnards had a habit of running and trying to get on the helicopters."[11]

Howard, helping to move bodies and direct the loading, was suffering. Although the extraction chopper was only about twenty-one yards from him, it seemed as if the distance were as long as a football field when he was dragging dead soldiers to the chopper.[12]

As the first CH-34 pulled away, another Kingbee moved

right in and began loading the majority of the platoon's surviving Yards. Once it was fully loaded, the pilot lifted out and pulled clear of the LZ as machine-gun bullets punched through the aluminum underside of his CH-34.

Once the final 219th Kingbees were gone, Bob Howard was left on the ground with only Jerome Griffin, Bob Gron, and a pair of their indigenous troopers. The last chopper coming in to pull them was a Huey slick. Its pilot hovered low over the LZ, but he did not quite place his skids on the ground because of the uneven terrain. As the Huey bounced slightly up and down, trying to remain level under gunfire, Spec-4 Gron was challenged with getting his shorter Montagnards on board. At times, the Huey lifted up chest high above the ground, its rotor fanning out the tall grass on either side.

Gron, who stood nearly six feet three, used his height advantage to help push his smaller comrades up into the open door. Once they were loaded, it was his turn. "I wanted to help get Howard in the helicopter, because his foot was wounded," Gron recalled. "He wouldn't have anything to do with that." By SOG team custom, the most senior members of a recon team or platoon were always the last men out. Howard was not leaving yet. So Gron reached up and grasped a handle behind the pilot's seat. Placing one knee and a foot on the skid, he slung his rifle up, holding on with one hand.[13]

The Huey's door gunners were blazing away with their machine guns at approaching enemy troops. Safely on board, Gron knelt to offer a helping hand to his two superiors, Sergeants Griffin and Howard. But they were frozen in place. Gron heard Howard suddenly shout out in agony.

"No! No! No!"

Confused, Gron saw that Griffin and Howard were refusing to climb on board. They were yelling back and forth to each other, pointing at an object in the tall weeds nearby. Gron shouted for the pilot to switch on his spotlight. And then, as the pilot let his chopper drift over slightly so that the rotor wash parted the tall grass, he saw it. Now visible to Gron in the spotlight was a body. It was their own Lieutenant Jerson, whose body had apparently been shoved off the first Kingbee by frightened men wanting to lighten their load.

"Howard had seen them push him off," Gron later recalled. "The first chopper had a Vietnamese crew on it and no Americans. If there had been an American on that bird, the guy who did it would have had a gun upside his head."[14]

Leave no man behind. It was a cardinal rule in Special Forces. Only under the most dire circumstances was a fellow Green Beret left on the ground. And even in those situations, Bright Light teams were always sent back in to attempt to recover their own.

Bob Gron jumped down off the Huey and rushed forward to assist Griffin and Howard. Ignoring enemy fire, the trio tugged and lifted Jerson's body up into the UH-1. Their ride out was not leaving without the lieutenant on board. Gron then scrambled back into the chopper and helped pull Sergeant Griffin in next.

Bob Howard was the last man out, in line with SOG tradition. He struggled to put weight on his tattered ankle; then strong hands grasped his fatigues and helped pull him into the Huey. Gron shouted at the pilot to go, and their mighty chopper was instantly lifting upward and away from the Laotian hell below.

Once on board, Sergeant Howard kept a tight grip on Lieutenant Jerson's body. The realization that his mission commander had perished hurt him far worse than any of his own wounds. "I'm not one about crying, but I was emotional at that time," he later admitted. "I was crying because the lieutenant was dead." As the pilot lifted away, he reached back with one hand to try to console the grieving sergeant. Struggling with his emotions, Howard simply pushed the pilot's arm away.[15]

Once his Huey had safely cleared the enemy gunfire, Howard finally collapsed in a heap on the floor, his own blood spreading across the slick steel. To platoon mate Gron, the acting platoon commander appeared to be somewhat dazed, perhaps suffering from a mild concussion from his head wound. Howard was still alert, but he was mentally and physically spent, having endured hours of fighting, crawling, and suffering. His prayers had been answered. His efforts during the past four-plus hours had saved the lives of two Americans and many of his indigenous team members.

Howard was scarcely conscious, fading in and out from exhaustion, stress, and pain. His small platoon had survived the unthinkable. After-action analysis of the Bright Light team's battle would later compile the best tally possible.

Army officials estimated that Howard and his men had killed twenty-five confirmed NVA soldiers, and estimated that at least twenty-five more had perished, but this could not be confirmed.

Another fifteen North Vietnamese were estimated to have been wounded, and the aerial strikes were modestly assumed to have killed and wounded at least fifty more enemy soldiers.[16]

Covey Rider Terry Hamric had nothing but praise for the acting platoon leader, who had worked with him throughout the firefight over the radio. "At all times, Sergeant Howard was extremely calm in the face of the enemy," Hamric stated in his report. "He kept us constantly informed of the enemy and friendly situation. It was only through his courageous and determined efforts that the air strikes were successful and the majority of the platoon was saved."[17]

Howard's two surviving fellow Green Berets were equally impressed with the courage that he had displayed throughout their ordeal.

"He limped among us, issuing orders and directing our fires with determination," Gron soon testified to intelligence officers. "Through leadership, determination, and devotion to duty, Sergeant Howard saved the platoon." Griffin added, "Even though wounded himself and in great pain, he didn't stop to administer first aid to himself nor would he allow any of us to help him. He told us there were others we could help."[18]

The eyewitness statements of both Specialist Fourth Class Bob Gron and Sergeant Jerome Griffin concluded with a common statement regarding Robert Howard.

Howard's actions and display of courage throughout that afternoon and evening "were above and beyond the call of duty."

★ SIXTEEN ★

COMPANY COMMAND

It was already the early-morning minutes of New Year's Eve 1968 when the Kingbees and the Huey returned to the Dak To staging area. The base was on full alert, as the Bright Light drama had been playing out over the radio for all to hear. Numerous personnel and medical staff from the 4th Infantry Division base were waiting, even FOB-2 base commander Roy Bahr.

Throughout the previous afternoon, Bahr and his staff had carefully monitored the Bright Light team's battle. For hours, they had helped orchestrate the air support and evac personnel who ultimately saved much of Bob Howard's platoon. Nothing else mattered during that time. Two new Green Berets freshly initiated into MACV-SOG, Sergeants John St. Martin and Dan Lindblom, had just landed at Kontum that day. "We were trying to figure out what was going on," St. Martin recalled. "No one paid much attention to us on December 30. The next day, Dan and I simply pitched in to help off-load men when the helicopter landed at Kontum with some of Howard's platoon."[1]

At Dak To, Bahr watched as the body of Lieutenant Jerson was carefully removed from the Huey, along with the men who were most seriously wounded. Howard was hustled into an emergency triage area, where the remnants of his tattered and bloodied fatigues were cut away. Surgeons set to work immediately, stitching his wounds and removing shrapnel from his body. They worked on his lacerated head, fingers, leg, thighs, groin, right foot, and torso while checking him carefully for other wounds.

The other two surviving Green Berets, Bob Gron and Jerome Griffin, were flown back to FOB-2 in company with the body of Lieutenant Jerson. Kontum's medical staff there would prepare it for proper transportation back home for burial. Intelligence officers began taking statements from the SOG warriors, trying to piece together the hectic series of events that had transpired overnight.

"It was well in the morning hours by the time they finished," Gron recalled. "I remember laying down on a cot to get a few winks. Someone finally woke us up so we could go get something to eat. Then they took me and Griffin back to our Yard camp near the base."[2]

That night, at the base club, dozens of Green Berets downed drinks in remembrance of Bob Scherdin and Jim Jerson. At FOB-2 Kontum, there was a solid custom of singing a tribute to mourn the recon company's losses. The tune they used was an American folk song, "Old Blue," the tale of a possum-chasing dog that died and went to heaven. "Dug his grave with a silver spade, lowered him down with a silver chain," they sang. The chorus read "Old Blue, you're a good dog, you." Captain Ed Lesesne led the next stanza: "Link by link, I lowered the chain, and with each link, I called his name." In place of Blue's name, the Kontum recon men sang out the names of others from their base who had perished in combat: Reno, Fawcett, Laws, Sain, and many others. As tears flowed, the litany continued, now with fresh names on the list.[3]

"Scherdin and Jerson, too. Hey, Blue, you're a good dog, you."

Captain Lesesne bore the burden of these losses with a heavy heart. But he was filled with pride for the outstanding valor displayed by members of the Bright Light team who had attempted the recovery of Scherdin. His intelligence officers had collected statements from many of those involved, including Griffin, Gron, Covey pilot Lyle Hill, and Covey Rider Terry Hamric. Griffin and Gron were each written up for Bronze Star Medals with the V device for valor. From the data collected on the performance of Robert Howard, Lesesne had no hesitation.

Lesesne began writing Howard up for the Medal of Honor. He had already done so once before, in the wake of the SLAM VII mission. For that mission, the Army had reduced Howard's recommendation to a Silver Star. Lesesne was aware that Howard had also seen his first Medal of Honor submission downgraded to a Distinguished Service Cross. He hoped the third time would be the charm for his brave sergeant.

Medal of Honor paperwork was rarely processed quickly. It could take six months to multiple years to clear all the approval levels. Once again, Howard's third submission would hit delays due to the ongoing war. By the spring of 1969, MACV-SOG command in Saigon had concurred with the recommendation received from Lesesne and Colonel Bahr of FOB-2. The paper trail proceeded during the next couple months, endorsed by both Lieutenant General Michael S. Davison and Admiral John S. McCain Jr.

On March 28, 1969, Major General Leo B. Jones of the U.S. Army approved the highest award he was authorized to, a second Distinguished Service Cross, which would be represented on Howard's uniform in the form of a First Oak Leaf Cluster. While the MOH process played out, the Army wished to at least acknowledge SFC Howard's heroism with the second DSC serving as a temporary placeholder.[4]

DURING THOSE EARLY months of 1969, Howard was far from idle. His company commander, Captain Lesesne, was stunned by how quickly he returned to duty. Howard had been sent to the 71st Evacuation Hospital in Pleiku for medical treatment after surviving his Bright Light mission. But he remained there for only a few days. Once his most serious wounds had been sewn up, the restless recon sergeant simply refused to remain bedridden. "He checked himself out and came back to base," Colonel Roy Bahr recalled.[5]

John Plaster, now assigned to RT New Mexico, spotted Howard clad in hospital pajamas standing before the base recon office, chatting with Ed Lesesne. "He bore several bandages and looked exhausted, but it was really him," Plaster recalled. "What a morale boost. All of us looked up to Howard. He was the gallant knight whose shining example inspired all the young squires."[6]

Howard told Plaster that he feared Army doctors might ship him back to Japan again for his recovery. He instead went AWOL from the hospital and hitchhiked aboard a Huey returning to Kontum. Howard told Lesesne that he was perfectly content with letting the senior Special Forces medic at FOB-2, SFC Lou Maggio, remove the dead tissue around his wounds and pull his stitches.

"As soon as I can find a fresh set of jungle fatigues, I'll be back on duty!" Howard declared.

In his element once again, Howard resumed working as his body healed. The war in Vietnam required the special skills of his recon base, and he intended to contribute. His position as the recon company training NCO required him to work closely alongside Master Sergeant Lionel Pinn, a seasoned World War II veteran who was the base's senior noncommissioned officer. Their personalities were similar. Pinn loved to join teams across the fence for combat, and he had collected numerous Purple Hearts. Like Howard, he was a fitness fanatic. Although husky and forty-five years of age, he could still run with the best of them. Some called Pinn "Chief" because of his Native American heritage, while others preferred "Choo-Choo" or "Chooch"—a nicknamed derived from his ability to run with a lit cigar, his smoke trailing behind him.[7]

In mid-January, the identity of FOB-2 changed. Overnight, signs were pulled down and replaced by new ones sporting the acronym CCC, standing for Command and Control Central.

Kontum would now answer directly to SOG headquarters in Saigon. In similar fashion, the forward operating base at Da Nang became Command and Control North (CCN) and Ban Me Thuot was now Command and Control South (CCS).

Howard had only recently returned when Colonel Bahr's new CCC camp faced more heart-wrenching losses. On the morning of January 29, 1969, Recon Team New Mexico failed to respond to radio calls from their position within Laos. Howard, Lesesne, and Master Sergeant Pinn worked to organize a Bright Light team, led by Lieutenant Tom Jaeger, who had just returned from leave. Jaeger's team soon found that the recon team had been overrun, and all three Green Berets had been killed. The youngest member of RT New Mexico, John Plaster, was devastated. Due to overcrowded choppers, he had been left behind when the team was inserted. Bob Howard would soon assign Plaster to a new team, RT Illinois.

Colonel Bahr forbade Howard from straphanging with any teams by the spring of 1969 as his Medal of Honor submission ran its course. Still, enemy action found its way to SFC Howard and the men of CCC at times. Around 0400 on March 2, the Kontum warning siren began to wail as an NVA sapper attack on the base commenced. Howard and his comrades raced into action, snatching up weapons and manning mortars as B-40 rocket-propelled grenades rained down on the base.

One RPG ripped through a Green Beret team room, hitting two young sergeants with shrapnel. The attack was over soon enough, but it was the first serious assault on the compound. Howard and his fellow leaders thereafter put new emphasis on nightly security patrols outside the CCC perimeter to prevent other insurgents from slipping in close enough to launch attacks.

Word of SFC Bob Howard's brave missions was already making him something of a SOG legend. During the first week of March 1969, prior to any announcement of a service medal for his December 30 mission, a reporter from *Pacific Stars and Stripes* magazine interviewed him. At that time, he was allowed to disclose what was known: He had received the nation's second-highest award for heroism, the Distinguished Service Cross. He had also received the Bronze Star, four Army Commendation Medals, two Air Medals, the Combat Infantryman Badge, and five Purple Hearts. The Vietnamese had also shown their appreciation to Howard by awarding him the Vietnam Cross of Gallantry, with both a Silver Star and a Bronze Star.[8]

Regarding his wife, Tina, and their two daughters back home in Rogers, Texas, Howard stated, "She handles the girls perfectly. They all understand how I feel about my job as a soldier and, fortunately, things have worked out real well." Playing to his desire for increased American support for the Vietnam War, Howard added about his NVA enemy, "I honestly feel we are slowly beating him, hurting his supply channels and at least slowing down his movements."

The *Stars and Stripes* reporter then asked Howard why he was on his third tour in Vietnam when most soldiers were content to return home after completing twelve months. "I guess it's because I want to help in any way I can. I may as well be here, where I can use my training," Howard said. "I have to do it. It's the way I feel about my job."

In March 1969, command of the Kontum base passed from

Colonel Bahr to Lieutenant Colonel Frederick Abt, a gray-haired Korean War veteran with blue-gray eyes and a solid command personality. Like Bahr, new base commander Abt respected the eagerness of Bob Howard, but similarly refused to let him partake in missions across the fence. So Howard worked closely with Chooch Pinn, training the teams and recommending when blooded Green Berets were experienced enough to take their own team leadership positions.

One of the most taxing missions for CCC during this time was Operation Nightcap, an offensive aimed at shutting down NVA convoys along Highways 96 and 110 in Laos. Lieutenant Colonel Abt's staff put together a SLAM mission that commenced on March 15 to handle the highway-roadblocking task. The multiday battle that ensued required steady resupply runs from choppers. They ferried in food, water, and ammunition, and hauled out wounded men. The CCC force destroyed several NVA trucks, created plenty of enemy casualties, and disrupted North Vietnamese traffic along the major route for more than a week. Four Kontum Green Berets would earn Purple Hearts, and five Montagnards perished in the endeavor, but the SLAM mission was enough of a victory that SOG command would order two more roadblock operations within the next year.[9]

Recon company master sergeant Chooch Pinn, knowing his tour in Vietnam was ending, received permission from base XO Clyde Sincere to run one last mission in April 1969. His fifteen-man Mike Force (Mobile Strike Force Command) team soon found itself in a severe firefight and had to call in a Prairie Fire emergency. Every member of the team was wounded before they were pulled out on strings, with Chooch Pinn hanging limp in his harness. He survived, and he would later be pinned with his eighth Purple Heart. His first had been earned in 1944 during World War II.[10]

Pinn rotated home to recover from his wounds. His position as the recon company first sergeant was handed off to a man he respected for having an almost equal number of Purple Hearts: Bob Howard. Bob's wounds from December were well healed, and his body was in top physical shape once again. He worked his men hard on immediate action drills—how to get out of life-or-death combat scenarios against the enemy. He was also a stickler on running, and he insisted that his company remain equally fit.

Some complained that their new first sergeant had a death wish: One well-placed NVA mortar could have easily taken out the entire company of Green Berets as they jogged along Highway 14 near Kontum. But no one was bold enough to confront this tough old veteran to his face. Only when NVA snipers later began firing at vehicles along Highway 14 did Howard show enough concern that he began jogging with a loaded weapon.[11]

As the senior noncom of the recon company, Howard had authority to reorganize teams and promote able men into leadership positions. During the spring of 1969, he was approached by two Green Berets of RT New York, one-one Sergeant John St. Martin and one-two Sergeant Ed Wolcoff. In confidence, they related serious allegations about the conduct of their one-zero while on duty. Howard absorbed their input and dismissed his recon men with "Let me handle it." Nothing more was said, but the one-zero was quietly reassigned to Okinawa.[12]

The next day, St. Martin was approached by SFC Howard. Powerfully built and strong-willed, St. Martin had shown great courage in the field thus far with RT New York. But the twenty-year-old Californian was not prepared for his recon sergeant's next orders.

"John, I want you to take over the team," said Howard.[13]

"Bob, I don't think I can handle the job," St. Martin protested. "I don't have enough experience."

"Well, I think you can, and I think you do," Howard said in his Alabama drawl. "So I'd like you to take it."

Howard knew a qualified team leader when he saw one, and he quickly convinced St. Martin that he could handle RT New York. His newest one-zero promised to do his best, and he would live up to that word. St. Martin and others promoted into one-zero positions by Howard respected him immensely.

John Plaster, who had run numerous missions and been promoted to sergeant by the summer of 1969, was finally deemed worthy of leadership in early August. Plaster returned from his latest mission with RT Illinois deadly sick with bacillary dysentery, a disease that made him so ill he lost twenty-two pounds in less than a week. During his recovery, he was visited in his hospital bunk by SFC Howard. The first sergeant explained that Plaster's one-zero was being sent to instruct at the in-country Recon One-Zero School, and his team would be handed off.[14]

"RT Illinois is yours now. You're one-zero, John," said Howard. "Take a couple of weeks and just train."

Nine months into running recon from CCC, Plaster had

finally graduated to commander of his own team. And the senior NCO selecting him was a recon man he hoped to emulate in the field. "It was like I had a first-round pick in the NFL draft," Plaster remembered.

As the training NCO of the recon company, SFC Howard routinely took teams out to the Kontum firing range to let them demonstrate their various immediate action drills. It was a learning experience for his junior Green Berets, as each one-zero developed various methods for how his team should respond to unexpected, potentially deadly enemy assaults. During one such exercise, an enemy sniper took a shot at the Americans from long range. "The firearm discharged a ways off and we then heard the bullet pass by," recalled Ed Wolcoff. Although the distance far exceeded the reach of his weapon, Wolcoff was called on by Howard to return fire with his B-40 rocket launcher.[15]

"Fire the damn thing!" Howard ordered.

Wolcoff duly put his B-40 at a forty-five-degree angle and fired it. Howard was disgusted that the limited range of the rocket had no effect, nor did the rounds fired into the jungle by other Green Berets. No one was hurt, but the incident further fueled Howard's desire to make sure his men were fully trained for any potential danger.

In the summer of 1969, Howard was decorated with his second Distinguished Service Cross. The presentation was made by Lieutenant General Frank T. Mildren, deputy commanding general of the U.S. Army in Vietnam. Howard stood stiffly at attention, showing no emotion as Mildren pinned the Oak Leaf Cluster to his first DSC. Howard despised all the attention as

In this photo taken by one-zero John St. Martin, recon first sergeant Bob Howard is with his Green Berets during helicopter rappelling training at Kontum in March 1969. Seen left to right are: Charles Erickson, Howard, Walter Horion, Ron Gravett, Dan Lindblom (with a CAR-15), and David Kirschbaum.

John St. Martin

base photographers snapped pictures of him. He was more than happy to simply return to his job of leading the recon company as soon as all the fuss was over.

His SOG recon soldiers worked at a relentless pace through the summer. Several teams attempted to pull off an NVA prisoner snatch during their operations, but no one from SOG had successfully captured a live enemy prisoner since Bob Howard had in November 1968. The next team to finally do so was headed by SSG David Gilmer, the one-zero of RT Texas.

Inserted into Laos near Highway 110, Gilmer's team assaulted a seven-man NVA patrol moving along a jungle trail. They moved in quickly and subdued one young soldier with minor leg wounds who was pretending to be dead. Gilmer dispatched other NVA troopers with his CAR-15 as RT Texas gagged and handcuffed their prisoner and hustled him toward a nearby LZ. A half hour later, Huey slicks scooped up the team and headed straight back to the CCC compound.

Gilmer and his team emerged from the choppers and readily accepted the celebratory beers pressed into their hands by fellow Green Berets. Bob Howard pushed through the men and pulled the terrified young North Vietnamese prisoner from the Huey. He scooped up the slight man, carrying him like a child in his bearlike arms. Trailed by armed SF men, Howard hauled the handcuffed POW to the base medics to have his shrapnel removed. The NVA soldier would face SOG intelligence officials, but not before Howard had him medically assessed.

Dave Gilmer's team was praised for their successful prisoner grab. Like Bob Howard before them, each Green Beret involved in the mission received a two-hundred-fifty-dollar cash bonus and R & R leave in Taiwan. Weeks later, Howard was notified of his own special bonus. His superiors had recommended him for promotion to officer, which would be preceded by a lengthy leave to visit his family. His orders were set for the third week of August, so the recon company commander spent that time preparing to pass off his unit into good hands.

The man selected by Howard and Lieutenant Colonel Abt was Master Sergeant Norm Doney, the former one-zero of RT Florida. Doney had nearly pulled off his own prisoner snatch in May after disabling a lone NVA with a suppressed .22-caliber pistol. But an NVA counterassault wounded Doney with shrapnel and forced him to gun down his would-be prisoner as the NVA soldier leaped for his automatic weapon.

During Howard's final two weeks at Kontum, another of his one-zeros attempted to pull off a prisoner snatch. On August 12, Sergeant John St. Martin's RT New York was in Laotian target area Tango 7, snooping on a major NVA headquarters near Highway 110. After calling in a bomb strike on the enemy buildings, St. Martin led his eight-man recon team forward to attack three surviving NVA soldiers spotted in the compound. "I was probably too aggressive in that situation," he later admitted. "I was trying to grab three North Vietnamese soldiers, but I didn't see their other guy."[16]

Bullets from the AK-47 of a fourth NVA trooper ripped through St. Martin as he moved forward. One bullet shattered his right ankle. Another slammed into his right thigh. A third hit his abdomen, shredding his gall bladder, liver, and intestines. His RT New York teammates, Ed Wolcoff and John Blaauw, spent the next hours trying to keep St. Martin alive while fighting off NVA attacks and calling in air strikes. Weighing more than two hundred pounds, St. Martin was an extreme challenge for Wolcoff to drag to an acceptable extraction point. Ed administered morphine to his one-zero, and helped push his intestines back into place with the use of St. Martin's web gear belt and jungle undershirt.

Finally extracted on strings by Hueys under heavy NVA gunfire, RT New York was raced back to Dak To for medical attention. Due to heavy rain and cloud cover over Dak To, the pilot was forced to fly to Kontum; St. Martin was then flown to the Pleiku hospital. "I lost seven pints of blood," recalled St. Martin, whose life had been saved by the courage of his team. After emergency surgery at Pleiku, St. Martin was still recovering when his recon company first sergeant paid him a visit the next day. "I later realized the irony of the situation," said St. Martin. "When I arrived at Kontum in December 1968, Bob Howard was fighting to survive his Medal of Honor mission. Eight months later, one of Bob's last acts on his tour of duty was to come visit me while I was fighting to survive."

Howard had never forgotten the SOG colonel who cared enough about one of his recon sergeants in 1965 to visit him in the hospital. Four years later, Howard was in his own position to express gratitude and sympathy to one of his wounded recon men. "I was pretty bad off, and I struggled to understand his words," St. Martin recalled. "But Bob had tears in his eyes as he grabbed my hand and squeezed it."

Bob Howard's third tour of duty in Vietnam ended the following week, on August 23, 1969. His return flights via Japan landed him Stateside in California days later. Prior to securing a final flight back home to greet his family in Texas, he was briefed on a tragedy that had befallen another of his former Green Berets during the past week.

On August 26, Staff Sergeant Ken Worthley's RT Florida was in trouble. Tracked by NVA forces for more than a day, Worthley's team was assaulted by a sizable force as Huey slicks worked to extract them. He was carrying important intelligence documents lifted from an NVA officer his team had killed. But after strapping into his harness to be pulled through the triple canopy, Worthley was shot through the neck. His body was returned to base and prepared for return to his home in Sherburn, Minnesota.[17]

Learning that the body of one of his team leaders was in transit back to the States, Howard put off his own home leave by three days. His final mission at the close of his third tour of duty was to pay respect. Howard accompanied the coffin back to Minnesota, where Kenneth Wayne Worthley was buried with honors. Howard presented the flag from Worthley's coffin to his grieving parents.

MORE THAN TEN months had passed since Robert Howard had seen his wife and daughters. The last time he had returned Stateside, he was recovering from serious battle wounds. This time the wounds he received during his Medal of Honor mission were now just more scars on his body.

Bob did not mention that he had been written up for the Medal of Honor again. For the time being, he was content to enjoy time with his kids before launching into his next military journey: becoming an officer.

Following his leave, Howard returned to duty at Fort Bragg, North Carolina, where his family lived with him in nearby Spring Lake. His exploits in the field were well-known by this time. Howard had been the subject of two different feature articles in 1969 in *The Green Beret,* an authorized monthly magazine of the 5th Special Forces Group. The October issue detailed his December 1968 mission, and a sketch of Howard was featured on the magazine cover.

Three months after his return from the war, Howard formally received his commission as a first lieutenant, effective December 6, 1969. Upon accepting it, he quickly immersed himself in the officers' courses required of all new infantry lieutenants.

Howard's Basic Infantry Officer Course ran from December 7, 1969, to February 23, 1970. After graduation, on March 20, he moved into the Army Ranger Course. This demanding program was considered one of the most difficult in the military, as the men were taught combat tactics, physical fitness, and effective leadership skills. The seven-week course was grueling, and many well-seasoned men were simply unable to finish it. But Bob Howard aced his Ranger training with flying colors, completing it on May 16, 1970, as that session's distinguished graduate.

Lieutenant Howard's next training was a five-week Platoon Leader Course, followed by a three-and-one-half-week Jungle Operations Course in the Panama Canal Zone. Fort Sherman, located at Toro Point at the northern end of the canal, had been used as the U.S. Army's Jungle Operations Training Center since 1951. The unforgiving terrain was used to indoctrinate trainees like Bob Howard on the geography, animal species, and weather conditions soldiers would face in tropical environments far removed from their homeland. For him, warfare operations in trying jungle worlds had become old hat, and he graduated with ease.

By the time he returned to Fort Bragg, Howard was a year removed from the Vietnam War. He was offered extended leave with his family, but the military had not paid for a year of his advanced training without a payoff. In October 1970, Lieutenant Howard had new orders: He was being sent back to

Vietnam for his fourth tour of duty. His service would continue with MACV-SOG.

His superiors knew where he fit best, and Howard was all too happy to learn that he would again be returning to his familiar forward operating base at Kontum in the Central Highlands of South Vietnam. When he arrived on October 24, 1970, he found much had changed. Lieutenant Colonel Fred Abt had been transferred to other duties, and base command of CCC was now under Lieutenant Colonel Edgar McGowan, a forty-eight-year-old former World War II Airborne veteran of the Pacific War.

There were plenty of fresh faces about the recon base. Most of the one-zeros Howard had helped train during the summer of 1969 had rotated back home or to new assignments. One of the few exceptions was Sergeant John Plaster.

Plaster was pleasantly surprised when his team returned from a four-day patrol near the Vietnam-Laos border. As he stepped from the chopper onto the CCC helipad, his team was greeted by their recon company first sergeant, Henry Gainous, a former one-zero. Standing beside Gainous was Bob Howard, sporting his trademark squint and a sly smirk.[18]

"Well, my eyes ain't playin' tricks," said Howard. "It's really you, John! I can't believe you're still here."

Sergeant Plaster bypassed the cold beers being handed out, instead accepting a fifth of Jack Daniel's that Howard offered him. After taking a healthy chug from the bottle, Plaster introduced the other Green Berets from his recon team. It was only then that the one-zero noted a first lieutenant's bar shining on Howard's collar.

"I stood at attention and saluted him," Plaster recalled. "I was so proud of him. Howard returned my salute though later he confessed he was embarrassed to be a shavetail lieutenant and could hardly wait to make captain."[19]

Plaster enjoyed catching up with Howard. The two would remain close friends, even as Plaster transitioned the following month from team leader into a Covey Rider role in which he would fly cover for other Special Forces teams for many months. One of the senior Covey Riders training Plaster was Larry "Six Pack" White, another of Howard's old friends. On their last mission together, Larry had collected four bullets in his body. Like Howard, he could not be kept from recon duty, and he was once again back at Kontum.

Although limited to in-country duties, Howard never missed the chance to test new weapons. His favorite gun was a modified M14 assault rifle complete with a forward grip and duplex round capabilities. With one round nested behind another in a single cartridge, the twenty-round magazine of Howard's M14 was capable of dispatching forty rounds. One afternoon, Howard spotted RT New York one-zero Ed Wolcoff walking past the recon headquarters building with an odd weapon.[20]

"Whatcha got there, Ed?" Howard called.

Wolcoff proudly displayed a modified bolt-action, lightweight 12-gauge shotgun fitted with a three-round magazine that he had obtained from a trip to the MACV-SOG arsenal at the Saigon headquarters.

Inspecting the unique shotgun, Howard said, "Let me keep this."

Wolcoff protested that his recon CO could order a whole

batch of them from Saigon, but the stern squint from Howard that he received was enough to convince him to let it go. Days later, Wolcoff found that his lieutenant was eager to conduct a long-distance open-road run outside the base with his new lightweight weapon.

Howard's role with CCC was that of commanding the entire recon company. During his evening hours, he frequented the base club with his fellow Green Berets. Howard's interest was not in downing ample quantities of liquor. He sipped coffee most nights while smoking his trademark Lucky Strikes and absorbing the latest mission details that flowed from his men.

AS THE RECON company commander, Lieutenant Howard did not tolerate nonsense.

Events across the fence sometimes led to tensions, and it took a strong arm to keep order and control. Staff Sergeant Mike Sheppard had a confrontation with one of his junior team members one night. During a mission months before, Sheppard had tried to save a wounded Montagnard in the middle of a firefight. Several rounds hit the Yard, killing him. Hearing his former teammate bragging in the bar about receiving a Bronze Star for "helping" Sheppard with the indig was too much.[21]

Sheppard confronted him and leveled him with a solid punch. An hour later, the other man, a sergeant first class, stomped into a Kontum village bar just outside of FOB-2. Sheppard was seated with his recon company commander, enjoying a drink with Howard. The two had become close friends, often playing in volleyball tournaments with each other during downtime.[22]

"Where's Sheppard at?" the SFC demanded as he entered the bar.

"He's right over here," barked Howard. "What do you want?"

A heated confrontation in which the SFC brandished a .45-caliber pistol ensued. Sheppard went for the .38-caliber in his pocket, but Lieutenant Howard was quicker. He jumped up and slugged the angry SFC. "He knocked him unconscious, but the .45 the sergeant first class was carrying to shoot me with went off when Howard hit him," Sheppard recalled. "I later dug the slug out of the wall in the village bar, made a plaque, and presented it to Howard, truly the bravest of the brave."

Howard immediately returned to base and explained the situation to his base commander, Lieutenant Colonel McGowan. He worried that his CO might press charges against him for punching one of his recon men, but Howard was greatly relieved when McGowan stated that Howard had instead prevented a shooting. McGowan and Howard remedied the situation by transferring the other Green Beret out of CCC.

By December 1970, Howard received noticed of his promotion from first lieutenant to captain. Meanwhile, Staff Sergeant Billy Greenwood was tapped to take on the role of company first sergeant, or senior company noncom. He had been serving as boss of the Dak To launch site, but he accepted the newly opened role. First Lieutenant Steve Hatch, one-zero of RT

Kentucky, recalled, "Greenwood and Howard had very similar personalities and became a tight team. They complemented each other well."[23]

Dan Ster, the one-zero of RT Nevada, remembered Howard as a quiet man. "When there was a dangerous mission to go on, he would want to go on it because he was someone who had been through it and done it. It was his DNA. This was what he was supposed to do." But Howard was still unable to join the fight due to his pending Medal of Honor paperwork. "He was put on stand-down. He was not allowed to go back into the field," Ster recalled. "He really had no way of getting rid of his anxiety sitting back at camp. I don't think he really knew how to relax, just walking around camp."[24]

During this period, Captain Howard kept busy. He met teams as they returned from their missions. He helped handle all the post-mission briefings and frequently visited the Dak To launch site. "He was trying to stay active by staying close to the action," said Ster. Howard often hit the recon company with challenging situations to test their mental abilities.

"I almost got relieved because I'd put salt in shotgun shells and shoot the troops, and burn 'em a little bit," Howard later related. "But it didn't hurt 'em. It would get their attention, you know." Howard would also put short fuses in grenades so they would go off prematurely. He demonstrated how to toss them quickly, simulating the worst-case scenario of having to toss away an enemy grenade that had landed near a soldier. Howard's methods might have seemed unorthodox and dangerous to some, but he truly believed he was instilling survival instincts in his young SF soldiers.[25]

Howard was equally tough on new groups of SF-qualified indigenous troops who arrived to blend into his recon teams. At one point when his company was at full strength, he received about eighty Montagnards. "Bob started them on a very robust physical fitness routine," recalled one-zero Ed Wolcoff. "His purpose was to whittle out those who were not physically fit or did not have the passion and resolve. He ran those guys to death." At the end of his days of brutal endurance challenges, Howard had cut the class size in half.[26]

First Lieutenant Steve Hatch felt that Howard was "a soldier's soldier." He simply expected the best from everyone, but he did so from a desire to help keep them alive when the shooting started. "If you weren't a hundred percent on everything you did, he had no use for you," Hatch later stated. "He could be very demanding. But if you were gung ho and did your job, he was very easy to get along with."[27]

Being on stand-down did nothing to sway Howard's desire to help his company's Green Berets when they were in peril. RT Montana one-zero Mike Sheppard's team was called upon for Bright Light duty to recover the body of an FOB-2 one-one who had been killed during an in-country patrol. As Sheppard and his Yards piled into a waiting Huey, he was surprised by one of its occupants.[28]

Already seated in the back was Captain Howard sporting a sheepish grin. Upon hearing the report that one of his men needed assistance, he had raced to his bunk and grabbed his ready rucksack and CAR-15. He knew he was acting against his standing orders.

"Bob, what are you doing here?" asked Sheppard.

"One of our men is down. I'm going in with you to get him," said Howard.

"Jesus Christ, you can't do that!" Sheppard protested.

Just as he spoke, Lieutenant Colonel McGowan raced up to the chopper to see his team off. Spotting his recon company commander geared up and ready to go, the FOB-2 leader became enraged.

"Get your ass out of there immediately!" he shouted.

Howard climbed out of the helicopter, but his willingness to ignore orders to go in for one of his men was not forgotten. "That's the kind of guy he was," Sheppard recalled.

As the Vietnam War rolled into early 1971, the number of deployed Special Forces troops was being steadily reduced. Salem House operations (previously known as Daniel Boone operations) into Cambodia by U.S.-led teams had already been forbidden on July 1, 1970, with the exception of POW missions or crash-site investigations. Detachment B-52, Project Delta, had been inactivated on June 30. During the fall of 1970, more 5th SFG personnel were removed, and the group was officially notified to stand down for deployment no later than March 31, 1971. On February 8, American Special Forces troops were ordered to cease participation in Prairie Fire operations into Laos.[29]

The slow withdrawal of MACV-SOG forces would take place through most of 1970, but the orders were particularly frustrating to men like Bob Howard. Just days before being ordered out of Laos, Howard would lose another man from his company, David "Lurch" Mixter, the athletic, six-foot-six assistant team leader of RT Colorado. Mixter was killed in an RPG attack, and his body was left behind when his team was hastily extracted under fire. The Bright Light team Howard sent in to retrieve Mixter found only a partial body that had been crudely hacked apart by NVA forces. The likable young soldier from a prominent New England family would prove to be SOG's final recon man MIA in Laos.[30]

Captain Howard was still troubled by the loss of Mixter when he stopped by the base bar several nights later to check in on his men. There he found a visiting recon man showing others a copy of the latest *Stars and Stripes* newspaper. One of its headlines bore the grim news of the reduction of the 5th Special Forces Group in Vietnam by two thousand Green Berets. The first of several cutbacks, this reduction would be a certain boost for NVA efforts in Cambodia and Laos, the recon men griped. One of the disgusted Green Berets pinned the *Stars and Stripes* issue to a window screen at the bar.[31]

Howard turned and left in anger. He returned with an automatic rifle and emptied a magazine safely above everyone's heads, riddling the paper with bullets. As the newsprint pieces drifted down like snow, Howard silently turned and walked away.

★ SEVENTEEN ★

THE MEDAL OF HONOR

February 1971

Brilliant red explosions momentarily lit the compound as mortars exploded during the early-morning hours. Dirt and debris rained down with each enemy round. Excited voices shouted commands to one another through the din of battle.

North Vietnamese sappers were assaulting the SOG compound with machine guns and fin-stabilized 122mm rockets launched from portable tripod stands. Lieutenant Steve Hatch raced to a mortar pit to help direct counterfire toward the NVA rocket men. Part of his job with the Kontum recon company was handling the base's canine, an Akita that Hatch sometimes took across the fence on patrols. "This dog could hear stuff that we humans simply couldn't hear," he recalled. His dog was racing about barking as the explosions erupted. Hatch was horrified to see his canine suddenly drop to the ground with a chest wound from shrapnel. Ignoring orders to stay put, Hatch leaped from the mortar pit and raced to retrieve his wounded dog. He pulled her to safety within the pit and began medical treatment on his Special Forces canine.[1]

As the NVA rockets began exploding within the CCC compound, Captain Bob Howard was also forced to race for cover in one of the mortar pits. As he jumped over a barrier, an NVA bullet struck him in the heel of his right foot. Despite the throbbing pain, he remained in position, shouting orders to his recon company gunners and mortarmen. He was uncertain how many insurgents were assaulting his base. It was not the first time that CCC had been targeted by sappers, but this attack was stronger than previous efforts.

Howard's wound was not severe. At the moment, he was angry—angry that he had been hit, and angry that the enemy was so bold as to attack an MACV-SOG camp. He now found an additional reason to be disturbed.[2]

The CCC operations officer leaped into his mortar pit and announced, "Captain, there's an urgent call for you!"

Howard immediately waved the other man off, shouting that he was in the middle of directing a defensive fight against the NVA. He had no time for telephone calls.

"But, sir, it's General Westmoreland. He's on the 312, and he wants to talk to you."

"What, does he want to know about this battle, or what?" asked Howard.

"No, sir. He wants to talk to you. He's got a special message for you."

Howard grumbled and then cautiously limped his way to the CCC tactical operations center, where a young soldier was manning the Army TA-312 field telephone. The size of a shoebox, the green battery-operated military phone was connected by two wires to a field generator; it had a black handset to listen or speak into.

Snatching up the phone, he said, "This is Captain Howard."

"Bob, how ya doing?" said the general.

"Sir, the situation is pretty damn bad here, plus my foot hurts. I just got shot in it. But how are you doing?"

"Bob, congratulations," said Westmoreland after a brief pause. "I've just been told that you're going to receive the Medal of Honor, and that you're to be in Washington, DC, on February 27."

"Well, General," said Howard, "I don't think that's possible. The enemy's got us—"

Westmoreland jumped back in, cutting Howard off. "Well, I hear you guys are in a little trouble over there, but I've got ahold of General Abrams, and he's gonna get you outta there."

"Well, you're gonna have to hurry up, because the mortar rounds are coming in pretty heavy over here."

"Well," said the general. "We'll get the 4th Infantry Division down there and we'll get you out."

"Okay, sir."

Howard turned to his commanding officer, Lieutenant Colonel Galen Wayne "Mike" Radke, a forty-one-year-old Missourian with sixteen years of Army leadership who had recently taken command of FOB-2 from Lieutenant Colonel McGowan. Handing him the field phone, Howard said, "The general wants to talk to you."

Radke spoke with Westmoreland for a few minutes, hung up, and then addressed Howard. "Captain, I don't want you going back out on the perimeter," he said. "I want you to stay right here. We're going to get the airfield secured and we're going to fly you out of here."

Howard protested. "I've got a damn company out here, Colonel! We've got the enemy that's maybe gonna attack the camp. Somebody needs to be in charge of them!"

"I'll take care of that," the colonel replied.

Howard remained around the TOC only long enough to have medics tend to his wounded right foot. Then he quietly slipped out and returned to directing his troops in securing their perimeter. Mortar rounds and small-arms fire continued to erupt through the morning hours. Howard was in his element, and Lieutenant Colonel Radke knew well enough that he was not a man to sit idly by during a battle.

Radke returned and told Howard, "They're going to land General Abrams's aircraft at Kontum. They've got the airfield secured, and they're going to fly you back to Saigon. But we've got a problem. The enemy is between us and the airfield."

The colonel then stated that he was going to send a team with Howard. They would move him by truck to the airfield and get him extracted. In short order, Howard was loaded on a sand-bag-reinforced deuce-and-a-half truck for the ride out to the airstrip. En route, the sergeant driving the vehicle announced to his captain that the NVA had captured the bridge across the Dak To River, which they had to traverse.

The sergeant said that he was still willing to give it a shot.

"I don't care," said Howard. "Just drive through and let's see if we can get this truck across."

The sergeant barreled across the compound in the truck as

small-arms fire chattered from enemy soldiers. Bullets sprayed dirt, but Howard's team managed to avoid getting anyone shot in the process. As they pulled onto the airfield, the twin-prop Beechcraft aircraft of General Creighton Abrams, commander of all U.S. forces in Vietnam, had just landed. Two colonels exited the plane. They appeared surprised at the appearance of the dirty, unshaven, blood-splattered officer limping forward with a bandaged foot.

"Are you Captain Howard?" one asked.

"Yes, sir."

"We've got to get you to Saigon. Let's go."

Howard hopped up the steps into the small military transport plane and took a seat. As he looked out the window, he could still see soldiers dashing about in the distance as they fired at NVA sappers. *I can't believe this is happening to me,* he thought. *I'm leaving my men in battle because the Army wants to give me an award.*

The general's plane lifted off without incident on February 12. Upon landing at Tan Son Nhut Air Base an hour and a half later, Howard was greeted by another group of colonels. After a surgeon treated his wounded foot, the men escorted him to a trailer near General Abrams's command headquarters. He was told to shower up and shave while a Class C uniform was measured up for him to wear. Howard protested that he had left so fast that he hadn't even had time to grab his shaving kit or anything other than the soiled uniform he was wearing.

After being reassured that he would be provided with everything he needed, Howard was left to clean up. During that time, he became sick. He couldn't believe what was happening to him. He had no desire to fly to Washington to receive another medal. His head reeled with the thoughts of his company being left under siege, and it made his stomach turn.[3]

Howard was emotional. In his heart, he didn't feel he deserved the Medal of Honor for his late December 1968 mission. His colonel had sent him in to retrieve a team member who had been captured or killed. In the end, he had not returned with the missing Green Beret. A cloud of guilt hung over Howard.

To further upset his uneasy stomach, he was informed that General Abrams was throwing a special dinner that evening with his top officers present.

"I don't want a dinner," Howard protested. "If you're going to take me to Washington, let's just go as soon as you can. But give me a chance to get a proper uniform before I go back."

After showering, he stretched out to rest on a bunk in the air-conditioned trailer. In short order, he was presented with a laundered pair of fatigues on which a pair of captain's bars had been freshly sewn. But his stomach was still churning. Howard did not have high respect for Abrams, whom he believed did not have a full appreciation for the work that MACV-SOG recon men were doing. And he had no desire to hobnob with a bunch of Vietnam brass at any fancy dinner party.

Howard's opinion changed when General Abrams appeared at his trailer a short time later. He hugged Howard warmly and said that he had set a great example for all the officers and men in Vietnam. Abrams wanted Howard to meet his staff, and he told him the dinner was being thrown in his honor.

"I really appreciate that, sir, but I'm sick and I just don't feel much like eating."

"You do what you want to do," said Abrams. "But you're going to be there."

"Yes, sir."

Despite his disdain for being honored, Captain Howard became more comfortable during the evening ceremony and even a bit embarrassed. Abrams gave a speech in which he praised the service of Howard in Vietnam and noted how he had been given a direct commission as an officer. "He knew more about me than I knew about myself," Howard recalled. "I kinda felt good. I would have felt better if he had presented me the Medal of Honor."[4]

Bob Howard was flown out of Tan Son Nhut on a commercial Continental Airlines flight. Although riding in first class while other soldiers flew coach, he was still sick to his stomach during the entire flight.

He landed in Oakland, California, where he was greeted by another procession of high-ranking Army officers. He was given another khaki uniform and prepared for another lengthy flight to Washington, DC. Upon landing, he was thrilled to find that the military had flown his family up from Texas to greet him.

As he departed from his plane, Howard was greeted by his wife, Tina; his daughters, Denicia and Melissa; and his wife's favorite aunt, Annie Marie (Shiplett) Punchard, who had been assisting her niece with raising the young Howard children. The family was driven to downtown Washington and checked into the luxurious Madison Hotel on 15th Street NW. They were escorted by a public relations colonel who was in charge of providing for their needs, but Howard was quickly irked by his instructions. With days to spend before the pending White House ceremony, he was told that his family was not to eat in the main restaurant, the Montpelier, and not to use room service. The government could not pay for that.

Aside from grappling with a senior escort who seemed interested only in minding his budget, Howard was soon faced with a new dilemma. A group called the Weather Underground had set off a bomb in the U.S. Capitol building in protest of ongoing U.S.-supported bombings in Laos. Triggered in a bathroom near the Senate, the bomb did not kill anyone but did create an estimated three hundred thousand dollars in damage. With Washington in a lockdown mode, it was uncertain whether the public ceremony the following day could proceed or not.

For his children, visiting the nation's capital was a wonderful trip. For six-year-old Melissa, it was quality time with a father she had scarcely seen for much of her life. On the first night, her great-aunt Annie got lost in the posh hotel and knocked on doors in her attempt to find the right room. Annie was soon in the correct room after security was called by one of the famous guests staying there that night, actress Lucille Ball.[5]

The next morning, Howard decided he didn't care what his escort colonel had to say about room service. "If I was going to receive that high of an honor, I was going to dignify my damn family and eat in a hotel just like high-level people did," he recalled. So he let his wife, kids, and aunt order anything they wished and gave the tab to the government.[6]

When the escorting colonel showed up to run Howard through the day's schedule, Howard was fired up. "If you even mention me having room service, sir, I will personally be insubordinate and kick your ass," Howard barked. "I finally got something dignified in my life and my family is not going to be deprived of it. I don't want you to worry me about it, or my family about it. From now on, you don't tell me anything."

The colonel opted not to make a scene in front of Howard's family, and instead informed Howard that he would have a full schedule for the day. When Howard met with General Westmoreland that morning, he complained of his overbearing escort.

"By God, we'll get it sorted out," Westmoreland assured him.

Captain Howard was then taken to meet with the U.S. secretary of defense, Melvin Laird. He took the chance to make it known he was unhappy that he had been told to wear his dress blues to the White House.

"I will *not* go in to receive the Medal of Honor in dress blues," he stated. "I will wear a Class A uniform, which is what I think is formal. And I will also wear blouse boots because I was a Special Forces sergeant and a paratrooper."[7]

Laird agreed to the request. Howard was next escorted in to meet Secretary of the Army Stanley Resor, whose nephew David Mixter was still officially listed as missing in action in Vietnam. In their private meeting, Howard had the unpleasant task of detailing the Bright Light mission in which one of his men had found the severed remains of the young Green Beret who had been part of his company. Both men became emotional as Howard delivered the news.

By the time Howard was preparing to head to the White House, Westmoreland had put a different, less gruff staff officer in charge of escorting the family. From that point forward, his wishes for his family were granted fully without any further complaints. In fact, before the family departed from Washington that week, the new colonel honored them with a fancy dinner on the town and a night at the theater.

During the late morning of March 2, Howard and his family were transported from the Madison Hotel to the White House. Their vehicles and those ushering in other honorees were greeted by an Army band and President Richard Nixon. Howard learned that he would be decorated in a group ceremony, along with five other Army veterans and one Marine: Captain Harold Fritz, Platoon Sergeant Finnis McCleery, Staff Sergeant Don Jenkins, Sergeant Gordon Roberts, Specialist Fourth Class George Lang, and Captain Wesley Fox of the Marine Corps.

The honorees were lined up inside the White House, with their families gathered nearby. President Nixon then entered the room and addressed the group. "Ladies and gentlemen, it is a very great honor for Mrs. Nixon and me to receive you personally in this House that belongs to all of the American people, and also to participate in a ceremony which is the highest honor a president of the United States can participate in," he began. "And that is the Medal of Honor ceremony, for men who have served our country as these men who will receive this award have served it."[8]

Nixon added, "Words are very inadequate to add to deeds of self-sacrifice, deeds of very great bravery. The deeds speak for themselves."

Military officials then stepped forward to read the official citations for each Medal of Honor recipient. Bob Howard was second in line, following the presentation to Captain Fritz. As the words of his citation were read, he felt awkward about some of the praise. Even though the exact sequence of events as typed up in the MOH narrative did not match perfectly with his own recollections of how the mission went, he was nonetheless greatly honored.

He experienced uncertainty as the president reached out to shake his hand. *What am I doing here?* Howard wondered. His mind raced through all the other heroes who had fought and served without such honor. His uncle Palmer had been wounded in World War II. He thought of his father, his other uncles, and his great-grandfather, who had fought in World War I. He also thought of his loving granny Callie and the values of patriotism that she had instilled in him. And then his mind raced to how smooth and gentle Nixon's hand felt in his own husky, battle-weathered hand.

By the time the Medal of Honor and its pale blue ribbon were draped around his neck, Bob had turned white in the face from the nervousness of the moment.

"Captain Howard, are you okay?" President Nixon asked. "You're looking pale."[9]

"Sir, I don't know if I am going to faint or not, but I apologize for my looks," mumbled Howard. "I think my heart stopped beating."

Nixon leaned in and smiled as he adjusted the medal around Howard's neck. The president was close enough that their cheeks touched. He whispered in the captain's ear, "This great country appreciates you, Bob."

The ceremony then continued for the other recipients until the last had been properly decorated. Then the senior officer reading the citations added a final thought on the worth of the men gathered in the room. "Their conspicuous gallantry, undaunted concern for their comrades, and intrepidity at the risk of their lives above and beyond the call of duty are in keeping with the highest traditions of the military service, and reflect great credit on themselves, their units, and the armed forces of the United States."[10]

President Nixon then announced that his wife, First Lady Pat Nixon, wanted to receive everyone in the state dining room for coffee and refreshments. Each child and spouse was presented with an official presidential seal as a memento. As Bob stepped into the next room, his wife, Tina, grasped his hand with pride. Daughters Melissa and Denicia each wrapped themselves around one of their daddy's legs. Bob was still nervous and pale-faced as Aunt Annie came over to give him a warm hug.

As President Nixon passed by, his eyes met Howard's again. Nixon gave Howard a special look of acknowledgment with a sly smirk. That image of the president's personal grin of approval would stick with Howard for decades.[11]

Still somewhat in a trance, Howard watched the First Lady greet his family. Prior to this date, when his wife, Tina, and Aunt Annie had viewed Pat Nixon on television during her public appearances, they had always believed that she appeared

In the White House following Bob Howard's March 2, 1971, Medal of Honor presentation (left to right)*: Secretary of the Army Stanley Resor, President Richard Nixon, Bob Howard, Tina Howard, Denicia Howard, Melissa Howard, and Annie Punchard.*

Robert L. Howard Collection, courtesy of Melissa Howard Gentsch

somewhat stern. But that day, she offered hugs to both women and to Tina's two daughters. The First Lady then turned to speak to Bob, who still looked pale.

"Can I get you something?" she asked.

"I'd just like some coffee, ma'am," he said.

Pat Nixon quickly returned with a cup of coffee for Howard before moving on to greet the other families. When the ceremonies were complete, Bob had one more special request that he had asked of the officials taking care of his family. He wanted to visit the Tomb of the Unknown Soldier in nearby Arlington, Virginia, to pay his respects. Originally dedicated in World War I to commemorate America's unidentified World War I service members, the white marble sarcophagus stands atop a hill overlooking the nation's capital city. In 1956, President Dwight Eisenhower had approved the additional selection and interment of unknowns from both World War II and Korea. Plans were already being debated on adding a third crypt to the tomb to honor the remains of Vietnam War service personnel.

Howard's family was driven to Arlington that afternoon. Still wearing his pale blue ribbon and Medal of Honor, Captain Howard stood with his family before the eternal flame that

Shortly after the Medal of Honor ceremony, Bob Howard and his family stand before the eternal flame at President John F. Kennedy's grave in Arlington National Cemetery.

Robert L. Howard Collection, courtesy of Melissa Howard Gentsch

burns from the center of a five-foot circular granite stone at the head of President John F. Kennedy's grave. Howard then led his family to the Tomb of the Unknown Soldier to silently pay his respects. He had visited the memorial once with his grandmother shortly before her death, but never with his own family. He stood this day in solid gratitude for his family members who had served in the armed forces and for the many young men who had given their lives in service.

As he stood silently, his younger daughter, Melissa, nudged up beside him and gently took his hand. She could see her father was welling up with emotions, and he was a man who rarely displayed sorrow or tears. He looked down at his daughter, and she understood that the tomb had great meaning for him.[12]

"So you get it, don't you?" Howard asked as he put a hand on her shoulder.

"Yes, sir."

EPILOGUE

In four tours, Robert Howard had spent forty months of his life in combat duty in Vietnam. He had gone in as an infantryman with the 101st Airborne Division, and he emerged as a commissioned Special Forces officer. More than two years of this service time had been with MACV-SOG's elite covert group.

He would spend thirty-six years of his life in honorable military service. From 1971 to 1973, Captain Howard shared his combat experience as an Airborne instructor at Fort Benning, Georgia, before taking on new instructor's duties for Army Ranger courses. His time back in the United States afforded him the opportunity to make up for lost time with his family. But Howard was cautious in allowing his children much time in Alabama around their grandfather, who continued to struggle with alcohol.

As a parent, Bob Howard did not discipline his daughters

with physical punishment. He didn't have to. One stern grimace on his face was more than enough for one of his daughters to immediately realize when she was out of line. Nor would he tolerate anyone else physically disciplining his children. On one occasion at Fort Benning in the early 1970s, another officer whipped Howard's daughter with a belt for being too loud and disrespectful. Howard marched young Melissa to the officer's home, made her apologize, and then proceeded to teach "respect" to the officer in physical fashion. Leading Melissa back to their own home, Howard advised her to show proper respect in the future. The incident was finished in his mind, and it was never discussed again.[1]

By 1973, Captain Howard had earned a bachelor's degree from Texas Christian University in police administration. In 1974, he was in command of Company C, Airborne Rangers, 1st Battalion, 29th Infantry Division at Fort Benning. By year's end, he had been transferred to Fort Lewis, Washington, where he commanded Company A of the 2nd Ranger Battalion, 75th Infantry Regiment. Throughout his command, he trained right alongside his men, participating in their grueling runs and even their Airborne training.

During one of his night jumps with his company, Howard's equipment became fouled, and his parachute failed to open properly. His rate of descent was twice the normal speed. When he slammed into the ground, he was knocked totally unconscious. When he came to, he was more embarrassed than hurt. Two noncommissioned officers stood over Howard's body, debating on whether their captain was dead or not.[2]

"We can't lose that dumb son of a bitch," one of the sergeants remarked.

Pulling the parachute off his face and climbing to his feet, Howard remarked, "Man, if it gets any harder than this, I'm gonna quit!"

His squad leaders were stunned that Howard then proceeded to complete the twenty-six-mile road march back to Fort Lewis without further complaints about his injuries. During the last two miles, he put the company on double-time pace.

Howard served with the Army Rangers through the late 1970s, and he was promoted to major. On other assignments, he was a combat arms instructor at Fort Leavenworth, Kansas, where he had his men run seven miles or more almost daily. The only blemish on his record during this time was a report in 1978 that his hand brushed the face of a soldier who was not taking his training seriously. The physical means of handling recalcitrant soldiers that Howard had sometimes employed during the Vietnam War was an issue in the peacetime military. During the investigation, the soldier recanted his story, and the incident was dismissed.[3]

Howard instead employed less direct methods of making his point known to his troops. During one ten-mile run, a senior noncom failed to follow Howard's directions. When the run was complete, Howard told the Ranger that he would be joining him on a second ten-mile run. The soldier was physically spent late that day when they completed their second leg. Howard had no harsh words for him. His point made, he simply shook the noncom's hand and congratulated him on a job well done.

For the years 1979–1980, Howard received an award for the Most Outstanding Infantry Officer of the Command and General Staff College. He earned his master's degree in public administration from Central Michigan University in 1980, and he completed a Special Forces Officers' Qualification Course at Fort Bragg the following year. He earned a second master's degree from Central Michigan in 1981, and served as a Special Forces training instructor for years.

During these years, Howard's marriage to his first wife, Tina, became strained, and they divorced in May 1977. Four months later, he married Rona Rossyln Redfern, whom he had met at a church in Houston, Texas. By 1983, Bob and Rona Howard had become parents to two children, Rossyln Ann Howard and Robert Lewis Howard Jr.

As he raised two young children in his mid-forties, Howard often turned to his older daughter Melissa for advice. "I was the one from day one that he would talk to and confide in," she recalled. "We became more like contemporaries during that time." Melissa was one of the few people in his life who could speak sternly to Howard about his actions and get away with it.[4]

Although he had gone to great lengths to keep his children distanced from many of his own family members, Howard was still compassionate. He helped his father, Charlie, when he could financially, and he covered the costs of his father's funeral in Opelika, Alabama, when he passed away in March 1982.

Howard was very protective of his children, as future son-in-law Frank Gentsch found out when he called on the colonel in Houston to ask for his daughter Melissa's hand in marriage. A rookie police officer in Waco, Gentsch knew little more than that Howard had served in the Army. "When I went to shake his hand, I shook the biggest hand I had ever shaken," Frank recalled. After some small talk, the colonel asked his daughter to excuse herself from the room.[5]

"I know why you're here," Howard started.

Gentsch proceeded to ask for the colonel's permission to marry his daughter. Howard, "with a Clint Eastwood smirk" and piercing blue eyes, looked the young man straight in the face and gave a firm reply.

"I give you my permission, but know one thing. If you *ever* do anything to harm my daughter, they will never find your body."

With the hair standing up on the back of his neck, Gentsch realized the colonel meant every word he had spoken. "I also knew that he loved his daughter so much."

During his later years of service from 1983 to 1990, Howard held commands in Korea and Germany. From July 1989 to June 1990, he was the second commander of the Special Operations Command Korea (SOCKOR) headquarters, located at Camp Humphreys near Seoul in South Korea. Captain Paul Wiseman, an intelligence officer, met Howard in 1990 when he was selected to become Howard's special intelligence officer for SOCKOR. "The only words he offered to me were 'Don't screw up. Don't do anything dumb,'" recalled Wiseman.[6]

During his time in Korea, Howard fell in love with a beautiful young woman named Sun Young In. Two years later, she would move to be with him in Texas, where the colonel's final duty was that of a special assistant to the commander of the 5th U.S. Army headquarters at Fort Sam Houston in San Antonio, Texas.

One of his softer sides, known only to his family, was that Bob Howard was a gardener. In his own way of showing love, he would sometimes arrive at his family's homes to plant rose-bushes. Daughter Melissa knew that her father found comfort in the solitude of his gardening. "He got peace from it, which was the antithesis of what he was known for," she recalled. Her father had conquered his own demons. "He knew alcoholism ran in the family," Melissa said. "He had had his own bouts over the years, but he swore it off in 1992." She found he was a man of his word, so she was greatly alarmed that July of 1992 when her father called asking her to bring him a bottle of Crown Royal.

Melissa pushed back, but her father insisted. It was July 11, his birthday and that of his granddaughter Holley. When Melissa arrived, Howard's wife, Rona, was equally annoyed to see the bottle. Howard took it and placed it on the mantel beside four other unopened liquor bottles.

"What are you doing, Daddy?" Melissa asked.

"Melissa, it takes more than five bottles of alcohol to tempt me," he pronounced.

His daughter could assume only that five was a significant number to the colonel, representing overseas tours of duty. "He was essentially giving the middle finger to his demon," she recalled. "True to his word, he didn't touch them. He dumped all five in the trash that day."[7]

Colonel Robert Howard was honorably discharged from the U.S. Army on September 28, 1992, after thirty-six years of service. He then went to work for the Department of Veterans Affairs in San Antonio, and he would remain in government employment another fourteen years. His marriage to his second wife, Rona, was already on the rocks, and their divorce was finalized on October 21, 1992, in Harris County, Texas.

Starting a fresh chapter in his life, he married Sun Young less than six months later in San Antonio on March 1, 1993. While working for the VA, Howard was actively involved in military organizations, attending various commencements and other ceremonies. He was also unafraid to speak out on controversial issues, including 1986 congressional hearings regarding POWs and MIAs still unaccounted for in Southeast Asia. Although urged to remain quiet by some, Colonel Howard testified about problems in the reporting and documentation of these service members; some of his statements were made behind closed doors.

One of the organizations that held special meaning to him was the Congressional Medal of Honor Society, chartered in 1958 to preserve the stories of veterans through outreach and education initiatives. Howard served as an officer for many years, and he was often seen alongside the U.S. president for annual ceremonies held at Arlington National Cemetery each May. During the late 1990s, he became close friends with a fellow Vietnam War Medal of Honor recipient, Gary Littrell, who was serving as the society's president while Howard was vice president. Littrell and Howard were contacted by the Armed Forces Entertainment network in Washington, DC, and asked if they could get together a group of Medal of Honor recipients who would like to visit the troops. "He wanted to be back in uniform so bad," said Littrell. "When he was talking to the troops, it was leadership. It was positive motivation. It was as if he was their colonel. They really appreciated him being there."[8]

Each year, Howard and Littrell toured the U.S. bases in Iraq and Afghanistan; they spoke to soldiers and thanked them for their efforts to fight the global war on terrorism. Speaking before soldiers of the 1st Infantry Division in Baghdad, Howard encouraged the men to stay in contact with their loved ones back home. Asked how American troops kept their motivation during the Vietnam War, Howard replied, "We had no choice but to stay motivated as leaders. As for our soldiers, we reminded them that God and country came before our needs."[9]

During one of his overseas tours to visit the troops, Howard had the pleasure of visiting with his son, Robert Jr., who was serving with the 173rd Airborne Brigade Combat Team in Afghanistan. Colonel Howard had been present in July 2006 when his son graduated from infantry school. Addressing the graduates, he related that his son had once asked him, "Dad, would you want me to go to war?"

"Son, I don't want you to go to war," his father said. "But if you decide to go to war, I'll be the proudest father in the United States of America."

As he spoke to the graduating class, the colonel pronounced them to be the fittest men the U.S. Army could produce. "We are looking at the finest that America has got right here, dedicated to the principles that we live for, dedicated to the preservation of lives and liberty and the justice for me to stand up here."

As Colonel Howard completed his speech, he said that he

was privileged to have been born an American and to have served the greatest nation in the world. "God bless you and your service." Pointing his right index finger toward those men, Howard advised, "Never surrender your weapons, and face the enemy!"

Sergeant Robert Howard Jr. was later selected for Special Forces training, but he left the service before completing it, and he was later seriously injured in an accident. He passed away in February 2022, at the age of thirty-eight, due to heart failure.

In April 2009, Gary Littrell, Bob Howard Sr., and other Medal of Honor recipients were on their sixth such overseas tour, one that would prove to be Howard's last. From his home in San Antonio, he had been secretly battling for several years with his toughest opponent, cancer. Howard kept this fact hidden from his family, but his body was growing frail during his last year. On March 25, he participated in a public ceremony on National Medal of Honor Day with other MOH recipients at Arlington National Cemetery. Those present to see President Barack Obama lay a wreath at the Tomb of the Unknown Soldiers noted that Colonel Howard's face was thin and sickly. His once husky body was shedding pounds quickly.

Howard received treatment quietly in his local San Antonio hospital. Shortly before Thanksgiving in 2009, he finally made the call to alert his daughter Melissa in Waco. Her family hurried to his side and soon convinced him to go home with them. Melissa and her daughter Tori rode back to Waco with her father and Vietnam Medal of Honor recipient Mike Thornton, a close friend of Howard's.

Suffering from terminal pancreatic cancer, Colonel Howard

was admitted to St. Catherine Center in Waco to live out his final weeks. Although weak and bedridden, he still had enough strength to pull one of his trademark stunts: slipping out of the hospital when he wasn't being watched. When his family learned that he was making his way to the Crying Shame, a local bar across the highway from St. Catherine, they were initially worried. "We found that he did not drink a drop," recalled Melissa. "He would just go there to drink coffee and talk with other retired men, just to be away from the hospital. When he made a vow, he would stick with it."[10]

By mid-December, Howard's body was failing fast. As the word spread, he had more Special Forces veterans and Medal of Honor Society comrades wishing to pay their final respects than St. Catherine's staff could handle. Melissa stayed with him around the clock, refusing even to go home to shower for several days. She carefully monitored the visitors he wished to see. Despite his frail condition, he managed to pull himself upright in his bed and look his friends square in the eye as they spoke with him. Fellow Vietnam MOH recipient Clarence Sasser was among those with whom he enjoyed visiting.

From his dying bed, Colonel Howard took time to make sure his uniform was properly prepared. Among the friends who slipped past the no-visitors sign to see him one day were a civilian friend and two SOG veterans. Howard modeled the fresh Class A uniform—provided to him by Fort Hood (now Fort Cavazos) near Killeen—he wished to be buried in. It was now decorated with rows of medals he had earned, including the DSC, plus the Medal of Honor that would be worn around his neck. He then asked SOG veteran Martin Bennett to touch up the polish on his jump boots, and Howard proudly saluted his buddies before returning to bed upon their departure. [11]

Robert Howard passed away two days prior to Christmas, on December 23, 2009. OakCrest Funeral Home in Waco prepared and held the colonel's body at no cost to the family until arrangements could be made for his final interment in Arlington National Cemetery. Due to numerous requests from friends and family who would not be able to travel to Arlington, Howard's son-in-law Frank Gentsch arranged closed-casket visitation periods at OakCrest. Two months would pass before Colonel Howard's body was moved from Texas. At the time of his passing, Robert Howard was survived by four children (Denicia, Melissa, Rosslyn, and Robert Jr.) and four grandchildren (Victoria, Holley, Isabella, and Robert Lewis "Tre" Howard III).

Gentsch contacted the superintendent at Arlington to help fulfill the colonel's dying wish. "He wanted to be buried in Section 7-Alpha, so he could see the Tomb of the Unknown Soldier from his plot," Frank recalled. He was initially told that the section was full, and any remaining plots were reserved. Gentsch was persistent, and he managed to enlist the help of his Waco congressman, Chet Edwards, who was on Arlington National Cemetery's appropriations committee. "The following Monday, I received a call from Washington," he said. "They had found room for Colonel Howard in 7-Alpha."[12]

The service in Arlington was finally organized for February 22, 2010, with full military honors. Texas billionaire Ross Perot, a longtime supporter of POW/MIA and Medal of Honor initiatives, graciously offered to fly the Gentsch family, including Howard's grandchildren, to Washington. On a cold, overcast day with ten inches of snow on the ground, funeral services were conducted at the Memorial Chapel at Fort Myer. More than 350 mourners were in attendance, including two of Howard's children, Melissa and Robert. Lieutenant General John F. Mulholland, commander of the U.S. Army Special Operations Command at that time, escorted Melissa during the service. Howard's flag-draped coffin was drawn by horses to his final resting place, where a Special Forces detail delivered flags to the family, and members of the Airborne Association of San Antonio presented the family with a special commissioned portrait of the colonel.

Howard's headstone in Arlington National Cemetery credits him officially with the Purple Heart and seven Oak Leaf Clusters. Today, research by Frank Gentsch turned up only four of those Purple Heart general orders even though Howard's military discharge papers, DD214, clearly shows he received eight. The rest were lost to time, burned up in an archives fire in St. Louis or destroyed with other MACV-SOG records after the Vietnam War.

In addition to his Purple Hearts, Howard had been presented with the Medal of Honor, two Distinguished Service Crosses (the second being a placeholder while his Medal of Honor was approved), the Silver Star, four Legion of Merit awards, two Bronze Stars, four Army Commendation Medals for Heroism, three Air Medals, and the Combat Infantryman Badge. Howard's other awards included the Joint Service Commendation Medal, the Meritorious Service Medal (three awards), the Joint Service Achievement Medal, the Army Achievement Medal, the Good Conduct Medal (four awards), the National Defense Service Medal, the Army Forces Expeditionary Medal (three awards), the Vietnam Service Medal (with three stars for three campaigns), the Armed Forces Reserve Medal, the NCO Professional Development Ribbon (with two devices), the Army Service Ribbon, and the Army Overseas Service Ribbon.

Colonel Howard was also the recipient of five different unit citations and numerous foreign awards, including the Republic of Vietnam Wound Medal and the Vietnam Cross of Gallantry with Gold Star, Silver Star, and Bronze Star. With more than thirty total medals from his multiple tours in Vietnam, Howard might have been the most highly decorated American soldier since World War II. He was certainly the most highly decorated Green Beret.

Special Forces troops training in Kentucky and North Carolina are constantly reminded of Howard's duty and sacrifice. On July 3, 2013, Howard was honored at Fort Campbell, Kentucky, with the headquarters building of the 5th Special Forces Group (Airborne) being named after him. His daughter Melissa Gentsch and her family were on hand as the plaque commemorating her father was unveiled outside the entrance to Howard Hall. At Camp Mackall's Rowe Training Facility in North Carolina, a classroom was renamed Howard Hall in April 2017, in honor of Colonel Howard.

In 2014, Colonel Howard was honored with the Bull Simons Award, named after Colonel Arthur "Bull" Simons. The annual

Melissa Howard Gentsch—seen with her middle daughter, Holley, and youngest daughter, Bella—at the dedication of Howard Hall at the headquarters building of the 5th Special Forces Group at Fort Campbell, Kentucky, in July 2013.

ROBERT L. HOWARD COLLECTION, COURTESY OF MELISSA HOWARD GENTSCH

award recognizes recipients who embodied the skills, values, and true spirit of a Special Operations warrior. Howard was further honored that year in his home state of Alabama with the dedication of the Colonel Robert L. Howard State Veterans Home in Pell City, about a hundred miles northwest of his boyhood home in Opelika.

In recent decades, the colonel has been honored by other military organizations and bases. In 2010, Robert Howard was inducted into the U.S. Army Aviation Hall of Fame. In 2019 in

Tampa, he was posthumously inducted into the USSOCOM Commando Hall of Honor. On April 16, 2021, the Special Operations campus in Korea was named in honor of Colonel Howard. Due to COVID restrictions, the family was unable to attend, but the ceremony was live streamed. Among the United States Forces Korea component commanders on hand to dedicate the campus to Robert Howard was General Robert B. Abrams, whose father had taken care of extracting Howard from combat in Vietnam in 1971 for him to receive his Medal of Honor. A special plaque honoring Howard was unveiled on the outside of the operations headquarters building at Camp Humphreys.

Special Forces officers unveil a plaque honoring Colonel Howard in 2021 when the base headquarters building at Camp Humphreys in South Korea was renamed in his honor. Second from left is General Robert Abrams.

Robert L. Howard Collection, courtesy of Melissa Howard Gentsch

Robert Lewis Howard's exemplary service to the United States of America is evident from the dozens of military awards he received in his career. His actions inspired many future leaders. As I close out this narration of Howard's military service, it is only fitting to give the final words to his comrades in arms and to his family.

He was a man of action. He didn't like to sit around. When it came time to do something, he always stepped up to the plate. By force of personality, he dragged a lot of people with him, and he made a lot of people better people.[13]

—Daniel J. Ster, one-zero, CCC *Kontum*

Bob Howard and his deeds were what helped a lot of new guys not be scared when they joined the company. We trusted that if we got into trouble across the fence, Howard would come in after us.[14]

—Louis J. DeSeta, recon Green Beret, FOB-2 Kontum

Bob was the epitome of a professional soldier warrior. His mission was priority. He led from the front, and he cared about his men. He expressed confidence as he taught us younger people things to keep us alive.

—John M. St. Martin Jr., one-zero, FOB-2 Kontum

Never once did I ever know him to do anything that solely benefited himself. He wouldn't try to promote himself. He never put himself in positions where he'd get admiration. The man was always supportive of the troops and primarily supportive of the mission.[15]

—Major John L. Plaster, one-zero, CCC *Kontum*

Colonel Howard always in my presence was the utmost professional, yet the most humble of any of us senior officers that I had ever come across. He had one thing in his office. It was a picture of Audie Murphy. On the corner of that photo in its frame was a set of Audie Murphy's dog tags, given to him by Audie Murphy's family. He pointed it out one day and said, "You know, I'm just a soldier. That man right there was a hero."[16]

—Captain Paul Wiseman, U.S. Army

Bob Howard was a shining example of what every Special Operations *operator should be.*[17]

—Sergeant Major Joe J. Walker,
one-zero, FOB-2 and CCC *Kontum*

He ran toward *the enemy at all times.*

—Captain Johnnie B. Gilreath, one-zero, FOB-2 Kontum

Bob Howard was a guy that I would want on any mission, whether it was a recon team, a platoon, or a company-sized mission. He felt at home there. Regardless of what the mission was, there was no fear. He was always the first to volunteer. Whenever we were attacked, he was always in the thick of it.

He was a phenomenal guy, because his lack of fear kept him in control.[18]

—Lieutenant Colonel *Thomas W. Jaeger, FOB-2 and* CCC *Kontum, Distinguished Service* Cross *recipient*

Toughest man I ever met in my life. He was a soldier's soldier.[19]

—Gary Littrell, Medal of Honor recipient

Howard was like a one-man Army, and his actions were of the highest caliber of bravery.[20]

—Stephen Roche, FOB-2 Green Beret

My father never asked anyone to do anything that he wouldn't do himself. He knew that real strength came from within. Granny Callie's words from his childhood stuck with him: "Run towards your problems, not away." From her, he learned honor, faith, respect, and perseverance. He lived through things he should not have survived. One of his favorite little phrases seems to fit with that: "I ran with the devil, but God always had my back."

—Melissa Howard Gentsch, daughter

★ ACKNOWLEDGMENTS ★

Telling the story of Bob Howard's beyond-the-call-of-duty service is possible due to the contributions of many. The cloak-and-dagger world of MACV-SOG in Vietnam was closely guarded for decades, and the Green Berets who participated on these missions were not allowed to publicly reveal their exploits until the late 1990s. Major John Plaster's 1997 book, *SOG: The Secret Wars of America's Commandos in Vietnam,* opened the door for other veterans to begin telling some of their stories.

For Colonel Howard, I have relied on his official military records and citations to frame the key dates of his service. His heroism on many of his missions was recounted by dozens of SOG veterans I had the pleasure to interview in the past decade. My uncle-in-law, George Wilson Hunt, was a recon team commander in 1968 and he knew Howard. At Special Forces reunions, Wilson introduced me to many FOB-2 veterans who kindly shared their experiences. Howard's own videotaped narratives for the Congressional Medal of Honor Society and the Pritzker Military Library were key sources for his personal achievements in combat.

Several MACV-SOG historians helped provide me with vital primary documents and photos. Jason Hardy, who has spent decades carefully compiling histories of the SOG teams, put me in touch with other veterans who knew Bob Howard. Historian Steve Sherman, owner of a vast archive of SOG data that he has published, was a great asset in providing records and award citations for me to analyze. Joe Parnar and Bob Dumont, coauthors of books on the Kontum recon company in which Howard served, provided other key contacts and first-person narratives.

I must also thank my friend Shawn Sherrill, a former Marine sergeant, who went out of his way to help copy other important papers. Natasha Ford of the J. L. Throckmorton Library at Fort Bragg, North Carolina, made arrangements for Shawn to review microfilm of the *Fort Bragg Paraglide* newspaper from 1968 and to copy the images needed.

Melissa Howard Gentsch and her husband, Frank Gentsch, patiently dug through scrapbooks of her father's service to provide photos for the book. Melissa and Frank have read through this manuscript to ensure that Howard's personal life and military service have been recorded as accurately as possible at this late date. Their years of effort to retrieve all Colonel Howard's valor award citations, such as paperwork for each of his Purple Hearts, have hit dead ends in certain cases. The covert nature of MACV-SOG operations, and the destruction of many of these records at the end of the Vietnam War, left gaps that could be filled in only with personal interviews of other veterans.

Lieutenant Colonel Tom Jaeger, who commanded a lengthy recon mission involving Howard, was a key contributor. Jaeger carefully read through my compilation of their SLAM VII mission and provided detailed edits to make sure everything was as accurate as possible. John Stryker "Tilt" Meyer, a former one-zero and author of several books on MACV-SOG, also reviewed this manuscript for accuracy. Tilt put me in touch with Alan R. Wise, who allowed me to include one of his photos of SOG team weapons in this book. Former one-zero Ed Wolcoff and Kristen Bouchard, daughter of SOG veteran Daniel Lindblom, helped put me in touch with John St. Martin and others who knew Howard. Lieutenant Colonel Wolcoff and Master Sergeant Jack Crossman, U.S. Army (ret.), each helped point out some of my errors in ranks, terminology, and tactics in their readings of an early version of this text.

I must also thank my agent, Jim Donovan, for his careful review and editorial suggestions for this manuscript. Brent Howard of Penguin Random House was eager to bring Bob Howard's story to print. Grace Layer provided an expert review of the manuscript and her editorial team at Dutton/Penguin helped produce this work in the most professional manner.

In the recounting of Howard's Medal of Honor mission from December 1968, I have followed the sequence of events as he later stated them to have occurred. He was quick to say that the eyewitness accounts accompanying his MOH citation did not properly follow the order in which certain events transpired. In the end, any mistakes in this biography are regretted but my hope is that this work will help honor one of America's great heroes. Robert Howard was a man who ran straight toward his greatest challenges without an ounce of fear. My thanks go out to all who helped in this so that others can understand a little more about this kind family man and valiant warrior.

★ GLOSSARY AND ABBREVIATIONS ★

AA:	antiaircraft.
AHC:	assault helicopter company.
Arc Light:	code name for a B-52 strike.
ARVN:	Army of the Republic of Vietnam (South Vietnamese Army).
BDA:	bomb-damage assessment.
Bra:	target area in southern Laos, so named because at this point Highway 96 crossed a double bend in the Dak Xou River that resembled a woman's brassiere when viewed from the air.
Bright Light:	SOG code name for a cross-border rescue-reaction team.
C and C:	command and control.
CAR-15:	Colt Commando (carbine version of the M16).
CBU:	cluster bomb units.
CCC:	Command and Control Central (Kontum); previously FOB-2.
CCN:	Command and Control North (Da Nang).
CCS:	Command and Control South (Ban Me Thuot).

Claymore M18:	a directional antipersonnel mine.
CO:	commanding officer.
Covey:	a U.S. Air Force detachment flying radio coverage, usually in Cessna O-1 Bird Dog, Cessna O-2 Skymaster, or North American OV-10 Bronco aircraft.
Daniel Boone:	SOG code name for Cambodian cross-border operations (later changed to Salem House).
Douglas A-1 Skyraider:	ground-attack aircraft.
DSC:	Distinguished Service Cross.
FAC:	forward air controller.
Fast mover:	jet aircraft.
FOB:	forward operating base, a permanent SOG camp that housed and trained SF troops.
FOB-2:	located at Kontum from May 1966 into 1971.
Hatchet Force:	code name for a SOG element specializing in search-and-destroy missions. Two or more Hatchet Force platoons combined were referred to as a Hornet Force or Havoc Force. Platoon-sized elements comprised four to five Green Berets and thirty to forty-two indigenous troops.
Huey:	nickname for Bell UH-1 Iroquois turbine-powered transport helicopter.
Kingbee:	code name for Sikorsky H-34 and CH-34 helicopters of South Vietnamese Air Force (VNAF) units that supported SOG cross-border operations.
Leghorn:	SOG radio relay and signal intercept site in southern Laos.
LZ:	landing zone, a site for a helicopter to land.
MACV-SOG:	Military Assistance Command, Vietnam—Studies and Observations Group.
McGuire rig:	swing seat attached to a rope and lowered from a helicopter hovering over treetops. Used for emergency extractions; also known as "strings."

Medevac:	medical evacuation of injured personnel.
Montagnards:	indigenous South Vietnamese hill tribesmen recruited as mercenaries for SOG units.
NCO:	noncommissioned officer.
Nickel Steel:	code name for operations straddling the western demilitarized zone, the dividing line between North and South Vietnam.
NVA:	North Vietnamese Army.
One-one:	SOG code name for recon team assistant team leader.
One-two:	SOG code name for recon team radio operator.
One-zero:	SOG code name for recon team leader.
Prairie Fire:	SOG code name for Laotian operations area; replaced the Shining Brass code name in 1967. Also used as a code word to request emergency extraction of a recon team.
RON:	remain overnight.
RPG:	rocket-propelled grenade.
RT:	recon team. A SOG team generally included three U.S. Special Forces men and between three and nine indigenous members.
Salem House:	SOG code name for Cambodian operations (replaced the Daniel Boone code name in 1969).
SF:	Special Forces.
SFG:	Special Forces Group.
Shining Brass:	SOG code name for Laotian operations area (see Prairie Fire).
SLAM:	search, locate, annihilate, monitor. A mission by a full company-sized element of Hatchet Force platoons.
Slick:	Huey helicopters that carried cargo or personnel.
SOG:	Studies and Observations Group, the Vietnam War's covert special warfare unit.
ST:	spike team; later referred to as recon teams (see RT).

TAC air: tactical air support.

VC: Viet Cong (indigenous South Vietnamese Communist guerrillas).

VNAF: South Vietnamese Air Force.

XO: executive officer.

Yard: American slang for Montagnard tribesman.

ENLISTED RANKS

Private first class	(PFC; E-3 pay grade)
Corporal	(E-4 pay grade)
Specialist fourth class	(spec-4; E-4 pay grade)
Specialist fifth class	(spec-5; E-5 pay grade)
Sergeant	(E-5 pay grade)
Staff sergeant	(SSG; E-6 pay grade)
Sergeant first class	(SFC; E-7 pay grade)
First sergeant	(E-8 pay grade)
Master sergeant	(E-8 pay grade)
Sergeant major	(E-9 pay grade)

★ MILITARY AWARDS FOR ROBERT LEWIS HOWARD ★

Medal of Honor

Distinguished Service Cross with one Oak Leaf Cluster (two awards)

Silver Star Medal

Legion of Merit (four awards)

Bronze Star Medal with Combat "Valor" Device (four awards)

Bronze Star for Meritorious Achievement

Purple Heart with seven Oak Leaf Clusters (eight awards)

Army Meritorious Service Medal (three awards)

Air Medal (three awards: one for heroism and two for aerial achievement)

Joint Service Commendation Medal

Army Commendation Medal with three Oak Leaf Clusters (four awards) with Combat "Valor" Device

Army Commendation Medal for Meritorious Achievement with two Oak Leaf Clusters (three awards)

Joint Service Achievement Medal

Army Achievement Medal

Good Conduct Medal (four awards)

National Defense Service Medal

Armed Forces Expeditionary Medal with two Oak Leaf Clusters (three awards)

Vietnam Service Medal with three Service Stars (three campaigns)

Armed Forces Reserve Medal

NCO Professional Development Ribbon with two devices

Army Service Ribbon

Army Overseas Service Ribbon

UNIT CITATIONS

Army Presidential Unit Citation with Oak Leaf Cluster (two awards)

Meritorious Unit Commendation

Navy Valorous Unit Commendation

Republic of Vietnam Cross of Gallantry Unit Citation with Palm

Republic of Vietnam Civil Action Unit Citation with Palm

FOREIGN AWARDS

Vietnam Cross of Gallantry with Gold Star (corps citation)

Vietnam Cross of Gallantry with Silver Star (division citation)

Vietnam Cross of Gallantry with Bronze Star (regiment/brigade citation)

Vietnam Cross of Gallantry with Palm (First Oak Leaf Cluster)

Republic of Vietnam Armed Forces Honor Medal, First Class

Republic of Vietnam Civil Actions Medal, First Class

Republic of Vietnam Wound Medal

Republic of Vietnam Staff Service Medal, Second Class

Republic of Vietnam Campaign Medal with 1960 Bar

Republic of Korea Order of National Security Merit (Samil Medal)

BADGES

Combat Infantryman Badge

Aircraft Crewman Badge

Master Parachute Badge

Pathfinder Badge

MILITARY AWARDS FOR ROBERT LEWIS HOWARD

Air Assault Badge
Expert Infantryman Badge
Vietnamese Ranger Badge
Army Ranger Tab
Special Forces Qualification Tab
Thai Master Parachute Wings
Vietnamese Master Parachute Badge
French Parachutist Badge
Korean Master Parachute Badge
Thai Balloonist Badge

MEDAL OF HONOR CITATION

Date of Action: December 30, 1968

The President of the United States in the name of The Congress takes pride in presenting the MEDAL OF HONOR to

FIRST LIEUTENANT ROBERT L. HOWARD
UNITED STATES ARMY

FOR SERVICE AS SET FORTH IN THE FOLLOWING CITATION:

For conspicuous gallantry and intrepidity in action at the risk of his life above and beyond the call of duty. 1st Lt. Howard (then Sfc.) distinguished himself while serving as platoon sergeant of an American-Vietnamese platoon which was on a mission to rescue a missing American soldier in enemy-controlled territory in the Republic of Vietnam. The platoon had left its helicopter landing zone and was moving out on its mission when it was attacked by an estimated two-company force. During the initial engagement, 1st Lt. Howard was wounded and his weapon destroyed by a grenade explosion. 1st Lt. Howard saw his platoon leader had been wounded seriously and was exposed to fire. Although unable to walk, and weaponless, 1st Lt. Howard unhesitatingly crawled through a hail of fire to retrieve his wounded leader. As 1st Lt. Howard was administering first aid and removing the officer's equipment, an enemy bullet struck one of the ammunition pouches on the lieutenant's belt, detonating several magazines of ammunition. 1st Lt. Howard momentarily sought cover and then realizing that he must rejoin the platoon, which had been disorganized by the enemy attack, he again began dragging the seriously wounded officer toward the platoon area. Through his outstanding example of indomitable courage and bravery, 1st Lt. Howard was able to rally the platoon into an organized defense force. With complete disregard for his safely, 1st Lt. Howard crawled from position to position, administering first aid to the wounded, giving encouragement to the defenders and directing their fire on the encircling enemy. For 3 and one half hours 1st Lt. Howard's small force and supporting aircraft successfully repulsed enemy attacks and finally were in sufficient control to permit the landing of rescue helicopters. 1st Lt. Howard personally supervised the loading of his men and did not leave the bullet-swept landing zone until all were aboard safely. 1st Lt. Howard's gallantry in action, his complete devotion to the welfare of his men at the risk of his life were in keeping with the highest traditions of the military service and reflect great credit on himself, his unit, and the U.S. Army.

DISTINGUISHED SERVICE CROSS CITATION

Date of Action: November 21, 1967

SERGEANT FIRST CLASS ROBERT L. HOWARD
UNITED STATES ARMY

CITATION:

The President of the United States of America, authorized by Act of Congress, July 9, 1918 (amended by act of July 25, 1963), takes pleasure in presenting the Distinguished Service Cross to Sergeant First Class Robert Lewis Howard (ASN: RA-14628152), United States Army, for extraordinary heroism in connection with military operations involving conflict with an armed hostile force in the Republic of Vietnam, while serving with Command and Control (Central), 5th Special Forces Group (Airborne), 1st Special Forces. Sergeant First Class Howard distinguished himself by exceptionally valorous actions on 21 November 1967, as Special Forces Advisor to a joint American and Vietnamese reconnaissance patrol conducting a search mission near the Laotian border. His patrol discovered a huge rice and ammunition cache surrounded by an enemy bunker complex. Sergeant Howard led a small team to provide security while the remainder of the unit began to destroy the stored supplies. His team encountered four

North Vietnamese Army soldiers, and Sergeant Howard killed them with a fierce burst of rifle fire. He and his men were immediately pinned down by a murderous curtain of fire which erupted from a nearby enemy machine gun position. With complete disregard for his safety, Sergeant Howard crawled toward the emplacement and killed a North Vietnamese sniper who was firing at him as he maneuvered. He then charged the bunker, eliminating its occupants with rifle fire. A second machine gun position unleashed a savage barrage. Sergeant Howard moved his troops to a covered location and directed an air strike against the fortified bunker. While assessing the bomb damage, Sergeant Howard was fired upon by North Vietnamese soldiers in the bunker who had survived the blasts. Pinned down directly outside the strongpoint with a blazing machine gun barrel only six inches above his head, he threw a hand grenade into the aperture of the emplacement, killing the gunners and temporarily silencing the weapon. He then dashed to his team's location and secured a light anti-tank weapon. As the enemy machine gun resumed firing, Sergeant Howard stood up amid a withering hail of bullets, fired his weapon, and completely demolished the position. His fearless and determined actions in close combat enabled the remainder of the patrol to destroy the enemy cache. Sergeant First Class Howard's extraordinary heroism and devotion to duty were in keeping with the highest traditions of the military service and reflect great credit upon himself, his unit, and the United States Army.

MILITARY AWARDS FOR ROBERT LEWIS HOWARD

SILVER STAR

Date of Action: November 12–20, 1968

SERGEANT FIRST CLASS ROBERT L. HOWARD
UNITED STATES ARMY

CITATION:

The President of the United States of America, authorized by Act of Congress, July 9, 1918, takes pleasure in presenting the Silver Star to Sergeant First Class Robert Lewis Howard (ASN: RA-14628152), United States Army, for gallantry in action while engaged in military operations involving conflict with an armed hostile force in the Republic of Vietnam, while serving with Headquarters and Headquarters Company, 5th Special Forces Group (Airborne), 1st Special Forces. Sergeant First Class Howard distinguished himself by exceptionally valorous actions from 12 to 20 November 1968, during an operation deep within enemy-held territory. As his platoon was being inserted into the area, it came under heavy fire from all directions. Sergeant Howard leaped from his helicopter before it touched down and began to return fire, providing protection for his men while they dismounted and moved safely off the landing zone. Seeing two enemy soldiers in a wood line, he charged their position and killed them both. When the unit was attacked by a company-size force on the night of 16 November, he went to each platoon member, encouraging them and directing their fire while completely exposing himself to the communists' barrage. Two days later while Sergeant Howard was leading the point element, the platoon was ambushed by an estimated two North Vietnamese Army companies. He skillfully maneuvered his men so that the enemy was caught in a deadly crossfire and the ambush was broken. The following day, Sergeant Howard had again taken the point element when he observed an estimated battalion-size ambush. Although wounded in the initial exchange of fire, he exposed himself to the aggressors to place effective fire on them and enable his platoon to take cover. Moving from position to position, he administered first aid to the wounded and set up a landing zone so that they could be evacuated. As the first ambulance helicopter came in, it was struck by hostile machine gun fire and burst into flames. Sergeant Howard, although wounded a second time, ran one hundred and fifty meters to where the ship had crashed and rescued a trapped pilot from the blazing wreckage. Once the entire crew was free from the aircraft, he led them back to the platoon while providing covering fire. Three hours later another helicopter succeeded in landing and the casualties were evacuated, but Sergeant Howard refused to leave. The next morning, he saw three North Vietnamese soldiers maneuvering towards his element and immediately opened fire, killing two of them and capturing the third. Sergeant First Class Howard's gallantry in action was in keeping with the highest traditions of the military service and reflects great credit upon himself, his unit, and the United States Army.

★ NOTES ★

CHAPTER ONE: "RUN TOWARDS YOUR PROBLEMS"

1. Bissell, "Fort Campbell."
2. Gentsch and Gentsch, telephone interview.

CHAPTER TWO: AIRBORNE

1. Smith, *The Greatest Hero America Never Knew*, 11.
2. Robert L. Howard Collection, personal narrative.
3. Robert L. Howard Collection, personal narrative.
4. "Robert L. Howard: Medal of Honor Series."
5. Gentsch and Gentsch, telephone interview.
6. Gentsch and Gentsch, telephone interview.
7. "Robert L. Howard: Medal of Honor Series."
8. "Robert L. Howard: Medal of Honor Series."
9. Gentsch and Gentsch, telephone interview.
10. Robert L. Howard Collection, personal narrative; Carland, *United States Army in Vietnam*, 37.

CHAPTER THREE: INTO THE GRAVE

1. Clodfelter, *Mad Minutes and Vietnam Months*, 25.
2. Clodfelter, *Mad Minutes and Vietnam Months*, 26.
3. Clodfelter, *Mad Minutes and Vietnam Months*, 27.
4. "Robert L. Howard: Medal of Honor Series."

5. Carland, *United States Army in Vietnam*, 37–38.
6. "Robert L. Howard: Medal of Honor Series."

CHAPTER FOUR: SPECIAL FORCES

1. In interviews, Robert Howard never specifically named this Special Forces sergeant. He said that he had met the man in Airborne training, that the man stayed in service for more than thirty years, and that the man had been killed in Desert Storm. Of fourteen Army veterans killed in the Persian Gulf War who were old enough to have served in Vietnam, only a few of them were found to have served in the U.S. Army during the Vietnam War. With the help of MACV-SOG and Special Forces historian Stephen Sherman, the author was able to find only one man who was known to have served with the 5th Special Forces Group. John Joseph Collins perished in 1991 during Desert Storm as a fifty-five-year-old chief warrant officer.
2. Robert L. Howard Collection, personal narrative.
3. "Project Delta."
4. "Robert L. Howard: Medal of Honor Series."
5. Gentsch and Gentsch, telephone interview.
6. Robert L. Howard Collection, personal narrative.
7. "Robert L. Howard: Medal of Honor Series."

CHAPTER FIVE: FOB-2 KONTUM

1. Moore, *Uncommon Valor,* 89; Jaks, telephone interview.
2. "Robert L. Howard: Medal of Honor Series."
3. "Colonel Robert L. Howard, 2014 Bull Simons Award Recipient."

CHAPTER SIX: STRAPHANGER

1. Messer, telephone interviews. The date of Howard's first recon mission being May 15, 1967, is based on the third Army Commendation Medal he received in 1968.
2. Plaster, *SOG: A Photo History,* 88, 105.
3. Messer, telephone interviews.

CHAPTER SEVEN: DISTINGUISHED SERVICE

1. "5th Special Forces Group Decorations"; "Gary Zukav with Fellow Veterans (Part I)," video.
2. Moore, *Uncommon Valor,* 91–94.
3. Plaster, *SOG: The Secret Wars,* 70.
4. Plaster, *SOG: The Secret Wars,* 129.
5. Plaster, *SOG: The Secret Wars,* 204.

6. White, telephone interviews.
7. White, telephone interviews.
8. Plaster, *SOG: The Secret Wars*, 150.
9. McCarley, telephone interview.
10. McCarley, telephone interview.
11. Williams, telephone interview; Gilreath, telephone interviews.
12. Greco, *Running Recon*, 54.
13. "1967 Gladiators–Cougars."
14. Plaster, *SOG: The Secret Wars*, 204.
15. Williams, telephone interview.
16. Williams, telephone interview.
17. Robert L. Howard Collection, Purple Heart citations.
18. Robert L. Howard Collection, medical and military records; "Recon Courage Under Fire."
19. Plaster, *SOG: The Secret Wars*, 205.
20. Gilreath, telephone interviews.
21. Robert L. Howard Collection, Distinguished Service Cross citation.

CHAPTER EIGHT: PURPLE HEARTS

1. Moore, *Uncommon Valor*, 99–100, 103–5.
2. Robert L. Howard Collection, medical and military records.
3. Gillespie, *Black Ops Vietnam*, 123–26, 142.
4. Plaster, *SOG: The Secret Wars*, 88–89.
5. Prados, *The Blood Road*, 248; Willbanks, *The Tet Offensive*, 54–55.
6. Plaster, *SOG: The Secret Wars*, 197.
7. DeLong, *War Heroes*, 82.
8. "Robert L. Howard: Medal of Honor Series."
9. "Robert L. Howard: Medal of Honor Series."
10. Dunlap, Army Commendation Medal for Heroism for March 30, 1968.
11. Moore, *Uncommon Valor*, 148.
12. Robert L. Howard Collection, medical and military records.
13. Wilson Hunt, personal interviews.
14. Parnar and Dumont, *SOG Kontum*, 21.
15. DeSeta, telephone interview.
16. McCarley, telephone interview.
17. McCarley, Bronze Star citation.
18. Robert L. Howard Collection, Army Commendation Medal for Valor citation.
19. Parnar and Dumont, *SOG Kontum*, 9–10.
20. Parnar, June 6, 2023, email.
21. "Sergeant Is Cited for Valor."
22. Lindsey, "Sergeant Wins Medals," 1.
23. Robert L. Howard Collection, personal narrative; Robert L. Howard Collection, medical and military records. In the personal narrative, Howard mistakenly stated that he was sent back home due to wounds from his

mission "in November of 1967." In reality, he remained at Kontum for six more months, receiving decorations for his valor in action on various dates from May 13, 1967, through May 14, 1968. He stated that after being in the Japanese hospital, he "ended up in Fort Bragg, North Carolina, in the 6th Special Forces Group. And I stayed there for three months and recovered and then they sent me back to Vietnam again." Howard's service records show that he was sent home from Vietnam in June 1968 and returned to FOB-2 in October 1968.

CHAPTER NINE: THIRD TRIP TO VIETNAM

1. "Sergeant Is Cited for Valor"; Lindsey, "Sergeant Wins Medals," 1.
2. Robert L. Howard Collection, Distinguished Service Cross citation.
3. Robert L. Howard Collection, personal narrative.
4. McCarley, telephone interview.
5. Walker, telephone interviews.
6. Plaster, *SOG: A Photo History,* 187–90.
7. Walker, telephone interviews.
8. Dumont and Parnar, *SOG Medic,* 83.
9. Swain, personal interviews.

CHAPTER TEN: SLAM SEVEN

1. Moore, *Uncommon Valor,* 47–48, 75.
2. Joe Walker statements from "Colonel Robert L. Howard, 2014 Bull Simons Award Recipient."
3. Jaeger, telephone interviews.
4. Jaeger, telephone interviews.
5. Jaeger, telephone interviews and email.
6. Robert L. Howard Collection, Silver Star commendation.
7. Parnar and Dumont, *SOG Medic,* 83.
8. Parnar and Dumont, *SOG Kontum,* 105.
9. Dorff, telephone interview.
10. Walker, telephone interviews.
11. O'Daniel, telephone interview; Farrell, telephone interview.
12. Parnar and Dumont, *SOG Medic,* 85.
13. Kendall, November 14, 1968, diary entry.
14. Parnar and Dumont, *SOG Kontum,* 107.
15. Parnar and Dumont, *SOG Kontum,* 106–7.
16. Parnar, August 22, 2023, email.
17. Jaeger, telephone interviews.
18. Jaeger, telephone interviews and email.
19. Jaeger, email; Dumont and Parnar, *SOG Medic,* 86; Dumont and Partner, *SOG Kontum,* 109–11.
20. Swain, personal interviews.

CHAPTER ELEVEN: "LET'S JUST SPRING THE AMBUSH"

1. Parnar and Dumont, *SOG Medic*, 86–89.
2. Parnar and Dumont, *SOG Kontum*, 114.
3. Jaeger, telephone interviews.
4. Jaeger, email.
5. Swain, telephone interview.
6. Swain, personal interviews.
7. Parnar and Dumont, *SOG Kontum*, 117.
8. Parnar and Dumont, *SOG Medic*, 90.
9. Jaeger, telephone interviews.
10. Parnar and Dumont, *SOG Kontum*, 118.
11. Jaeger, telephone interviews; Bingo, personal interview.
12. Hoeck, "Shot Down," 1–2.
13. Hoeck, "Shot Down," 2–5.
14. Parnar and Dumont, *SOG Medic*, 92.
15. Jaeger, telephone interviews.
16. Jaeger, telephone interviews.
17. Jaeger, telephone interviews.
18. Parnar, August 22, 2023, email; Nozzi, "Major Howard," 48.
19. Parnar and Dumont, *SOG Medic*, 93–94.
20. Parnar and Dumont, *SOG Kontum*, 134.
21. Gron, telephone interviews.
22. Roche, telephone interviews.
23. Robert L. Howard Collection, Silver Star commendation (Roche eyewitness statement).
24. Jaeger, telephone interviews.
25. Parnar and Dumont, *SOG Medic*, 94.
26. Gillespie, *Black Ops Vietnam*, 144.
27. Plaster, *SOG: The Secret Wars*, 208.
28. MACV Command History, Annex F, 1968.
29. Robert L. Howard Collection, Silver Star commendation.

CHAPTER TWELVE: SIX PACK'S RETURN

1. Parnar and Dumont, *SOG Kontum*, 136.
2. Gron, telephone interviews.
3. Plaster, *SOG: The Secret Wars*, 147.
4. Plaster, *SOG: The Secret Wars*, 147.
5. Plaster, *SOG: The Secret Wars*, 147.
6. "Colonel Robert L. Howard, 2014 Bull Simons Award Recipient."
7. Plaster, *SOG: The Secret Wars*, 213.
8. Clough, Robert E, Air Medal citation, dated April 8, 1969.
9. Plaster, *SOG: The Secret Wars*, 213.
10. Robert L., Howard Collection, Purple Heart citations. Howard's paperwork lists Purple Hearts issued on both December 8, 1967, and December 8, 1968,

with the same details. The first date is likely an error, as Howard was wounded on December 10, 1967.

11. Greenwood account from Bottoms, "Medal of Honor Recipient"; "Colonel Robert L. Howard, 2014 Bull Simons Award Recipient."

CHAPTER THIRTEEN: THE SCHERDIN BRIGHT LIGHT

1. Plaster, *Secret Commandos*, 38.
2. Plaster, *Secret Commandos*, 38.
3. Plaster, *Secret Commandos*, 39.
4. Parnar and Dumont, *SOG Kontum*, 159.
5. Parnar and Dumont, *SOG Kontum*, 158–59.
6. Plaster, *Secret Commandos*, 39.
7. "Recon Courage Under Fire."
8. Robert L. Howard Collection, personal narrative.
9. Gron, telephone interviews.
10. Robert L. Howard Collection, personal narrative.
11. Robert L. Howard Collection, personal narrative.
12. Robert L. Howard Collection, Recommendation for award of the Medal of Honor (Gron eyewitness statement); Gron, telephone interviews.
13. Robert L. Howard Collection, Recommendation for award of the Medal of Honor (Griffin eyewitness statement).
14. Gron, telephone interviews.
15. Robert L. Howard Collection, personal narrative.

CHAPTER FOURTEEN: "GIVE ME YOUR WEAPON!"

1. "Robert L. Howard: Medal of Honor Series."
2. "Robert L. Howard: Medal of Honor Series."
3. Robert L. Howard Collection, personal narrative. It should be noted that in his interviews, Robert Howard later insisted that the sequence of events that he was recalling of this mission did not follow the official Medal of Honor citation that the U.S. Army had documented. Based on Howard's personal testimony and a review of the eyewitness statements of other survivors, the author is following Howard's sequence of events in this narration.
4. "Recon Courage Under Fire."
5. Robert L. Howard Collection, personal narrative.
6. Gron, telephone interviews.
7. Robert L. Howard Collection, personal narrative.
8. "Recon Courage Under Fire."
9. "Robert L. Howard: Medal of Honor Series."
10. "Recon Courage Under Fire."
11. Robert L. Howard Collection, Recommendation for award of the Medal of Honor (Griffin eyewitness statement).

12. Robert L. Howard Collection, Recommendation for award of the Medal of Honor (Griffin eyewitness statement).
13. Robert L. Howard Collection, personal narrative.
14. Gron, telephone interviews.
15. "Robert L. Howard: Medal of Honor Series."
16. Robert L. Howard Collection, Recommendation for award of the Medal of Honor (Gron and Griffin eyewitness statements).
17. Robert L. Howard Collection, Recommendation for award of the Medal of Honor (narrative description).
18. Robert L. Howard Collection, personal narrative.
19. Gron, telephone interviews.
20. Gron, telephone interviews.
21. Robert L. Howard Collection, Recommendation for award of the Medal of Honor (Griffin eyewitness statement).
22. Robert L. Howard Collection, personal narrative.

CHAPTER FIFTEEN: "IT SEEMED LIKE A LIFETIME"

1. Robert L. Howard Collection, personal narrative.
2. Robert L. Howard Collection, Recommendation for award of the Medal of Honor (Hill eyewitness statement).
3. Gron, telephone interviews.
4. Robert L. Howard Collection, personal narrative.
5. Robert L. Howard Collection, Recommendation for award of the Medal of Honor (Hill eyewitness statement).
6. Robert L. Howard Collection, Recommendation for award of the Medal of Honor (narrative description).
7. Gron, telephone interviews.
8. Haskew, "The Claymore vs. the M14."
9. "Robert L. Howard: Medal of Honor Series."
10. "Robert L. Howard: Medal of Honor Series."
11. Gron, telephone interviews.
12. Robert L. Howard Collection, personal narrative.
13. Gron, telephone interviews.
14. Gron, telephone interviews.
15. Robert L. Howard Collection, personal narrative.
16. Robert L. Howard Collection, Recommendation for award of the Medal of Honor (narrative description).
17. Robert L. Howard Collection, Recommendation for award of the Medal of Honor (Hamric eyewitness statement).
18. Robert L. Howard Collection, Recommendation for award of the Medal of Honor (Gron and Griffin eyewitness statements).

CHAPTER SIXTEEN: COMPANY COMMAND

1. St. Martin, telephone interview.
2. Gron, telephone interviews.
3. Plaster, *Secret Commandos*, 41.
4. Robert L. Howard Collection, Distinguished Service Cross (First Oak Leaf Cluster) citation.
5. Bahr, telephone interview.
6. Plaster, *Secret Commandos*, 43.
7. Pinn, *Hear the Bugles Calling*, 17, 20, 58.
8. "'I Just Do My Job,'" 1A.
9. Moore, *Uncommon Valor*, 288–92.
10. Pinn, *Hear the Bugles Calling*, 189–93.
11. Plaster, *Secret Commandos*, 163.
12. Wolcoff, telephone interviews.
13. St. Martin, telephone interview.
14. Plaster, *Secret Commandos*, 149.
15. Wolcoff, telephone interviews.
16. St. Martin, telephone interview.
17. Worthley, Silver Star citation, October 14, 1969; Plaster, *Secret Commandos*, 154–55.
18. Plaster, *Secret Commandos*, 264.
19. Plaster, *Secret Commandos*, 265.
20. Wolcoff, telephone interviews.
21. Greco, *Running Recon*, 212.
22. Sheppard, telephone interview.
23. Hatch, telephone interview.
24. "Colonel Robert L. Howard, 2014 Bull Simons Award Recipient."
25. "Robert L. Howard: Medal of Honor Series."
26. Wolcoff, telephone interviews.
27. Hatch, telephone interview.
28. Sheppard, telephone interview.
29. Kelly, *Vietnam Studies*, 177–78.
30. Plaster, *SOG: The Secret Wars*, 317.
31. Plaster, *Secret Commandos*, 302.

CHAPTER SEVENTEEN: THE MEDAL OF HONOR

1. Hatch, telephone interview.
2. Unless otherwise noted, Robert L. Howard Collection, personal narrative and "Robert L. Howard: Medal of Honor Series" are the key sources for the section that follows.
3. Robert L. Howard Collection, personal narrative.
4. Robert L. Howard Collection, personal narrative.
5. Gentsch and Gentsch, telephone interview.

6. "Robert L. Howard: Medal of Honor Series" is the primary source for the section that follows.
7. Robert L. Howard Collection, personal narrative.
8. Richard Nixon Presidential Library, audio of Medal of Honor ceremony.
9. "Recon Courage Under Fire."
10. Richard Nixon Presidential Library, audio of Medal of Honor ceremony.
11. Robert L. Howard Collection, personal narrative.
12. Gentsch and Gentsch, telephone interview.

EPILOGUE

1. Gentsch and Gentsch, telephone interview.
2. "Robert L. Howard: Medal of Honor Series."
3. Smith, *The Greatest Hero America Never Knew*, 42.
4. Gentsch and Gentsch, telephone interview.
5. Gentsch and Gentsch, personal interview.
6. "Colonel Robert L. Howard, 2014 Bull Simons Award Recipient."
7. Gentsch and Gentsch, telephone interview and personal interview.
8. "Colonel Robert L. Howard, 2014 Bull Simons Award Recipient."
9. Roberts, "Medal of Honor Recipients Visit Soldiers."
10. Gentsch and Gentsch, personal interview.
11. SOG Chronicles, "MACV-SOG."
12. Gentsch and Gentsch, personal interview.
13. "Colonel Robert L. Howard, 2014 Bull Simons Award Recipient."
14. "Colonel Robert L. Howard, 2014 Bull Simons Award Recipient."
15. "Colonel Robert L. Howard, 2014 Bull Simons Award Recipient."
16. "Colonel Robert L. Howard, 2014 Bull Simons Award Recipient."
17. "Colonel Robert L. Howard, 2014 Bull Simons Award Recipient."
18. Jaeger, telephone interviews.
19. "Colonel Robert L. Howard, 2014 Bull Simons Award Recipient."
20. Robert L. Howard Collection, Silver Star commendation (Roche eyewitness statement).

★ BIBLIOGRAPHY ★

INTERVIEWS AND ORAL HISTORIES

Bahr, Roy W., Colonel, USA (ret.). Telephone interview with author, January 3, 2017.

Bingo, Michael J., Jr., Sergeant Major, USA (ret.). Personal interview with author, October 21, 2014.

DeSeta, Louis J. Telephone interview with author, June 10, 2023.

Dorff, Anthony C., Staff Sergeant, USA (ret.). Telephone interview with author, April 3, 2015.

Farrell, Alan F. Telephone interview with author, April 2, 2015.

Gentsch, Melissa Howard, and Frank Gentsch. Telephone interview with author, April 25, 2023, and subsequent email correspondence, April 25 to June 10, 2023. Personal interview with author, June 2, 2023.

Gilreath, Johnnie B., Jr., Colonel, USA (ret.). Telephone interviews with author, January 15 and 16, 2015.

Goth, Stephen M. Personal interview with author, October 21, 2014. Telephone interviews with author, September 29, 2016, and May 15, 2023.

Griffith, Richard J. Telephone interview with author, January 6, 2015, and personal interview with author, August 29, 2015.

Gron, Robert M. Telephone interviews with author, April 4, 2015, and April 8, 2023.

Groves, William J., Jr. Personal interview with author, October 21, 2014.

Hatch, Steve. Telephone interview with author, May 8, 2023.

Hunt, George Wilson. Personal interviews with author, July 24–25, August 14, and August 18, 2014, and January 15, 2015.

Jaeger, Thomas W., Lieutenant Colonel, USA (ret.). Telephone interviews with author, January 15, 2015, and May 11 and May 29, 2023, and email, August 22, 2023.

Jaks, Frank, Major, USA (ret.). Telephone interview with author, October 26, 2016.

Lesesne, Edward R., Colonel, USA (ret.). Email correspondence and personal interviews with author, August 13 to 21, 2014.

McCarley, Eugene C., Lieutenant Colonel, USA (ret.). Telephone interview with author, March 16, 2015.

Messer, Joseph. Telephone interviews with author, December 16, 2014, and April 19, 2023.

O'Daniel, Lloyd G., Master Sergeant, USA (ret.). Telephone interview with author, August 6, 2014.

Parnar, Joseph F., USA (ret.). Personal interview with author, October 19, 2016; telephone interviews with author and email correspondence from 2014 to 2016, June 6, 2023, and August 22, 2023.

Plaster, John L., Major, USA (ret.). Personal meeting, August 29, 2015.

Roche, Stephen M., Sergeant, USA (ret.). Telephone interviews with author, March 26, 2015, and May 16, 2023.

Sheppard, Michael M., Sergeant, USA (ret.). Telephone interview with author, August 30, 2023.

St. Martin, John M., Jr., Sergeant, USA (ret.). Telephone interview with author, August 3, 2023.

Swain, Lee R. Personal interviews with author, October 21, 2014, and October 19, 2016, and telephone interview with author, April 20, 2023.

Walker, Joe J., Sergeant Major, USA (ret.). Telephone interviews with author, December 7, 2014, and January 19 and July 19, 2015.

White, Larry M., Command Sergeant Major, USA (ret.). Telephone interviews with author, September 20, 2016, and April 9, 2023.

Williams, Larry D., Sergeant First Class, USA (ret.). Telephone interview with author, January 16, 2014.

Wolcoff, Edward, Lieutenant Colonel, USA (ret.). Personal interview with author, October 22, 2014, and telephone interviews with author, January 22, 2015; March 12, 2018; and August 2, 2023.

ARTICLES / MEMOIRS / OFFICIAL REPORTS

"1967 Gladiators–Cougars," 57th Assault Helicopter Company. Accessed August 28, 2015. www.57thahc.com/unit_history.php?year=1967 (dead link).

"5th Special Forces Group Decorations." *The Green Beret Magazine: A Publication of 5th Special Forces Group (Abn)*, Vietnam. Vol. 4, no. 13 (April 1968).

Bissell, Major Brandon. "Fort Campbell 5th Special Forces Operation Complex Memorialized as Howard Hall." Clarksville Online, July 11, 2013. Accessed May 5, 2023. https://www.clarksvilleonline.com/2013/07/11/fort-campbell-5th-special-forces-operations-complex-memorialized-as-howard-hall/.

BIBLIOGRAPHY

Bogguess, Sergeant First Class Rolland. "Green Beret Wins Second DSC." *The Green Beret* IV, no. 10 (October 1969): 19.

Bottoms, Mike. "Medal of Honor Recipient, Special Operations Legend Receives USSOCOM's 2014 Bull Simons Award." United States Special Operations Command, May 27, 2014. Accessed May 8, 2023. https://www.socom.mil/Pages/MedalofHonorrecipientSpecialOperationslegendreceivesUSSOCOMs2014BullSimonsAward.aspx.

Clough, Robert E. Air Medal citation, dated April 8, 1969.

Dunlap, Charles E. Army Commendation Medal for Heroism citation for March 30, 1968.

Haskew, Michael. "The Claymore vs. the M14 Mine in Vietnam." Warfare History Network, July 14, 2015. Accessed May 22, 2023. https://warfarehistorynetwork.com/the-claymore-mine-vs-the-m14-in-vietnam/.

Hoeck, Carl. "Shot Down" (personal narrative of November 1968 SLAM mission, 2014). Courtesy of Robert Dumont and Joseph Parnar.

"'I Just Do My Job,' Says 3rd-Tour GI," *Pacific Stars and Stripes*, March 8, 1969.

Kendall, William L. Personal diary/team notes written from September 1968 to January 1969. Courtesy of William L. Kendall.

Lindsey, Beverly. "Sergeant Wins Medals Including DSC." *Fort Bragg Paraglide* XXVIII, no. 41 (October 10, 1968): 1.

MACV Command History, Annex F. 1968. https://www.loc.gov/item/powmia/pwmaster_118923/.

McCarley, Captain Eugene C. Bronze Star citation for action on April 16, 1968. General Orders Number 831, May 27, 1968.

Nozzi, Specialist Fourth Class Sandra. "Major Howard." *Gung-Ho: The Magazine for the International Military Man,* December 1983.

Nuzzo, Specialist Fifth Class Ron. "Instant Replay." *The Green Beret* IV, no. 4 (April 1969): 7.

Plaster, Major John L. "The Humble Knight: Colonel Robert L. Howard 1939–2009." *The Drop* (Special Forces Association). Accessed May 6, 2023. http://www.professionalsoldiers.com.

"Project Delta: 5th Special Forces Detachment B-52." Accessed May 5, 2023. http://www.macvsog.cc/special_projects.htm#Project%20DELTA.

Robert L. Howard Collection. Army Commendation Medal for Valor citation for action on April 16, 1968. General Orders No. 934, June 5, 1968.

———. Distinguished Service Cross citation for actions on November 21, 1967. General Orders No. 2018, May 2, 1968.

———. Distinguished Service Cross (First Oak Leaf Cluster) citation. General Orders No. 1065, March 28, 1969.

———. Medical and military records.

———. Purple Heart citations for injuries sustained on November 21, 1967; December 8, 1967; and March 29, 1968.

———. Recommendation for award of the Medal of Honor, April 19, 1969. Including narrative description and Jerome Griffin, Robert M. Gron, Terry Hamric, and Lyle Hill eyewitness statements.

——. Silver Star commendation. General Orders No. 371, February 3, 1969. Including official citation, proposed citation, narrative description, and Stephen M. Roche eyewitness statement.

Roberts, Sergeant Dustin. "Medal of Honor Recipients Visit Soldiers in Iraq." U.S. Army, October 17, 2011. Accessed May 30, 2023. https://www.army.mil/article/19712/medal_of_honor_recipients_visit_soldiers_in_iraq.

"Sergeant Is Cited for Valor: Eight Awards Presented." Undated North Carolina newspaper clipping, circa October 1968, courtesy of Melissa Howard Gentsch.

SOG Chronicles. "MACV-SOG" (Robert L. Howard biographical sketch). Accessed June 5, 2023. https://sogchronicles.com/macvsog-cmoh/#Robert-Howard.

Worthley, Sergeant Kenneth W. Silver Star citation, October 14, 1969.

VIDEOS AND AUDIOTAPES

"Colonel Robert L. Howard, 2014 Bull Simons Award Recipient." USSOCOM History & Research Office. Accessed May 3, 2023. https://www.youtube.com/watch?v=WrwFlkGiARg&t=116s.

"Gary Zukav with Fellow Veterans (Part I)." Accessed June 29, 2023. https://www.youtube.com/watch?v=2wIixanWvVg.

"Recon Courage Under Fire" (Robert L. Howard, Medal of Honor recipient profile). Pentagon Channel. Accessed May 20, 2023; video no longer available. https://www.youtube.com/watch?v=feAu6erxn_M&t=342s.

Richard Nixon Presidential Library and Museum. Audio of Medal of Honor ceremony, March 2, 1971. Accessed May 6, 2023. https://www.nixonlibrary.gov/media/14782.

Robert L. Howard Collection. Personal narrative (AFC/2001/001/89693; videotaped oral history, collected September 18, 2003). Washington, DC: Veterans History Project, American Folklife Center, Library of Congress.

"Robert L. Howard: Medal of Honor Series" (videotaped interview with Ed Tracy, July 27, 2006). Chicago: Pritzker Military Library.

BOOKS

Carland, John M. *The United States Army in Vietnam—Combat Operations: Stemming the Tide May 1965 to October 1966*. Washington, DC: Center of Military History, United States Army, 2000.

Clodfelter, Michael. *Mad Minutes and Vietnam Months: A Soldier's Memoir*. New York: Zebra Books, 1988.

DeLong, Kent. *War Heroes: True Stories of Congressional Medal of Honor Recipients*. Westport, CT: Praeger, 1993.

Gillespie, Robert M. *Black Ops Vietnam: The Operational History of MACVSOG*. Annapolis, MD: Naval Institute Press, 2011.

Greco, Frank. *Running Recon: A Photo Journey with SOG Special Ops Along the Ho Chi Minh Trail*. Boulder, CO: Paladin Press, 2004.

Kelly, Colonel Francis J. *Vietnam Studies: US Army Special Forces, 1961–1971.* Washington, DC: Department of the Army, 2004.

Meyer, John Stryker. *Across the Fence: The Secret War in Vietnam*, expanded edition. Oceanside, CA: SOG Publishing, 2018.

Moore, Stephen L. *Uncommon Valor: The Recon Company That Earned Five Medals of Honor and Included America's Most Decorated Green Beret.* Annapolis, MD: Naval Institute Press, 2018.

Parnar, Joe, and Robert Dumont. *SOG Kontum: Top Secret Missions in Vietnam, Laos, and Cambodia, 1968–1969.* Philadelphia: Casemate, 2022.

———. *SOG Medic: Stories from Vietnam and Over the Fence*. Boulder, CO: Paladin Press, 2007. Havertown, PA: Casemate, 2022.

Pinn, Lionel F., Sr., with Frank Sikora. *Hear the Bugles Calling: My Three Wars as a Combat Infantryman*. Montgomery, AL: NewSouth Books, 2007.

Plaster, John L. *Secret Commandos: Behind Enemy Lines with the Elite Warriors of SOG*. New York: NAL Caliber, 2004.

———. *SOG: A Photo History of the Secret Wars*. Boulder, CO: Paladin Press, 2000.

———. *SOG: The Secret Wars of America's Commandos in Vietnam*. New York: Simon & Schuster, 1997.

Prados, John. *The Blood Road: The Ho Chi Minh Trail and the Vietnam War.* New York: John Wiley & Sons, 1999.

Sherman, Steve. *Who's Who from MACV-SOG*. Houston, TX: Radix Press, 1996.

Smith, Thomas Dale. *The Greatest Hero America Never Knew: The Extraordinary Life of Robert Lewis Howard, Professional Soldier.* Privately published, 2016.

Willbanks, James H. *The Tet Offensive: A Concise History.* New York: Columbia University Press, 2007.

Wolcoff, Lieutenant Colonel Ed (ret.). *Special Reconnaissance and Advanced Small Unit Patrolling: Tactics, Techniques and Procedures for Special Operations Forces*. Barnsley, South Yorkshire, England: Pen & Sword Military, 2021.